# Exploring Learner Language

Also published in
**Oxford Handbooks for Language Teachers**

ESOL: A Critical Guide
*Melanie Cooke and James Simpson*

The Oxford ESOL Handbook
*Philida Schellekens*

Teaching American English Pronunciation
*Peter Avery and Susan Ehrlich*

Success in English Teaching
*Paul Davies and Eric Pearse*

Doing Second Language Research
*James Dean Brown and Theodore S. Rodgers*

Teaching Business English
*Mark Ellis and Christine Johnson*

Intercultural Business Communication
*Robert Gibson*

Teaching and Learning in the Language Classroom
*Tricia Hedge*

Teaching Second Language Reading
*Thom Hudson*

Teaching English Overseas: An Introduction
*Sandra Lee McKay*

Teaching English as an International Language
*Sandra Lee McKay*

How Languages are Learned (3rd. edition)
*Patsy M. Lightbown and Nina Spada*

Communication in the Language Classroom
*Tony Lynch*

Teaching Young Language Learners
*Annamaria Pinter*

Doing Task-based Teaching
*Jane Willis and Dave Willis*

Explaining English Grammar
*George Yule*

# Exploring Learner Language

*Elaine Tarone and Bonnie Swierzbin*

OXFORD
UNIVERSITY PRESS

# OXFORD
UNIVERSITY PRESS

Great Clarendon Street, Oxford OX2 6DP

Oxford University Press is a department of the University of Oxford.
It furthers the University's objective of excellence in research, scholarship,
and education by publishing worldwide in

Oxford  New York

Auckland  Cape Town  Dar es Salaam  Hong Kong  Karachi
Kuala Lumpur  Madrid  Melbourne  Mexico City  Nairobi
New Delhi  Shanghai  Taipei  Toronto

With offices in

Argentina  Austria  Brazil  Chile  Czech Republic  France  Greece
Guatemala  Hungary  Italy  Japan  Poland  Portugal  Singapore
South Korea  Switzerland  Thailand  Turkey  Ukraine  Vietnam

OXFORD and OXFORD ENGLISH are registered trade marks of
Oxford University Press in the UK and in certain other countries

BOOK ISBN: 978 019 442289 5

DVD ISBN: 978 019 442290 1

PACK ISBN: 978 0 19 442291 8

Printed in China

ACKNOWLEDGEMENTS

Illustrations on page 162 by kind permission of Nora Wildgen.

Illustrations on page 163 care of OUP.

Photos on page 164 by kind permission of Elaine Tarone.

Figure 8.1 by kind permission of the Center for Advanced Research
on Language Acquisition (CARLA) at the University of Minnesota and
can be found in Allwright, D. (2001): 'Three major processes of teacher
development and the appropriate design criteria for developing and using
them', in B. Johnston and S. Irujo (eds.), *Research and practice in language teacher
education: Voices from the field: Selected papers from the First International Conference
on Language Teacher Education*. Minneapolis, MN; University of Minnesota,
Center for Advanced Research on Language Acquisition (CARLA).
More information about this CARLA publication can be found at:
http://www.carla.umn.edu/resources/working-papers/index.html

**With thanks to Grant and Tom**

# CONTENTS

# PREFACE

This book came about as a direct outcome of work sponsored by the Center for Advanced Research in Language Acquisition (CARLA), a US Department of Education Title VI-funded Language Resource Center housed in the Office of International Programs at the University of Minnesota. The first author began to see the need for this book as she co-taught, with Professor Maggie Broner, a CARLA Summer Institute titled 'Basics of SLA for Teachers,' using videos she'd adapted from Teemant and Pinnegar (2002). After she spoke in 2007 at CARLA's Language Teacher Education conference about the need to radically rethink the way SLA is taught, she realized she'd need to write an SLA textbook using the new approach. The second author is fascinated by the puzzles in learner language and has experienced the both the joys and the difficulties of bringing language learners and developing teachers together to examine language. For her, the videos on the DVD fulfill the need to bring the joys of real learner language to the SLA classroom without the logistical struggles.

We are grateful to the many people who helped us write this book. Most importantly, we want to recognize and thank the six language learners who graciously and courageously agreed to be videotaped for this book, at a time when their English language skills were much less developed than they are today. It is obvious that there would be no book without their cheerful willingness to be themselves as they allowed us to document their progress in learning the language. We also warmly thank the native speakers of English who agreed to be videotaped and provided us with insights into their own language use.

We are also deeply grateful to our graduate students, developing teachers who gave us many suggestions on how to improve the exercises in this book. Both the book and the exercises have benefited greatly from their comments, insights, and recommendations: from Hamline University, they are Michelle Asche, John Breyfogle, Amy Christianson, Linda Erickson, Michelle Fuller, Katie Grosse, Susan Johnson, Amna Kiran, Brooke Lundgren, Liz Meyer, Nicki Olalde, Greg Parker, Yoshiko Shakal, Jen Sherman, Katie Thorp, Claire Undis, Scott Williams, Andrea Wilson, and Kristen Young, and from the University of Minnesota, they are Yunseong Cheon, Dan Coplen, Anne Edvenson, Erica Finken, David Graber, Justin Haring, Susana Perez Castillejo, Rhonda Petree, Parthy Schachter, and Eugene Tsuprun. Others who gave us invaluable suggestions on the content of the book include Gwen Barnes-Karol, Martha Bigelow, and Maggie Broner. Mike Anderson provided essential moral support.

Thanks also to the very friendly and helpful librarians at the Franklin County Library in Eastpoint, Florida. Sorace et al. (1994) provided an early model for this book. Rich Reardon and his staff at the University of Minnesota did a terrific job of videography, and all the OUP staff were a pleasure to work with.

Finally: Karin Larson, the CARLA coordinator, sine qua non, envisioned this book several years ago, and patiently persisted in urging that it be written. This book owes its existence to Karin.

# LIST OF ACRONYMS

| | |
|---|---|
| CA | contrastive analysis |
| CBI | Content-Based Instruction |
| EFL | English as a foreign language |
| ESL | English as a second language |
| FL | foreign language |
| FLAC | Foreign Language Across the Curriculum |
| IL | interlanguage |
| IPA | International Phonetic Alphabet |
| LAD/LAS | Language Acquisition Device/Language Acquisition System |
| L1 | first language |
| L2 | second language |
| NL | native language |
| NS | native speaker |
| SLA | second language acquisition |
| TL | target language |
| TLU | target-like use |
| TTR | type-token ratio |
| UG | Universal Grammar |
| ZPD | Zone of Proximal Development |

# INTRODUCTION

Before you start reading this book, we invite you to open the DVD and click on 'Introduction', to begin your exploration of learner language.

---

**EXERCISE 0.1**          **Puzzles in Learner Language**

 DVD INTRODUCTION

## Exploratory Practice

Learner language is a constant source of interesting puzzles and problems for language teachers. Sometimes teachers are puzzled by a language structure they hear a student use, sometimes an often-used activity fails to help students acquire a new structure, or sometimes learners do unexpectedly creative things with their language. When teachers encounter such a puzzle in the classroom and desire deeper understanding of the situation, they may reflect on what has happened, they may take action to gain understanding, and as a result of that new understanding, they may change their classroom practices. In short, they may participate in Exploratory Practice (Allwright 2001, 2005; Allwright and Hanks, 2009), which is the framework we adopt in this book as we focus on the structure of learner language and the way it is acquired in the classroom.

## Learner Language as Object of Study

We believe that the job of language teachers is to facilitate language learning, and that to do their best in this job, teachers should know something about how second languages are learned, and how learner language is structured. And indeed, as part of their preparation for teaching, language teachers are usually required to take a course on second language acquisition (SLA) research. But how should such courses be structured if they are to truly engage and prepare teachers for careers of Exploratory Practice focused on learner language development?

Since Selinker first proposed the interlanguage hypothesis in 1972, learner language has been the object of research in its own right. It is worthy of study as an independent system, instead of always being compared negatively to the language spoken by native speakers (NSs). Many studies have been published by university-level researchers, describing the structure of learner language and documenting stages in its development. Explanatory theories of SLA have also been published to account for the patterns found in these studies of learner language. The number and complexity of publications in this field has increased exponentially from one year to the next. Introductory SLA courses and books typically present this scholarly research on second language acquisition in a form that is accessible to prospective language teachers and researchers. These books provide knowledge *about* research on SLA, and there are many currently available, including Ellis (1994, 2003), Doughty and Long (2005), Ellis and Barkhuizen (2005), Lightbown and Spada (2006), Saville-Troike (2006), Brown (2007), Gass and Selinker (2008), and Ortega (in press).

# Focus on Knowledge or Skills?

Introductory SLA books and courses, in their focus on knowledge about SLA, typically describe prominent SLA theories, research studies, and researchers whose findings have supported or contested these theories. To pass such courses on SLA, researchers and teachers in training show what they know about the theories and the research. It is argued that once teachers have internalized this body of knowledge about SLA research, they will be able to apply that knowledge in their own classrooms to improve the decisions they make in teaching language to their students. But Freeman and Johnson (1998), among others, have raised serious questions about the adequacy of this view of the knowledge-base for language teachers. This book responds to some of their concerns in the area of SLA.

We believe that introductory SLA courses should do more than impart knowledge about theories and research findings. They should also provide the skills that teachers and researchers will need to analyze learner language for themselves. Teachers will need those skills if they are to involve themselves in Exploratory Practice in their teaching. We have written this book, following principles articulated in Tarone and Allwright (2005) and Tarone (in press), to provide what we feel has been missing in introductory courses in SLA: basic skills and tools for the analysis of learner language. Students who have taken SLA courses should not just know facts about published SLA theories and studies; they should know how to study and understand the learner language that presents itself to them in their particular classrooms and communities. We would argue that the best SLA course for language teachers should include a substantial hands-on component providing instruction and practice in how to *do* simple learner language analysis at the local level.

The introductory SLA course designed both for researchers and teachers should contain both a Lecture component and a Laboratory component. In the Laboratory component, beginning researchers, prospective, and in-service teachers can learn to do their own descriptions of learner language, and interpret those descriptions in light of the more general knowledge gained in Lecture (Tarone, in press). Though it is not designed for teachers, some practice in learner language analysis is provided in Gass, Sorace, and Selinker (1999) using extensively edited transcripts of published data samples. This book and DVD provide opportunities for this kind of hands-on work in introductory SLA courses. In this book, in exploring and analyzing video samples of learner language at the descriptive level of a case study, prospective language teachers and researchers alike will come to understand in a much deeper way how students learn second languages, they will gain analytical skills that may be useful in assessment of learning in intact classrooms, they will practice using tools that will aid their analysis, they will develop skills to cope with the extensive variability found in learner language, and they will improve their ability to evaluate published research in this field.

# How to Use This Book

This book is accompanied by a DVD that you will need to view periodically in order to complete exercises provided in each chapter. The book and the videos on the DVD are designed to be used either as part of an introductory class on second language acquisition (SLA), or in self-study by individual learners. In either context, the book and videos are meant to be supplemented by readings from standard books on second language acquisition, teachers' lectures, and in-class discussions. Suggestions for these readings are provided at the end of each chapter, in the section called Further Reading.

Each chapter provides basic information about a way of analyzing learners and learner language; related books and articles providing in-depth information on the topic are cited throughout. Each chapter contains exercises in which readers describe the learners' characteristics or analyze the language those learners use. Each exercise may take a considerable amount of time to complete, particularly if the reader takes a thoughtful approach to it. For this reason, readers or course instructors should be strategic, selecting only those exercises that are most interesting and relevant to their own particular puzzles and problems.

## *The Speakers*

On the DVD, you will see six learners of English as a second language (ESL) and two native speakers (NSs) of English. The learners are typical of those seen in college and university ESL classes, in that they have begun their study of the language in formal classrooms, and range in age from 18 to 28. There are three pairs of learners: two NSs of Spanish from Mexico, two NSs of Chinese from the People's Republic of China, and two NSs of French from Central Africa. Each of the learners is shown on the video in six segments, performing a different speaking task in each segment. All the learners perform the same six tasks in DVD Segments 1–6. Each of the NSs of English is shown performing in DVD Segments 2–6. Transcripts of all the language samples on the video are provided at the end of the book, beginning on page 129.

## *The Tasks Used to Elicit Learner Language*

A useful discussion and classification of types of tasks used for collecting learner language samples is provided in Ellis and Barkhuizen (2005: 15–50). For this book, different kinds of 'clinical elicitation' tasks were used. Below we list those tasks, with the instructions given to the speakers and the way each task would be classified by Ellis and Barkhuizen.

### DVD Segment 1: Interview

This is an 'oral interview' task (Ellis and Barkhuizen 2005: 33). Each learner was asked the same questions in the same order, with follow up questions where needed:

- What is your native language?
- What other languages do you speak?
- Did you learn English in school in your home country?
- How old were you when you started learning English?
- Why did you start learning English?
- Can you describe a typical English class when you studied in your home country? What did the students do?
- What do you do now to learn English?
- Do you speak English with your siblings?
- If I were your English teacher, what would you want to tell me about yourself, about how you learn?

Only part of each interview is shown on the DVD; because some interviews were quite long, we selected portions from each one that contained interesting and representative samples of their language. If you are interested in seeing videos of oral interviews of middle school learners of ESL, along with rough transcriptions of the learners' speech, see Teemant and Pinnegar (2002).

### DVD Segment 2: Question Task

This task 'clinically elicits' a 'focused sample' (Ellis and Barkhuizen 2005: 31); the focus is on questions. Each learner was shown a set of pictures one by one. The interviewer said: 'Ask me questions about what you see in the picture, and I'll tell you the story. At the end, I will ask you to tell the story back to me'.

### DVD Segment 3: Retell Task

This task is an oral 'picture composition' task which has been partially rehearsed (Ellis and Barkhuizen 2005: 33). When each learner completed asking questions for the Question Task in DVD Segment 2, the interviewer said: 'Thanks. Now please tell the story back to me. You can look at the pictures'.

### DVD Segment 4: Narrative Task

This task is an unrehearsed oral 'picture composition' task (Ellis and Barkhuizen 2005: 33). Each learner was shown a set of four line drawings. The interviewer said: 'This set of drawings shows a series of events. Look at the drawings and think about what happened. Imagine that you saw the events and I did not. Tell me what happened here'.

### DVD Segment 5: Jigsaw Task

This task is an oral 'information gap' task (Ellis and Barkhuizen 2005: 31–2). A pair of learners sat facing each other. Each learner was given a photograph of a different house. The interviewer said: 'Each of you has a photograph of a house in Minnesota. I would like you to compare the houses by giving each other information about your photograph or by asking questions, but don't show the other person your photograph. For example, you could say, "This house has four windows", or you could ask, "Is that house in a city?" Start by briefly describing the pictures to each other. Then find three things that are the same and three things that are different'.

### DVD Segment 6: Comparison Task

This task is an 'opinion-gap' task (Ellis and Barkhuizen 2005: 31–2). The same pair of learners sat next to each other with their photographs on the table in front of them. Both learners could see both photos. The interviewer said: 'I would like you to talk about who might live in each house. For example, how many people do you think live in this house? What do you think their social class is? Are these typical houses in Minnesota? What do these kinds of houses tell you about American culture?'

## *The Written Task*

This task is a rehearsed written 'picture composition task' (Ellis and Barkhuizen 2005: 33). When each speaker finished the speaking tasks, he or she was given a short written task. The interviewer gave each one a pen and a piece of paper, and said: 'Now write down the story about what happened in the grocery store'.

## *The Organization of the Book*

This book is organized into an Introduction and eight chapters, listed in the Table of Contents. Chapters 1 and 2 introduce the learners and provide some research background. Chapter 1 focuses on individual differences in SLA, and Chapter 2 presents SLA theories that may be useful in explaining patterns in learner language. Chapters 3–7 each take a different approach to analyzing learner language. Each contains background information needed to respond to a set of exercises that structure the reader's analysis of learner language. At the end of each chapter is a list of further readings that we would recommend as companion pieces to the chapter in any standard introductory SLA course. Possible responses to the exercises in Chapters 1–7 can be found in the Answer Discussion section at the back of the book (see page 104).

### The Transcripts

At the end of the book, the reader will find transcripts of the learner language produced by each learner and NS in response to the tasks as well as copies of their written narratives (see Transcripts and Written Narratives, page 129). The transcripts are numbered by line so that you can refer to them easily in doing the chapter exercises. We used a 'broad' transcription (Ellis and Barkhuizen 2005: 28), intended to provide guidance to the readers of the book. The transcripts are as accurate as we could make them. However, like all transcripts, they record our perceptions of what the learners said in the videos. Although we have checked and double checked them, readers may hear the learner language on the videos differently than we did, and disagree with the way we have transcribed it. That is always the case with recordings and transcripts of learner language, which is inherently variable and indeterminate (Tarone 1983).

The transcripts do not provide any information on how words were pronounced. Readers will definitely need to view the videos to do exercises on learner language phonology. Those who can use the International Phonetic Alphabet (IPA) will find it useful for those exercises, but we have tried to design them so that the IPA is not required. In many cases, watching the learners' faces on the video will help you figure out how they are pronouncing particular sounds.

### The Prompt Cards Used on the DVD
Copies of the prompt cards used to elicit learner language for the various tasks on the DVD can be found in the Photocopiable Resources section at the end of the book on pages 162–4.

### References
All the works cited are in the Bibliography at the end of the book (see page 165).

### The Independent Research Project
Chapter 8 uses the framework of Exploratory Practice (Allwright and Hanks, 2009) to provide guidance for the reader in carrying out independent research projects in the classroom focused on learner language. Readers can do 'case studies', describing the language produced by a single individual learner or a small group of learners.

Different tasks are useful for eliciting different aspects of learner language, but the readers are welcome to use the tasks we did in eliciting the language on the DVD. This might be interesting from the point of view of comparison of the learner language produced by learners with different target languages, native languages, and proficiency levels. For that purpose, on pages 162–4 we provide Prompt Cards with the pictures and photographs used in collecting the learner language samples. Readers can use these with the same instructions we did, or change the instructions to target the structures of learner language that are of particular interest to them. There is also a sample consent form at the back of the book (see page 161) for readers to use with L2 participants in a research study.

## Summary

Learner language is fascinating in both its regularity and its infinite variety. We invite you to join us in exploring its characteristics. We hope that the methods and approaches we share with you here will be useful to you as you engage in Exploratory Practice in your classroom, or begin other research ventures. We start out by introducing you to the learners who graciously provided us with samples of their learner language.

# 1

# SECOND LANGUAGE LEARNERS

## Introduction

In this chapter, we will begin our exploration of learner language by considering the backgrounds, personal characteristics, and goals of **second language** (L2) learners. These can all have an important impact on learners' patterns of language acquisition. In this chapter we will:

- review what the research literature says about the impact of learners' varying aims and purposes for learning a language, and the influence of such individual characteristics of learners as motivation, personality, age, learning style, and learning strategies
- introduce you to six adult learners of English as a second language (ESL), ask you to explore who they are as people – their backgrounds, learning purposes, and individual characteristics – and think about the way these might affect their patterns of acquisition of learner language.

## Individual Differences in Second Language Learning

There is no such thing as a generic 'good second language learner', because there is no such thing as a generic learner. Each learner has his or her own unique aims and characteristics, many of which must unavoidably affect the way they approach the project of learning a second language. The linguistic forms the learner needs to know in the target language (TL), and the strategies needed for learning, will be different if his or her aims are, for example, to pass a grammar-based exam to fulfill a college requirement, to speak a few phrases to foster goodwill as a tourist, or to get a better job to achieve more economic security. And even when their aims and purposes are the same, learners may take different pathways to reach those goals because of their own unique constellation of individual characteristics. Among these individual differences in **second language learning** that have been the object of research in second language acquisition (SLA) are differences in the strength of learner motivation, in learner personality (for example, risk-taking versus cautious, extrovert versus introvert), age (during or after the **critical period**), learning styles (visual, auditory, tactile, analytic), and favored learning strategies (for example, memorization, mnemonics, reading aloud). We will consider each of these individual learner characteristics in turn below.

## Learner Aims and Purpose

Learners' aims and purposes in wanting to learn the same foreign language can vary quite a lot. For example, one group of Spanish speakers who are undergraduates in veterinary medicine in Mexico City may only aim to learn reading skills in English as a Foreign Language (EFL) in order to be able to read technical material in their field; they may need no other English language skills (Mackay 1981). But another group of Spanish speakers may be attending the same school and planning to travel in the US these students will then need to master speaking and listening skills so they can use conversational English to interact socially with American English speakers (Tarone and Yule 1989: 8). And still another group of Spanish speakers may be attending middle school in a city in the US where they need to use English for academic language functions such as comparing, inferring, and summarizing. Scholars say linguistic form follows communicative function; they mean that when the second language is used for different functions or purposes, the language forms that serve those purposes will also differ. Learners' differing aims and purposes lead them into different **discourse communities** that use differing varieties of the TL, so what it is that must be learned also varies from one community to the next.

In addition, even when they are entering the same discourse community, individual learners may define their learning aims and goals quite idiosyncratically. Even within a single foreign language class, one learner may have the goal of achieving native-like pronunciation, another may want to learn as many vocabulary words as possible, and yet another may want to master the nuances of the grammatical system. It is important for teachers and researchers alike to acknowledge the impact that these individual learning goals will have on what a learner actually ends up learning.

Scholarship in this area suggests that we can identify two broadly defined types of L2 learner in terms of their overall aims and orientation to the language they are learning (Ellis 1994: 508). The first type is the experiential learner whose primary aim is communication; the second type is the analytical learner whose primary aim is accuracy. An example of a communicatively oriented learner is Zoila, a 25-year old Spanish speaker learning English; she candidly reveals that for her, little English words like 'a', 'the', and 'do' are simply not important. She has no intention of trying to learn them. She can do without them, given that her aim is to 'continue my conversation'.

> **Zoila**   I never ... I never listen, you the ... the words little, uh, small words for continue my conversation.
> **Rina**    What, like what? ...
> **Zoila**   Ah, 'and', and 'that', mmm /ipidit/ (examples of 'little' words as observed by Zoila). You know? ... I'm hear and put more attention the big words. You know and ... something 'house'. I know 'house' is the casa for me. And ... little words is no too important for me.
>
> (Shapira 1978: 254)

Where Zoila is communication-oriented, refusing to use 'little words' prescribed by the grammar book, an accuracy-oriented learner might care more about being correct. Such a learner might self-correct and monitor his or her own accuracy more. Clearly, these different learning orientations, either to communication or accuracy, can also be used to describe different language classrooms and teaching approaches. The communication-oriented learner will probably feel more comfortable in a communicative or proficiency-oriented classroom, while the accuracy-oriented learner will prefer a grammar-focused classroom.

One factor that may affect a learner's orientation toward communication or accuracy is the learner's level of formal education and literacy. There is almost no published research on the relationship between learner orientation and either formal educational level or literacy level. We know that Zoila, who is quoted above, has little formal education, and her preference for a communicative orientation may have been influenced by her relative lack of exposure to school contexts that require accuracy. However, very little SLA research has been done on the impact of literacy level on adults' learner language and learning processes (one exception is Tarone, Bigelow, and Hansen 2009). For example, we know very little about whether a communication-focused or grammar-focused classroom is likely to be preferred by low-literate adult learners, or result in better SLA. Research on this topic, by teachers as well as researchers, is badly needed.

## Motivation
Learners also vary quite a lot in the type and amount of their motivation to learn the language. Language learning **motivation** is the intensity and persistence of a learner's desire to succeed. We infer that a learner is motivated when we observe that learner's willingness to exert effort towards attaining language learning goals. Clearly, whether that goal is to communicate or to be accurate, the amount of motivation the learner has will affect the outcome.

A very useful distinction that has been made is that between **extrinsic motivation** and **intrinsic motivation**. Extrinsic motivation is imposed on the learner by outside forces (grades, requirements), while intrinsic motivation comes from within the learner (desire for personal growth or cultural enrichment). This distinction is related to one made by Gardner and Lambert (1972) between **instrumental motivation** and **integrative motivation**. Instrumental motivation focuses on practical goals for language learning such as program or career requirements, and integrative motivation focuses on love of the language or identification with its community of speakers. Any individual's motivation to learn a language is very complex; it changes over time, and is very sensitive to a range of contextual and internal goals and factors. Contextual factors include whether those around the learner (including the teacher) are interested in the learning activities. If the teacher and those around the learner are engaged in the activity, this will help increase the learner's motivation to engage as well. Internal factors that affect motivation include the learner's assessment of the novelty and pleasure to be gained from the activity, whether the learner believes the activity's outcome will benefit him or her, and whether the learner's participation in the activity is consistent with his or her self and social image. In general, it appears that a classroom learner's **task motivation** – that is, interest and willingness to expend effort on any classroom **task** or activity – is related to that learner's long-term value placed on learning the language, his or her investment in the course, and his or her assessment of the interest level and importance of the particular task (Dörnyei and Kormos 2000).

## Personality

Different **personality** traits of L2 learners also can affect their success in mastering the linguistic features of the language. So, for example, some researchers have studied whether extroverts or introverts make better language learners. They have found that these particular personality traits do not seem to affect success; both extroverts and introverts can succeed in attaining their language learning goals, provided their motivation is strong enough.

Empathy appears to be a centrally important personality factor in language learning. Can the learner empathize with speakers of the TL, and see the world from their point of view? In the early 1970s, Guiora hypothesized that empathetic individuals have more fluid language ego boundaries – that is, they may be more willing to imagine being someone from the TL community, and more likely to pronounce the new language like them. Learners with less empathy, he hypothesized, may have solidified their **native language** (NL) ego boundaries and tend to hold on to their native pronunciation patterns, or accents, to differentiate themselves from speakers of the TL. To experimentally test this hypothesis, Guiora, Beit-Hallahami, Brannon, Dull, and Scovel (1972) tried to artificially increase the empathy levels of adult language learners by giving them half-ounce increments of alcohol in martinis. They compared these learners to other learners given non-alcoholic placebos, and found that the pronunciation of the learners who were given alcohol was in fact rated significantly more native-like with increasing increments – until the learners' consumption exceeded 1.5 oz. After that point their pronunciation deteriorated for other reasons. Though this study is now viewed as controversial, empathy is still felt to be an important individual variable in SLA.

**Risk-taking** is defined as an individual's willingness to try new things even if the attempt might lead to misunderstanding or loss of face. Confidence and self-esteem seem to be hallmarks of the risk-taker. By comparison, an individual who is less risk-taking by nature is more cautious in trying uncertain new ventures, preferring to wait until there is more evidence that the attempt will succeed. Trying to communicate using the linguistic features of a new language can be an uncertain and face-threatening venture that can, under some circumstances, lead to failure, miscommunication, or even embarrassment. Yet attempts to communicate in the face of possible failure are necessary if the L2 learner is to continue to develop new linguistic features of the language. Risk-taking is required if the learner is to try out new linguistic patterns in speaking or writing the language.

## Age

The age at which language learning begins is widely believed to have a particularly strong impact on pronunciation. Older learners almost always pronounce a second language 'with an accent'; as soon as they speak, they are identifiable as foreigners by members of the TL community. Scovel (2001: 113–16) reviews the research evidence and concludes that there are virtually no exceptions to the generalization that those who begin learning a language after puberty will have identifiable foreign accents, even though they may be perfectly intelligible and even eloquent in their mastery of syntax, **discourse** and vocabulary. This interesting learning outcome has been called the **Joseph Conrad phenomenon** in honor of the famous British author whose proficiency in English syntax and vocabulary far surpassed that of most **native speakers** (NSs), yet who retained a Polish accent his whole life (Scovel 1969). Joseph Conrad did not begin learning English until after the so-called **critical period** – the age period when the brain is supposed to be predisposed to success in language learning.

Does it matter that post-puberty learners can bank on ending up with a 'foreign accent'? Maybe not, since it appears that learners do continue to improve their ability in all other aspects of the second language throughout their lifespan. One can be perfectly intelligible, articulate, and persuasive in speaking with an accent. In an ideal world, accents should be viewed as assets that add interest and variety to one's speech, rather than as liabilities.

## Learning Styles and Strategies

Learners have different overall preferences in learning languages, and these can affect their learning outcomes. Examples of different **learning styles** include:

Sensory/Perceptual

- Visual: prefer learning through pictures, charts, reading material
- Auditory: prefer learning through lectures, tapes, conversation
- Tactile/kinesthetic: prefer learning through moving, manipulating, drawing

Cognitive

- Analytical: like to take things apart, notice grammar differences, prefer **contrastive analysis**
- Synthesizing: like to integrate information, notice similarities, summarize, identify key points
- Concrete/sequential: work best linearly with concrete examples
- Intuitive/abstract: work best with abstract models and rules

Learners with different sensory/perceptual learning styles may find themselves using associated **learning strategies** when they focus on internalizing a new vocabulary word or grammar rule. For example, a visual learner may find it useful to use the strategy of associating a new vocabulary word with a picture, while an auditory learner who encounters a new word while reading may want to repeat it out loud. An analytical learner may find it useful to focus on the differences between the grammar rules in the NL and the new one, while a synthesizing learner may prefer to focus on the similarities.

Learning style and strategy preferences may lead learners to notice different aspects of the second language, even when they are provided with exactly the same lesson material in the same classroom. And this can affect what aspects of the linguistic system they learn. A visual learner, for example, may emphasize the writing system of a second language and try to pronounce words the way they are written. If the writing system does not accurately reflect the way the language is pronounced (as with many words in English), it can cause so-called 'reading pronunciation' of the language: a mispronunciation of a word, or an inability to blend words together in a native-like way. Such visual learners may try to pronounce each vowel and consonant of the words the way they are written, in a phrase like 'Did you eat yet?' and not notice the way NSs reduce vowels and blend consonants in conversation, producing something like 'Jeet-chet?' (/ˈdʒiːtʃɛt/). On the other hand, a visual learner may be more likely than an auditory learner to notice and learn grammatical endings such as the final *–s* and *–ed* endings on verbs; such endings are clearly visible in writing, but because in aural input they are typically unstressed or blended at the ends of words, such endings may be less salient, or noticeable to the auditory learner than to the visual learner.

## Profile of the Six Learners

Six learners of ESL were interviewed and did several typical classroom tasks providing language samples that you can watch on the DVD that accompanies this book. In this chapter, we will introduce you to these six learners. Table 1.1 below provides you with some basic facts about their general background. Take a look at the table, and then listen to what they say about themselves in the interviews in DVD Segment 1 so you can get a sense of their individual characteristics as learners, including their general proficiency levels, overall orientations to language learning, personalities, and language learning histories.

*Rodrigo*

| Rodrigo |
| --- |
| Age: 28 |
| Native language: Spanish |
| Other languages: none |
| Studied English: three years in high school, starting age 14 |
| Native country: Mexico |
| Education: five-year law degree from university in Mexico City |
| Length of time in US: 36 days |
| Occupation in US: university intensive English program student |
| Living situation: American friends in suburbs |
| Relationship with other learners: Antonio's brother |

*Antonio*

| Antonio | |
| --- | --- |
| Age: 29 | |
| Native language: Spanish | |
| Other languages: some French | |
| Studied English: two to three years in high school, starting age 13 | |
| Native country: Mexico | |
| Education: five-year law degree from university in Mexico City | |
| Length of time in US: 22 days | |
| Occupation in US: university intensive English program student | |
| Living situation: American friends in suburbs | |
| Relationship with other learners: Rodrigo's brother | |

*Xue*

| Xue | |
| --- | --- |
| Age: 19 | |
| Native language: southeast China dialect | |
| Other languages: Mandarin Chinese, one semester of Japanese | |
| Studied English: ten years, starting age nine | |
| Native country: People's Republic of China | |
| Education: first or second year in college | |
| Length of time in US: 28 days | |
| Occupation in US: one-semester university exchange program | |
| Living situation: host family in suburbs | |
| Relationship with other learners: fellow student | |

*Chun*

| Chun | |
| --- | --- |
| Age: 18 | |
| Native language: Mandarin Chinese | |
| Other languages: none | |
| Studied English: six years, starting age 12 | |
| Native country: People's Republic of China | |
| Education: first or second year in college | |
| Length of time in US: 27 days | |
| Occupation in US: one-semester university exchange program | |
| Living situation: host family in suburbs | |
| Relationship with other learners: fellow student | |

*Catrine*

| Catrine |
|---|
| Age: 19 |
| Native language: French |
| Other languages: Lingala, Swahili |
| Studied English: about nine years, starting age ten |
| Native country: in Francophone Central Africa |
| Education: still in school |
| Length of time in US: 18 months |
| Occupation in US: senior in high school |
| Living situation: own family in suburbs |
| Relationship with other learners: Jeanne's sister |

*Jeanne*

| Jeanne |
|---|
| Age: 21 |
| Native language: French |
| Other languages: Lingala, Swahili |
| Studied English: six years, starting age 15 |
| Native country: in Francophone Central Africa |
| Education: high school graduate |
| Length of time in US: 18 months |
| Occupation in US: first or second year in community college |
| Living situation: own family in suburbs |
| Relationship with other learners: Catrine's sister |

*Table 1.1 Profiles of Six Learners*

---

**EXERCISE 1.1**

### Individual Characteristics of the Six Learners

DVD SEGMENT 1: INTERVIEWS

Watch at least two learners who have different language backgrounds in DVD Segment 1. (If you are in a class, different classmates can look at different learners and compare their findings with yours.) Answer the following questions about the L2 learners you chose to look at:

1  What is your general impression of each learner's English language ability? Describe that ability in terms of fluency, accuracy, pronunciation, or intelligibility.

2  Describe each learner's individual characteristics, as you can identify these in the information given in the interview. Document what you know about each of them in terms of:

  a  How long they have been learning English, and what kind of exposure to English they have had. Was it communication-oriented or accuracy-oriented?

b  Whether they began learning English before the end of the critical period
c  Educational and literacy level; present and past purposes for learning English
d  Whether their present orientation is to either communication or accuracy
e  Personality
f  Motivation
g  Learning styles and strategies
h  Other possibly relevant traits (for example, gender, birth order, cultural orientation, hobbies).

3  Compare the individual characteristics of the learners. How are these the same or different?

4  If you are taking a class, describe the individual characteristics of your learner(s) to the group or class. As a class, discuss all six learners, in terms of your answers to Question 3 above.

5  Going deeper: If you have access to Teemant and Pinnegar (2002), watch the video interviews with two pairs of learners: Spanish-speakers Barbara and Nikcole, and Japanese-speakers Mieko and Makoto. All four are English language learners in an American middle school. Consider their individual characteristics, in comparison with those of the learners on our DVD. What impact do age and maturity have on these learners' individual characteristics and the language they produce?

6  Going deeper: Reflect on the reaction of one of our students, who was in the Peace Corps and has taught ESL. He listened to Rodrigo's interview and was later surprised to learn that Rodrigo has a college degree. He realized that he had assumed from Rodrigo's accent that he was uneducated. This student was puzzled by his own reaction.

# Summary

In this chapter, we have reviewed some individual differences in the aims and individual characteristics of L2 learners, as these have been identified and studied in SLA research. We met six college-aged learners of ESL as they presented themselves in their interviews in DVD Segment 1, and we attended in some detail to what they told us about themselves. We considered their individual identities: who they are as social and emotional people and as learners of a second language and culture. We found that their personalities, individual circumstances, and perspectives on language learning were distinctive.

In Chapter 2, we will turn to a consideration of what is known, in general terms, about the language that is produced by L2 learners and we will explore some of the theories of SLA that have been proposed to account for the structure of learner language.

## *Further Reading*

**Brown, H. D.** 2007. Chapter 3 'Age and acquisition', Chapter 5 'Styles and strategies', Chapter 6 'Personality factors'. *Principles of Language Learning and Teaching* (5th edn.). White Plains, NY: Addison Wesley.

**deBot, K., W. Lowie,** and **M. Verspoor.** 2005. Unit A6 'Learners' characteristics'. *Second Language Acquisition: An Advanced Resource Book.* New York: Routledge.

**Ellis, R.** 1994. Chapter 11 'Individual learner differences'. *The Study of Second Language Acquisition.* Oxford: Oxford University Press.

**Gass, S. M.** and **L. Selinker.** 2008. Chapter 12 'Beyond the domain of language'. *Second Language Acquisition: An Introductory Course* (3rd edn.). New York: Routledge.

**Lightbown, P.** and **N. Spada.** 2006. Chapter 3 'Individual differences in second language learning'. *How Languages Are Learned* (3rd edn.). Oxford: Oxford University Press.

**Ortega, L.** In press. Chapter 2 'Age and L2 acquisition', Chapter 6 'Individual differences'. *Understanding Second Language Acquisition.* Hodder Arnold Publications.

# 2 SECOND LANGUAGE ACQUISITION RESEARCH

## Introduction

In the last chapter, we met six learners of English as a second language (ESL). We listened to what they told us about their language learning history and preferences, considered some of their personal characteristics, and formed a general impression of their proficiency in speaking English. In this chapter we will:

- review what is known about learner language: its autonomous and systematic nature, and the forces that shape it
- introduce the primary theories that have been proposed to explain second language acquisition (SLA)
- consider the implications of those theories with examples from the learner language produced by our six learners.

## Learner Language

### Input ≠ intake

(Corder 1967)

Input does not equal intake; in other words, the linguistic forms we teach a second language (L2) learner are *not the same as* the forms that learner learns. This certainly should not be news to language teachers. This fundamental mismatch between language teaching and language learning happens, not because of any failure on the part of either the student or the teacher, but rather because of the way the learner's brain is wired to learn language. Whatever the teacher's **syllabus** may be, learners have their own 'built-in syllabus' (Corder 1967). The goal of the study of learner language is to understand the nature of the 'built-in syllabus' that L2 learners follow, a syllabus leading them to first form unique linguistic rules to express given functions, and then over time to gradually change those rules in stages to become more like the rules the teacher originally had in mind.

The field of SLA research began in the late 1960s when a group of scholars decided that they should study the way learner language develops, instead of just accepting what current linguistic theory had to say about the way it ought to develop. Almost immediately, they found that their observations did not accord with the predictions of the theory that was generally accepted at the time. They began assembling a set of descriptions documenting the systematic development of a range of rules of learner language. Today, after several decades of research on SLA, current theories continue to try to explain or account for the linguistic shape of learner language. There are many accounts of those theories of SLA (for example, Ellis 1994; Brown 2007; Lightbown and Spada 2006: 29–52; Gass and Selinker 2008). But those theories, interesting and even entertaining though they may be, do not in and of themselves form the foundation of the field of SLA. That foundation is what we have learned about the way learner language forms and develops. This body of information about learner language is important to teachers and scholars alike. This book offers teachers analytical skills to help them add to this body of information as they study learner language at the local level, and thereby improve their understanding of a phenomenon that is central to their classroom.

## *Autonomy of Learner Language*

Native speakers (NSs) of any language tend to perceive learner language through the filter of their native language (NL) rules. From that perspective, what we, as NSs, seem to notice at first are ways the learner's language forms differ from our own. We call these deviant learner forms 'errors' or 'mistakes'. We may feel that our own language forms are systematic and usually 'follow the rules' (though we may not always be able to articulate just what those rules are), while we feel the learner's language forms are a motley, unsystematic collection of forms that are just … wrong. We know that our own language has its rules, and we know the learner's NL has its rules as well. But learner language seems at first like a collection of mistakes, most of them due to the influence of their native language.

However, research has shown that learner language is also rule-governed. It follows its own set of rules, which are different from the rules of the learner's **target language** (TL) and the rules of the NL as well. The linguistic system of learner language has been called **interlanguage**.

## *Interlanguage*

The term **interlanguage** (IL) was introduced by Selinker in 1972 to refer to the linguistic system we see when an adolescent or adult L2 learner tries to express meanings in a language he or she is learning (Selinker 1972). The IL is not produced when the learner focuses on grammatical accuracy, as when reciting memorized dialogues or doing form-focused drills. The learner's IL can only be observed when he or she is focused on the meaning of the message. The learner's linguistic system in that case is clearly different from both the linguistic system of the TL and the learner's NL system. It is autonomous; it is a rule system in its own right, and its rules can be described. An adult learner's IL starts out in a process of change over time. But Selinker claims that the learner's linguistic system typically **fossilizes**, meaning it stops developing at some point and permanently differs from the TL system. In this respect he says an adult's IL is very different from child language. Child language, produced in **first language** acquisition, always continues evolving and developing until it meets a native speaker standard. But according to Selinker, adults' ILs do not do this. Adult L2 learners' rule systems always fossilize so that they end up being in some way (though sometimes in very minor ways) different from the linguistic rule systems that NSs of the TL have.

Most teachers do not like to hear this message; teachers prefer to assume that continued learning is possible. They do not like Selinker's hypothesis that while some parts of an adult's IL will continue to grow and develop, other parts of it – typically, the pronunciation – cannot. If this is true, then it might be preferable to focus attention on those parts of IL that can continue to grow and change.

Some of the processes claimed to shape the rules of IL include NL transfer, overgeneralization, transfer of training, strategies of communication, and strategies of learning (Selinker 1972). Some of these processes may be at work in the ILs of our six learners.

The first process, **native language transfer**, occurs when learners use rules from their NL in trying to produce an utterance in a second language (L2). Transfer is particularly obvious in the early stages of acquisition, and in IL phonology, or pronunciation. In Exercise 2.1 at the end of this section, you can look for examples of transfer in the speech of one of the six learners.

A second process that shapes IL is **intralingual** in nature. Its source is the structure of the language being acquired. The most obvious type of intralingual error is **overgeneralization**: applying an otherwise correct TL grammar rule in the wrong contexts. Learners with all kinds of different NL backgrounds may still make the same intralingual errors. For example, any of our six learners of English who have correctly learned to form the past **tense** in English by adding –*ed* to the verb may occasionally produce the verb *\*gived*. All learners seem to go through this stage, even learners whose native languages also have irregular past tense forms. All learner language, both child language and adult IL, contains some rules formed in this way by overgeneralization.

A third process is **transfer of training**: IL rules can be unfortunate results of instruction gone wrong. For example, English language learners may use past perfect forms to refer to events that occurred in the distant past, as opposed to the recent past, because they have read in a grammar book that past perfect tense is used for 'past past' events. Or a learner may decide not to use request forms like 'Would you mind if …' because he or she has been taught that Americans value directness.

Many cognitive processes, in addition to NL transfer, appear to work together to produce the unique rules of IL. The important point for us, for now, is to recognize that there are features of IL that clearly are *not* due to NL transfer. After you look at NL transfer in Exercise 2.1, in Exercise 2.2 you can look for elements that are *not* due to transfer in the speech of one of the six learners.

**EXERCISE 2.1**

*Rodrigo*

**Transfer in Rodrigo's Speech**

 DVD 1.1: INTERVIEW (LINES 32–46)

Watch a segment of Rodrigo's interview, to identify linguistic elements in his speech that might be caused by his transfer of Spanish rules into his English. Refer to Rodrigo's Interview transcript (lines 32–46) to help you (see page 131). If you do not know Spanish, refer to a contrastive analysis (CA) between English and Spanish, such as Coe (2001) in Further Reading at the end of this chapter. Do you think that Rodrigo is transferring some Spanish into his IL?

---

**EXERCISE 2.2**

*Antonio*

**Features in Antonio's Speech *Not* Due to Transfer**

DVD 1.2: INTERVIEW (LINES 9–22)

Watch this segment of Antonio's interview, to identify linguistic elements in his speech that could not have been caused by transfer of Spanish NL rules. Refer to Antonio's Interview transcript (lines 9–22) to help you (see page 134). If you do not know Spanish, refer to Coe (2001). Are there aspects of Antonio's IL that could not have been due to NL transfer? What do you think might have caused those?

---

# Theories Explaining SLA

Several theories of second language acquisition (SLA) have now been proposed to account for the linguistic patterns observed in learner language. Knowing something about those theories can help us interpret and understand those patterns. Following Lightbown and Spada (2006), we group the theories of SLA into four types: behaviorist, innatist, cognitivist, and interactionist. These four types are listed in the historical order in which they have been popular in SLA research. In the next section, we will provide a brief account of each theoretical approach, and refer to some theories that fall in each category. We encourage you to read about these theories in more depth in works cited in the following discussion.

## *Behaviorist: Contrastive Analysis and Language Transfer*

**Behaviorist** theories view learning as a process of habit-formation. Learners' systematic productions of linguistic forms are considered to be habits, and the process of SLA is one in which old (NL) habits are being replaced by new (TL) habits. Habits change through practice, practice, practice. Errors must be prevented if possible, and stamped out immediately when they occur, before they become habitual. The audio-lingual teaching methodology, which emphasizes rote repetition and drill of decontextualized sentences, is founded upon behaviorist learning theory, and relies on predictions made by **contrastive analysis** (CA). Lado (1957) provided a clear statement of the logic of this theory. If learning is a process of replacing old habits (one's NL linguistic system) with new habits (the linguistic system of the TL), then all learning difficulties can be predicted by a systematic comparison of the NL and TL linguistic systems. In this view, linguistic difference = learning difficulty. Where the two linguistic systems are the same, as when both French and English have the same **phoneme** /b/, there will be no learning problem. But where the two linguistic systems are different, as when French has one kind of /r/ pronounced with friction, and English has another kind of /r/ pronounced as a glide, then we predict that there will be learning difficulty, both for French speakers learning English and English speakers learning French. And in many cases, the predictions made by CA are borne out. French speakers have no difficulty pronouncing English /b/ but typically have lots of difficulty pronouncing English /r/. (And when English speakers learn French, they have no trouble with /b/ but /r/ is hard.)

Difficulty is also predicted if NL and TL have the same form but it occurs in different positions in the word or syllable. For example, English and Vietnamese both have the sound /ŋ/ in syllable-final position, as in English 'long' and Vietnamese *Vang*, and as predicted by CA, that sound is not a problem for L2 learners in syllable-final position. But Vietnamese also has that sound /ŋ/ in syllable-initial position (*Ngo*), and English does not. As predicted by CA, we find that English-speaking learners of Vietnamese have a very hard time producing the sound /ŋ/ in syllable-initial position. These patterns of learning ease and difficulty are all a result of NL transfer, and have been claimed to support a behaviorist, habit-formation, theory of SLA.

But many predictions of behaviorist theory are not borne out by observations of learner language. Sometimes differences between the NL and TL do not cause difficulty at all. For example, the /ʒ/ sound that occurs in syllable-final position in both French (*rouge*) and English ('garage'), occurs in word-initial position only in French (*jamais*), but never occurs at the beginning of a word in English. In this way the distribution of French /ʒ/ seems to be exactly like that of Vietnamese /ŋ/. Nevertheless, English speakers have relatively little difficulty producing /ʒ/ in syllable-initial position (Brière, Campbell, and Soemarmo 1968). CA has no explanation for this and other examples where linguistic difference does not result in learning difficulty at all.

To add to the problem, there are famous examples of L2 learning difficulty in cases when both the NL and TL are the same. Where the linguistic rules are the same, behaviorist theory would predict no difficulty because the old and new habits are the same. But in such cases there sometimes is difficulty. One example is the marking of male and female gender on pronouns. Both English and French have subject pronouns marked for natural gender: French *il* and *elle* are used to refer to male and female humans, just like English 'he' and 'she'. The two languages have separate forms to refer to men and women, and so a behaviorist theory would predict there should be no learning problem. But both English learners of French and French learners of English do have difficulty learning to use the right pronouns to refer to male and female humans; both almost always overgeneralize the male pronoun, referring to Mrs. Smith as 'he' and Mlle. Marie as *il*. The predictions of a habit-formation, behaviorist theory of SLA are not supported by observations of actual learner language. So while it appears that habit-formation might be at work in some cases, it clearly is not in others. A behaviorist theory cannot predict all the patterns we observe in learner language.

**EXERCISE 2.3**

*Catrine*

**Overgeneralization of** /h/ **in Catrine's Speech**

DVD 3.5: RETELL TASK (LINES 1–4)

A behaviorist theory might have little difficulty explaining why Catrine drops /h/ from some words in this DVD segment. But can a behaviorist theory explain Catrine's overgeneralization of /h/ to words where it does not belong?

## *Innatist: Universal Grammar, the Monitor Model*

**Innatist** theories are based on the hypothesis that language learning results from an innate property of the human mind that is dedicated to language acquisition; this property is variously referred to as a Language Acquisition Device, LAD, a Language Acquisition System, LAS, or as Universal Grammar, UG (Cook 1993: 13–17). Innatist theories originate from Chomsky's (1957, 1959) position that behaviorism and habit-formation can never explain an individual's ability to be creative in generating new utterances they have never heard before. **Innatist SLA theories** state that because all L2 learners are innately endowed with the same Universal Grammar, their ILs should all evolve according to the same developmental sequences, regardless of their NL. For support, innatist SLA researchers point to research studies that document the same developmental sequences in the evolution of several structures of learner language (most notably questions and negation), with minimal influence from the NL of the learner.

Two innatist theories have been particularly influential: Universal Grammar (UG) theories, and the **Monitor model**. UG theories predict that interlanguage (IL) rules operate in ways similar to the rules in all natural languages, and explore in depth ways in which the acquisition processes of children acquiring a NL and adults acquiring an IL can be predicted by the same linguistic models. There are differences of opinion in UG theory about whether adult L2 learners have the same access to UG that they did as children; some UG researchers feel they do, but others feel that adults may only be able to access a part of that inborn human capacity for language acquisition.

The Monitor model (Krashen 1981, 1982, 1985) bases its five hypotheses on the central assumption that adult L2 learners are capable of completely accessing and reactivating the same LAD/LAS they used in acquiring a NL in childhood. Because it has had particular influence on language teaching, we will describe the five hypotheses of the Monitor model in more detail.

The first hypothesis is that learners internalize a second language in two ways – they can acquire it or they can learn it. In **acquisition**, L2 learners internalize TL forms unconsciously by using the same LAD they did when they acquired their NL as a child. In acquiring TL linguistic forms, learners are not conscious of them or analytical about their form. This body of acquired linguistic knowledge is used to generate new utterances in the IL. On the other hand, in **learning**, L2 learners consciously attend to the linguistic forms they hear or read, and consciously analyze the rules for combining those forms as they speak or write. Learned segments may also be memorized and used appropriately in conversation

as unanalyzed chunks of language, but these do not lea[c]
never occur in any form other than the memorized form

The second hypothesis is the **natural order** hypothesis. T[.]
when a second language learner acquires a new TL structu
the LAD, that new linguistic structure will evolve over tim[e]
order of acquisition that is unaltered by the NL of the learn
'built-in syllabus' consists only of those TL forms that have [b]
acquired; it does not include TL forms that have been consci[...]          [...]ed. Figure
2.1 shows the 'natural order' in which some **morphemes** are acquired in English
L2:

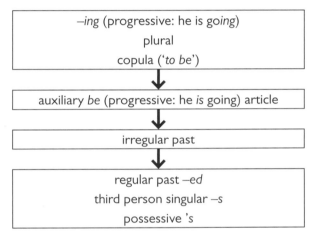

*Figure 2.1 Krashen's (1977) summary of second language grammatical morpheme acquisition sequence*

We see that some morphemes, such as the *–ing* in *playing*, are shown in Figure 2.1 as acquired early, and others, like the third person singular *–s* in *plays* are acquired late. Some predicted acquisition orders may surprise you. For example, irregular past verb forms like *went* are acquired before regular past verb forms with *–ed* like *wanted*. Why do you think these morphemes are acquired in this particular order? What makes some of them easy to acquire and others more difficult?

The third hypothesis is that linguistic information that is consciously learned is stored in the **Monitor**. The Monitor cannot be used to generate utterances; it can only be used to edit the form of utterances already generated by linguistic information that has been acquired. And there are tight restrictions on Monitor use. The Monitor can only be used by the learner to do this editing when there is a focus on accuracy, when there is enough time for the learner to 'look up' the information in the Monitor, and when the rule in question has in fact been learned. Only consciously learned language becomes part of the Monitor; language the learner acquires is stored in a different place. Krashen supports the **noninterface** position. That is, he believes that these two bodies of language knowledge – the acquired TL knowledge used to generate utterances, and the learned TL knowledge used to monitor utterances – do not affect each other at all.

Krashen says it is not possible for someone to consciously learn a new TL rule, and then have that rule somehow become a part of the acquired rule system.

The fourth hypothesis, called the **input** hypothesis, tells us what needs to happen for a second language learner to acquire a new rule. The new linguistic form must be part of comprehensible input that is provided to the learner. In other words, the learner must hear or read some TL input that contains the new form, and is made comprehensible by the context. For example, the learner might hear someone use the passive 'The bus was hit by a truck' while viewing a video of this event.

The fifth hypothesis is the **affective filter** hypothesis, which explains why sometimes L2 learners fail to acquire a new TL form, even with all the conditions for acquisition outlined above. The affective filter, which consists of a learner's attitudes and expectations, can block comprehensible input from reaching the LAD. If learners have negative attitudes and expect to be bored, or to fail, then we say they have a high affective filter, so high that it blocks out all the comprehensible input. If a learner has great attitudes and expectations, then we say that person has a low affective filter, meaning the learner is predisposed to let the comprehensible input in so as to reach the LAD.

Both UG and the Monitor model rely heavily on research studies that describe linguistic structures of interlanguage (IL) that go through a set sequence of developmental stages. Questions, negation, **relative clauses**, and possessive determiners do seem to evolve through developmental sequences. But there are very many linguistic structures of IL that have not been shown to do this, possibly because those structures have not been studied yet, or studied in the right way. And even where developmental stages have been identified, NL transfer can also be involved. So for example, in stage 1 negation in English the word 'no' or 'not' occurs in front of the verb, as in 'no open it' or 'he no want one'. If Spanish is the learner's NL, then NL transfer of the Spanish negation rule (place *no* before the verb) would result in exactly the same learner output as Stage 1 negation. Research shows that Spanish-speaking learners use Stage 1 negation much longer; for them, transfer combines with innate forces to reinforce this stage of negation.

---

**EXERCISE 2.4**

### Monitoring, Learned Chunks, and Morphemes in Rodrigo's Speech

**DVD 1.1: INTERVIEW**

Listen to Rodrigo's entire interview again. Can you find evidence of:

- monitoring
- production of learned chunks
- natural order morphemes?

*Rodrigo*

Can all these things be explained in terms of the Monitor model?

---

## *Cognitivist: Processability Theory, Connectionism*

**Cognitivist** SLA theorists do not hypothesize that the mind has a uniquely specified cognitive capacity to acquire language (an LAD or LAS). Cognitivists think that general cognitive processes used for all kinds of learning can also explain second language acquisition (SLA). Selinker (1972) took a cognitivist approach in stressing that IL could not be produced by a LAD, but rather resulted from five more general cognitive processes. Cognitivist SLA theory includes models that are empirically-based. One such model of the brain and neuronal functioning is provided by **connectionism**; see Ellis (2002) for a persuasive presentation of a connectionist model of SLA. Another model is **Processability Theory**, which claims that cognitive constraints on permissible changes in word order can account for developmental sequences in SLA. Processability Theory (Pienemann 1998) has been particularly influential in providing a theoretical foundation for research on developmental sequences in SLA. What unites these theories and causes us to classify them together is their general shared sense that behaviorism's process of habit-formation cannot explain all of SLA, and their consensus that there is no need to posit a unique specialized language capacity in the mind because general cognitive processes can explain everything we observe in learner language.

## *Interactionist: Focus on Form, Sociocultural and Sociolinguistic Theories*

The **interactionist** theories include **Focus on Form**, **sociocultural theory**, and **sociolinguistic** (variationist) **theory**. In general, what these theories have in common is their assertion that SLA results from learners' active **interaction** with other, usually more proficient, partners as they collaboratively carry out certain kinds of activities. All these theories disagree with Krashen's assertion that learners' passive reception of comprehensible input can drive SLA. Tasks and activities requiring real communication and also the use of particular linguistic forms are a top priority for interactionist theories, which stress that such activities do not just provide practice – they cause acquisition to occur. The interactionist theories all recommend the pedagogical use of communicative activities in the classroom (either in pairwork or groupwork). The key is that these activities be designed to encourage students to stay focused on meaningful communication while simultaneously using targeted linguistic forms.

In 1990, Schmidt posited that L2 learners must consciously notice a linguistic form in order to acquire it. Where Krashen had claimed that acquisition had to be unconscious, Schmidt claimed the opposite. Schmidt (2001: 5) defined **noticing** as a conscious focus on 'elements of the surface structure of utterances in the input'. A second language learner can be led to notice these elements in several ways: through producing IL output, attending to L2 input, or in interactions with others who provide corrective feedback. According to Schmidt, not everything learners notice is necessarily acquired, but every L2 linguistic form that is acquired has to have been noticed, at some point in time. Obviously, this assertion is diametrically opposed to claims in the Monitor model. Schmidt's Noticing

Hypothesis underlies Doughty's (2001) notion of **Focus on Form**, which language teachers have found to be very useful. In Focus on Form, learners must switch back and forth between a primary focus on meaning with occasional brief instances of noticing in a process that is claimed to lead to acquisition over time. See Doughty and Williams (1998) for an excellent set of studies on Focus on Form. It is worth mentioning here that interactionist claims have been based almost exclusively on research with educated, literate L2 learners. There is recent evidence that low-literate adults acquiring second languages may not notice forms in the same way that literate learners do (Tarone, Bigelow, and Hansen 2009).

**Sociocultural theory** that is based on the work of Vygotsky (1978, 1987) focuses on learners' conscious attention to linguistic form in interaction with more knowledgeable others who provide **scaffolding** in collaborative dialogue with them as they try to construct utterances containing linguistic forms they are in the process of acquiring. Such forms are said to be in the learners' **Zone of Proximal Development (ZPD)**, meaning the learner cannot produce them without scaffolding from more knowledgeable interactive partners. We see this dynamic of scaffolding and **co-construction** when a learner starts to produce a sentence, gets stuck on a linguistic form in their ZPD, and their interactive partner uses that form in completing their sentence. The learner notices and acknowledges the new form, and then tries to use it on his or her own, both immediately and later in the interaction. In such collaborative exchanges, sociocultural theorists argue, we can actually see L2 knowledge being co-constructed as acquisition takes place. Lantolf (2000) provides an excellent account of sociocultural theory in SLA. You can analyze a possible collaborative sequence in Exercise 2.5.

**Sociolinguistic (or variationist) theory** documents the interactive impact of a wide range of social and linguistic variables that systematically encourage or discourage a learner from producing a particular linguistic form. These variables range from the social role of the **interlocutor**, to the social context evoked by a particular task or activity, to the topic under discussion. Such sociolinguistic variables have been shown to have a systematic impact on the variants produced by a second language learner – as when, for example, Chinese-Thai bilinguals produce more Thai variants when conversing with an ethnically Thai interlocutor, and more Chinese variants when addressing an ethnically Chinese interlocutor (Beebe 1977). Variationist theory seeks to identify the social variables related to interlocutor, task, or topic that cause learners to attend to one linguistic form as opposed to another, or to discount corrective feedback provided by one interlocutor as opposed to another. See Tarone (1988, 2000) and Preston (1989, 2002) for accounts of variationist SLA.

**EXERCISE 2.5**

*Rodrigo*

**Rodrigo and Antonio's Collaborative Interaction**

**DVD 6.1: COMPARISON TASK (LINES 8–12)**

Watch Rodrigo and Antonio as they interact in DVD 6.1. Describe the way Rodrigo gets stuck on a linguistic form, and Antonio supplies that form. Can the idea of collaborative **scaffolding** account for this process? Do you think Rodrigo will acquire the new linguistic form? Why or why not?

# Implications of SLA Theories for Teaching

One of the enduring claims of SLA theory is that learners have two stores of knowledge about the TL: a relatively explicit, well-analyzed form of knowledge, and a relatively implicit, unconscious form of knowledge. Most SLA theories focus on the development of this second type of knowledge.

The learner's explicit knowledge consists of facts and rules about the language that they have consciously learned. This knowledge is formed in a sequence established by the teacher's and book's syllabus, and is used to edit utterances, to make them conform with what the learner was taught. The implicit knowledge base is used to produce utterances when the speaker is focused on meaning. This implicit knowledge follows its own internal developmental plan – it has a 'built-in syllabus' – and for this kind of knowledge base, input does not equal intake. Most current SLA theories, unlike the Monitor model, assume that there is a relationship between these two bodies of L2 knowledge, and that things consciously learned can become part of the implicit knowledge used to generate utterances.

From a pedagogical point of view, we argue that teaching and learning a second language should involve formation of *both* types of knowledge: explicit and implicit. Most learners in school settings need to have explicit knowledge about what is correct in the second language, in order to pass chapter tests in the book and most standardized language tests at the program level. They need to know explicitly what is correct, and be able to show that on a test. That explicit knowledge base will be useful to them in editing their writing and so on. But L2 learners also need implicit knowledge that enables them to unconsciously produce the linguistic forms of language when they are focused on meaning. *That implicit knowledge has its own independent logic.* Teachers and learners need to know that the order in which those implicitly developing forms develop is predictably going to be different from the order in which the explicit body of language rules is internalized. And that is no one's fault; it is the way the human brain is wired to acquire second languages. In this book we will focus on the development of implicit learner language, and the way it can interact with the learner's explicit knowledge.

# Summary

In this chapter we have considered some theoretical constructs that will help us in our exploration of learner language. We discussed the construct of learner language, not as a collection of errors, but as an autonomous linguistic system: an

IL. We then turned to a brief description of central theoretical approaches in SLA research, and explored some pedagogical implications of those theories.

In Chapter 3 we will begin our exploration of the linguistic form of learner language, identifying errors learners make in producing particular TL forms, as well as instances in which they get those forms right.

## *Further Reading*

**Brown, H. D.** 2007. Chapter 10 'Theories of second language acquisition'. *Principles of Language Learning and Teaching* (5th edn.). White Plains, NY: Addison Wesley.

**Coe, N.** 2001. 'Speakers of Spanish and Catalan' in M. Swan and B. Smith (eds.). *Learner English: A Teacher's Guide to Interference and Other Problems.* Cambridge: Cambridge University Press.

**Gass, S. M.** and **L. Selinker.** 2008. Chapter 6 'Formal approaches to SLA', Chapter 8 'Looking at interlanguage processes', Chapter 10 'Input, interaction and output'. *Second Language Acquisition: An Introductory Course* (3rd edn.). New York: Routledge.

**Larsen-Freeman, D.** and **M. Long.** 1991. Chapter 7 'Theories in second language acquisition'. *An Introduction to Second Language Acquisition Research.* New York: Longman.

**Lightbown, P.** and **N. Spada.** 2006. Chapter 2 'Explaining second language learning'. *How Languages Are Learned* (3rd edn.). Oxford: Oxford University Press.

**Ortega, L.** In press. Chapter 9 'Contemporary SLA theories'. *Understanding Second Language Acquisition.* Hodder Arnold Publications.

# 3 EXPLORING ERRORS AND INTERLANGUAGE

## Introduction

In Chapter 2, we explored the nature and characteristics of learner language and the forces that shape it, and reviewed the major theories that have been proposed to explain second language acquisition (SLA). Now we begin our exploration of the linguistic characteristics of learner language. Our primary focus is on gaining some insight into the systematic linguistic forms that make up the learner's language – forms at the level of pronunciation (**phonology**), grammar (**morphology** and **syntax**), and vocabulary (**lexicon**) – in order to provide teachers and researchers with tools for Exploratory Practice. In this chapter, we will:

- record our overall impressions of the English language proficiency level of two language learners and use two procedures of error analysis to do a deeper analysis of their errors in morphology and syntax
- identify some of the limitations of error analysis as a tool for looking at learner language by analyzing two learners' errors in pronunciation
- re-analyze these learners' production of two English phonemes using an interlanguage (IL) analysis tool called target-like use (TLU)
- use TLU to describe the six learners' patterns of correct and incorrect usage of third person singular –s, and the relationship of those patterns to their apparent proficiency levels.

## First Impressions of Learner Language

We will begin by looking at the interviews of two learners: Xue and Rodrigo. Recall that Xue is an undergraduate on a semester abroad from the People's Republic of China. Rodrigo earned an undergraduate degree in law and political science in Mexico, and is studying English because he would like to get a master's degree.

First, we will ask you what you have noticed about their learner language already. Fluent speakers of English may find that certain features of learner language just 'jump out at them'. Usually these are features that 'sound different': elements of foreign accent, or grammatical **errors**. A busy teacher may also have first impressions of learners in their class simply on the basis of exchanging a few words with them.

---

**EXERCISE 3.1**

*Rodrigo    Xue*

**First Impressions of Rodrigo's and Xue's Proficiency and Learner Language**

DVD 1.1 AND 1.3: INTERVIEWS

Without going back to look at the interviews again, what do you recall about Rodrigo's and Xue's language?

1  Did either of them seem to be more proficient in English than the other? Which one? What made you think that?

2  Jot down some notes about the features of their learner language that you remember, the ones that seemed to 'jump out' at you. Were there instances of 'foreign accent'? Grammar error?

---

# Error Analysis

As a language teacher, you may have noticed that it is the errors in English form that 'jump out' at you – are most noticeable – when you first listen to the form of a learner's language or when you correct a student's writing. Perhaps the first thing that we do as teachers when we start to analyze a learner's language is an **error analysis**. We make a note of the errors in form that we hear in the speech of our students or we identify the errors in a student's writing. Learner language is a linguistic system that is in the process of formation, and learners are typically uncertain of many of the rules they use. Learner language is a very imprecise tool for them to use in realizing intended meanings. For this reason, it is not always easy to figure out exactly what the learner intended to say in producing a given error, and so it is not obvious how to correct it. But let's start with a detailed error analysis of two learners' language, so that we can see what we can learn from analyzing learners' errors, and what the limitations of error analysis might be.

## *Error Analysis of Rodrigo's and Xue's Learner Language*

As a language teacher, you may have noticed errors in the English of Xue and Rodrigo as you listened to what they had to say in their interviews. Maybe you noticed when Xue said 'Chinese are always focus on grammars', or when Rodrigo said, 'in Mexico no is good'.

Researchers have worked out a procedure for analyzing learner errors. Following a simplified version of Corder (1974), we suggest you follow this procedure in doing your error analysis:

### 1 Identify the errors

Prepare a reconstruction of the sample as you think it would have been produced by the learner's NS counterpart under similar circumstances. (For example, if the learner is a teenager speaking in a particular social situation, their counterpart is a

NS teenager speaking in the same situation. Sometimes you may need to make two or three possible reconstructions, because you do not know the learner's intended meaning, and you have to guess. Do not worry when this happens; indeterminacy is a basic characteristic of learner language.) Then compare the learner's production to the reconstruction(s), identifying which part of each learner utterance differs from the reconstructed version(s). Your reconstructions of one of Xue's errors might look like this:

2    Mm, because our school force us to learn English because um it's, it's a trend
2a   Mm because our school forced us/ because it was/ a trend
2b   because it was a requirement at our school/ because it was/ popular
2c   because it was required at our school to learn English/, because it was/ a fad

## 2 Explain the errors

You will have to make a decision about each difference your reconstruction has identified. Do you think it is an **error** (systematic) or a **mistake** (a one-time slip like one that a NS might make)? Since we only have a few language samples, it will be hard to be sure, but see if you can find evidence for one or the other. If you decide it is an error, identify possible causes for the error, such as native language (NL) transfer, intralingual error, induced error, **communication strategy**, and so on. Be open to the possibility that a single error may have more than one cause. For example, native language transfer and overgeneralization of NL rules may both be forces that lead the learner to make a given error.

---

**EXERCISE 3.2**

*Rodrigo*    *Xue*

### Error Analysis: Rodrigo and Xue

**DVD 1.1 AND 1.3: INTERVIEWS**

Watch Rodrigo's and Xue's Interviews in DVD 1.1 and 1.3 while you read the first 25 lines of the corresponding transcripts (see pages 130–31, 139).

1  Mark all the errors you hear on a photocopy of the transcript. Following the guidelines above, an error is something that is different from your reconstruction of the utterance as you think an equivalent NS would have produced it. So, for example, a sentence fragment is not an error because NSs speak in fragments. A colloquial expression is not an error if an equivalent NS (for example, same age and educational level) would use it. If the same error occurs twice, count it as two tokens of the same error.

2  Fill out Table 3.1 for at least six each of Rodrigo's and Xue's errors. Try to include examples at each level: phonology, morphology, syntax, and vocabulary.

   a  In Column 1, indicate the line number where you found the error.

   b  In Column 2, copy the error and the words that immediately preceded and followed the error, and make a note on whether it is an error of phonology, morphology, syntax, or vocabulary (for example, line 1, this house /dɪs aus/, phonology).

   c  In Column 3, indicate your reconstruction(s) of the learner's erroneous utterance. If there is more than one possible reconstruction, list them.

   d  In Column 4, indicate possible causes of the error. To find out if the cause might be NL transfer, you may need to consult a resource providing **contrastive**

> **analyses**, such as Swan and Smith (2001); consult Chang (2001) for Xue's, and Coe (2001) for Rodrigo's errors.

3  If you want to, you can enter similar information on other errors you have found for Rodrigo and for Xue on a separate piece of paper, using the format in Table 3.1.

4  Now reflect on what you see in your data analysis by considering the following questions. (If you are doing this work in a class, compare your answers to these questions with a classmate and explore why your answers might have differed).

   a  Compare the learners' errors. Did one of these learners seem to make *more* errors (in terms of either types or tokens) than the other, or make *different types* of errors than the other? Explain.

   b  What psycholinguistic processes might have caused their errors? Where their errors were different, was this because of the influence of their differing NLs, or for some other reason? Where their errors were the same, why do you think this was?

   c  Is number of errors a good measure of proficiency? How about type of error?

   d  What did you learn from this error analysis that you might be able to use if you were Xue's or Rodrigo's English teacher?

| **Name of learner:** *Rodrigo* | | | |
|---|---|---|---|
| **Line number** | **Phrase with error (phonology, morphology, syntax, vocabulary)** | **Target language reformulation(s)** | **Cause of error** |
|  |  |  |  |
|  |  |  |  |
|  |  |  |  |
|  |  |  |  |
|  |  |  |  |
|  |  |  |  |
|  |  |  |  |
|  |  |  |  |
|  |  |  |  |
|  |  |  |  |
|  |  |  |  |

| Name of learner: *Xue* | | | |
|---|---|---|---|
| **Line number** | **Phrase with error (phonology, morphology, syntax, vocabulary)** | **Target language reformulation(s)** | **Cause of error** |
| | | | |
| | | | |
| | | | |
| | | | |
| | | | |
| | | | |
| | | | |
| | | | |
| | | | |
| | | | |
| | | | |
| | | | |

*Table 3.1 Error Analysis/Contrastive Analysis (EA/CA) Form*

## Error Analysis of Two Learners' Pronunciation

You probably noticed that Xue and Rodrigo had some pronunciation errors. Pronunciation is often the most noticeable feature of a learner's interlanguage (IL). This is often what we mean when we say someone 'has an accent'. Their pronunciation patterns or their **interlanguage phonology** may be different from the local standard. Perhaps their IL phonology is influenced by their NL phonology.

In Chapter 2, we discussed the influence of NL **transfer** on learner language. There are several areas where the sound system of English differs from that of Chinese (Chang 2001) and French (Walther 2001). We use this information to structure Exercise 3.3, focusing on Xue's pronunciation, and Exercise 3.4, on Jeanne's pronunciation. You can do either one, or both, depending on your interests.

**EXERCISE 3.3**

**Error Analysis: Xue's Pronunciation**

DVD 1.3: INTERVIEW

We begin by contrasting English and Chinese phonology to identify possible areas of learner difficulty:

- English has a (th) sound (both the voiced /ð/ as in 'this', and the voiceless /θ/ as in 'think'), but Chinese does not have either. We might expect Chinese learners of

*Xue*

English to have trouble with the English (th) sound.

- English has many words that end in consonant clusters (for example, 'hard', 'trend'), while Chinese has very few words that end in either consonants or consonant clusters. A Chinese learner of English might find final consonant clusters hard to pronounce.

Listen to Xue's pronunciation of voiced (th) /ð/ and of final consonant clusters in DVD 1.3. Xue occasionally produces /d/ for /ð/; she says /dey/ for 'they' in 'they don't really to, listen' (Interview transcript, line 20). See if you can find other cases where she pronounces words like 'this', 'that', or 'the' in a similar manner. (One of our students recommends watching Xue's mouth on the video to determine when she says /d/ and when she says /ð/.) Final consonant clusters may also be difficult for Chinese learners of English. Listen for Xue's pronunciation of words like 'hard', 'blackboard', 'world', and 'trend'. Photocopy and use Table 3.2 to list examples of words (with line numbers, and the preceding and following words) where Xue has difficulty with each phonological target: (th) /ð/ and final consonant clusters. If you are using this book in a class, discuss your findings with a classmate.

| Name: | | Name: | |
|---|---|---|---|
| **Phonological error:** | | **Phonological error:** | |
| | | | |
| | | | |
| | | | |
| | | | |
| | | | |
| | | | |
| | | | |
| | | | |

*Table 3.2 Phonological Errors in Context*

Photocopiable © Oxford University Press

---

**EXERCISE 3.4**     **Error Analysis: Jeanne's Pronunciation**

 DVD 1.6: INTERVIEW

We begin by contrasting English and French phonology to identify possible areas of learner difficulty:

- English has a (th) sound (both the voiced /ð/ as in 'this', and the voiceless /θ/ as in 'think'), but French does not have either. We might expect French-speaking learners of English to have trouble with the English (th) sound. As we did with Xue above, we will focus only on the voiced (th) /ð/ in words like 'that'. We will be particularly interested to see what phoneme Jeanne uses to substitute for /ð/. Substitutes could be either /d/ (as in 'dis' and 'dat') or /z/ (as in 'zis' and 'zat').
- The consonant sound /h/, as in English 'house', does not exist in French. A French-

speaking learner of English might omit the phoneme /h/ in such words. Watch Jeanne's interview in DVD 1.6. Photocopy and use Table 3.2 again, to identify places where Jeanne has difficulty producing both voiced (th) /ð/ and (h). When you are finished, compare your list with that of someone else in class. If you can, compare the types of errors made by Xue and Jeanne.

## *Limitations of Error Analysis*

Up to this point, we have looked at learner language in terms of the errors that we noticed in the speech of our English language learners. Among other things, we identified morphemes that the learners do or do not use. Next we consider morpheme usage in video segments you may not yet have watched. For example, Catrine does not always mark third person singular verbs with –*s*. In the Retell Task in DVD 3.5, she says (lines 8–9):

1   **C**  And now, he find his friend, he see his friend in the car, and he
       think his friend can give me … And, his friend stop …

When Catrine is writing the story (WR 4.5 Narrative Task), she does better (for example, she writes 'meets' in line 1), but sometimes makes the same error (lines 3–4):

3–4   **C**  And her friend's daughter reach in her bag.

Chun and Xue help each other during DVD 5.2: Jigsaw Task, to remember to mark plural nouns with –*s* (lines 3–5):

3   **C**  in the picture, they're just have the leaf.
      **X**  Leaves?
      **C**  Yeah. Leafs.

If you did Exercise 3.2, you watched the learners and read their transcripts to identify errors such as these, not just errors with omission of required morphemes but also errors of pronunciation, grammar (for example, word order, tense, and aspect), and vocabulary. You noted cases in which these errors could be traced to transfer from the learners' NLs. For example, Chinese grammar does not mark whether nouns are plural or not. Perhaps Chun and Xue have difficulty with this one point because of negative transfer from Chinese.

However, in Chapter 2 we made the point that learner language is not just a collection of errors and mistakes, but rather is best seen as a system of distinctive rules of phonology, morphology, syntax, and lexicon. Error analysis is just one way to look at learner language, but it has limitations. One limitation is that it leads us to ignore places where the learner seems to get a given form right. In other words, we only see half of the picture. If we can systematically identify those instances where a learner gets a form right, then we may have gained some pedagogical leverage in figuring out how to extend that accuracy to more problematic instances.

A complete description of learner language has to include all the possible instances of any given form – those that appear to be correct, as well as those that do not. Let's look at line 9 of Chun's Interview transcript, when she says:

9  **C**  Because we have the class.

In this clause, the form of the verb appears to be correct. But let's look at this line in context. It is the answer to a question by the interviewer (Interview, lines 8–9):

8  **I**  And why did you start [learning English]?

   **C**  Because we have the class.

Context shows us that Chun is referring to a past time, when she was in China. In this context, she should have used 'had'. If we look further, we see that Chun never uses the irregular past form 'had'; she always uses 'have,' for present as well as past time. You can see the pattern more clearly in Interview, lines 54–5: 'when I arrived here, I think I have a lot of words I don't know'. This example shows us one reason why error analysis – just counting errors – can be limiting; it can hide from us systematic patterns in learner language, such as the systematic way that Chun is using the word 'have'. It will be very helpful for Chun's teacher to understand this in order to know how and when to provide correction for this verb which is very frequently used in English discourse.

Another limitation of error analysis is that it only tabulates cases where the learner tried to produce a difficult form and failed. Error analysis does not identify cases where the learner avoided that form in the first place because it was difficult. Lightbown and Spada (2006: 82) put it this way:

> … learners sometimes avoid using certain features of language that they perceive to be difficult for them. This avoidance may lead to the absence of certain errors, leaving the analyst without information about the learners' developing interlanguage. That is, the absence of particular errors is difficult to interpret. The phenomenon of 'avoidance' may itself be a part of the learner's systematic second language performance.

An IL analysis can improve on error analysis both by helping us compare the correct and the incorrect attempts to produce a given linguistic feature, and by helping us to identify instances where the learner may be completely avoiding the production of a target linguistic feature because of its difficulty. There are many different kinds of IL analysis. We will begin in this chapter with one that is similar to an error analysis: a **target-like use analysis** (TLU) that counts both the errors and the correct uses of a form.

*Target like Use*

# Interlanguage (TLU) Analysis

Let's now return to our learner transcripts and do an IL analysis that counts both the correct and incorrect uses of a given form. What features of learner language should we look for, if we do not look first for obvious errors?

## *Pronouncing English Phonemes*

We will begin, in Exercise 3.5, by revisiting our earlier error analysis of Xue's pronunciation of English **phonemes**. This time, we will not just look at her errors; we will also look at contexts where she produced these phonemes accurately. A TLU analysis will enable us to identify new patterns; in some contexts learners will

produce those phonemes more accurately than in others. (See Ma...
approach to analyzing interlanguage phonology.)

**EXERCISE 3.5**

*Xue*

**TLU Analysis of Xue's Pronunciation of Voiced (th) /ð/**

DVD 1.3: INTERVIEW

In Exercise 3.3, we asked you to do an error analysis of Xue's production of voiced (th) /ð/. In this exercise, we will ask you to do a TLU analysis of her production of that same phoneme. In Table 3.3 below, list those incorrect and correct instances side by side. To identify contexts that favor correct, as opposed to incorrect, productions, include the sounds that preceded and followed the voiced (th) /ð/. Then, looking at the data you have entered in Table 3.3, answer the following questions:

1  What new information have you obtained about Xue's IL phonology by listing correct productions of voiced (th) /ð/ next to incorrect ones? Are there phonological contexts in which (th) /ð/ is produced more correctly than others? Specify.

2  If you like number crunching, you can derive a quantitative measure using the data in Table 3.3, with Pica's (1983) equation for target-like use or TLU: the number of correct uses in obligatory context divided by (the number of obligatory contexts) + (the number of incorrect contexts). It is a fraction in which the numerator is the number of correct uses in obligatory context, and the denominator adds together the number of obligatory contexts and the number of incorrect contexts. This equation provides a quantitative measure to compare learners in terms of how target-like their use of a linguistic expression is.

3  How does the new information provided by TLU analysis suggest a teaching strategy for (th) /ð/?

*43 instances of TH*
*none incorrect contexts*

| Name: | |
|---|---|
| **Incorrect form in context** | **Correct form in context** |
| | |
| | |
| | |
| | |
| | |
| | |
| | |
| | |

*Table 3.3 Correct and Incorrect Versions of Target Form*
Photocopiable © Oxford University Press

*This Activity is an Interlanguage Analysis.*

*We are going to do a TLU (Target Like Use) Analysis on a Second Language student, Xue's production of the phoneme "th"*
*We'll be recording the Incorrect and correct form of the phoneme "TH" in context. So jot down the words before + after*

*TLU analysis helps to identify patterns.*

## Correct and Incorrect Use of English Morphemes

In Exercise 3.6 below, we will ask you to look at the **third person singular morphemes** these learners use to mark present tense verbs, not just their incorrect uses, or errors, as we did in our general error analysis in Exercise 3.2 above, but also their correct uses of the third person singular morpheme –*s*. We will look at their verbs in DVD Segment 3: Retell Task.

| | |
|---|---|
| **EXERCISE 3.6** | **Third Person Singular –*s* on Present Tense Verbs** |

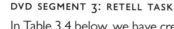

DVD SEGMENT 3: RETELL TASK

*Rodrigo*   *Antonio*

*Xue*   *Chun*

*Catrine*   *Jeanne*

In Table 3.4 below, we have created lists of all the third person singular present tense verbs (that is, verbs whose subjects can be replaced by 'he', 'she', or 'it') that were used by our six English language learners in DVD 3: Retell Task. In English, such verbs are typically marked with the final morpheme –*s*:

• In verbs like 'clean' as in 'he cleans the window'
• In **auxiliaries** like 'is' as in 'it is snowing'
• In **copula** 'is' as in 'he is a student'.

In English, the present tense is often used in telling stories; when used in this manner it is called 'the historical present'. While NSs may tell a story entirely in the present tense (or entirely in the past tense), it is also not unusual for them in telling a story to alternate between their use of the present tense and the past tense in a patterned way. For example, they may use one tense (usually past tense) to mark background information, and the other (usually present tense) for verbs that move the action of the story forward.

The shifts our English language learners make between present and past tense in telling stories may or may not be so systematic. This can make it hard to look only at third person singular present tense morphemes in these stories. We have tried to simplify your analysis of this form in Table 3.4 below by listing only those verbs clearly referencing present time in our learners' DVD 3: Retell Task.

| **Rodrigo** | | **Antonio** | |
|---|---|---|---|
| I | he is Ahmed | I | This guy is, Ahmed. |
| I | he's late | 3 | Ahmed, eh, try wake up |
| I–2 | he, eh, have he he, he has to, uh school | 3 | he's late |
| 2 | your class, is nine o'clock | 4 | it's, eight |
| 2–3 | he's, I don't know, sleeping | 9 | he have to, to take a, a bus |
| 5 | he is, n- anxious | 10 | he, don't, don't find |
| 7–8 | he is very, eh, anxious because it's late | 11 | he's late |
| 10 | he don't, don't take, your class | 11 | it's far |
| 10 | it's OK | 11 | it's winter |
| 12 | Mohammed, eh, smile | 12 | it's cold |
| 13 | he is inside the car | 14 | it's a, lucky |
| 13 | he clean, cleanest, up the window | 14 | it's, a, a, Ahmed friend? |

| | 16 | he say the, a, a ride? |
|---|---|---|
| | 16 | it's a lucky. Lucky man |
| | 17 | his friend, clean, the the window |
| | 17 | the snow, no allow the see? |
| | 20 | Ahmed is say, hello |

| **Xue** | | | **Chun** | | |
|---|---|---|---|---|---|
| | 6 | his room is so messy | | 1 | it's a winter morning |
| | 6 | then he go go outside | | 1 | the boy is a student |
| | 7 | it's snowing outside | | 2–3 | he's late |
| | 7 | he wants to take bus to school | | 2–3 | he's very hurry, to find the money |
| | 7–8 | he wants to find some change | | 4 | he very hurry to to catch the bus |
| | 8 | and he looking for change | | 5 | he want to uh take a take a ride |
| | | | | 7 | he just do this (gestures with thumb) |
| | | | | 9 | and then he think the car was, agree, |
| | | | | 9–10 | the driver want to take him to the school |
| | | | | 10 | so he get in the car |
| | | | | 10–11 | He get in the car but the driver get off the car |
| | | | | 11–12 | he want to, he just want to clean the windshield |
| | | | | 12–13 | the driver want to take him to the school |
| | | | | 15 | the driver just clean the the windshield |
| | | | | 18 | he's a little bit late |

| **Catrine** | | | **Jeanne** | | |
|---|---|---|---|---|---|
| | 3 | this is Ahmed. | | 3 | Ahmed is, wake up, late for school |
| | 3 | He just, wake up late for school | | 5 | In his way to, go to school, and, he find out |
| | 5 | Now he's looking for the keys | | | |
| | 5–6 | and he's wearing his jacket | | | |
| | 6 | it's, cold | | | |
| | 6 | It's Minnesota. | | | |
| | 6 | And now, uh, he miss the bus | | | |
| | 6–7 | and he's, trying to catch the bus | | | |
| | 7 | but it's too late | | | |
| | 8 | And now, he find his friend | | | |
| | 8 | he see his friend in the car | | | |
| | 8–9 | he think his friend can give me a ri-, can give him a ride | | | |

| 9–10 | And, his friend stop to clean, the snow | | |
| 10 | and he, get in the car | | |
| 10–11 | And now, he is happy | | |
| 11 | because he has a ride now. | | |
| 11 | And his friend, is, asking him | | |

*Table 3.4 Obligatory Contexts for Third Person Singular Present Tense Verb Morphology*

1 Analyzing the data in Table 3.4, in terms of both correct and incorrect uses of third person singular –s, what patterns do you see for each learner?
2 Is there a tendency to mark –s correctly on copulas or auxiliaries, but not on **main verb**s? Is this tendency the same for all six learners, or only for some? Describe it.
3 Is there a tendency to put the third person singular –s only on some main verbs and not others? What pattern do you see in this tendency among the six learners? This pattern is surprising; what can explain it?
4 Given their patterns of –s marking, what teaching approach would you use to teach the third person singular –s pattern to each of the six learners?

We conclude this chapter by inviting you to branch out on your own. Apply the approach we have been practicing in this chapter by searching in the transcripts of the interviews of at least two learners for their correct and incorrect uses of one other English morpheme. You could look at one of these: plural –s on nouns, copula 'be', or auxiliary 'be'. Use a contrastive analysis (CA) such as Swan and Smith (2001) to explain any patterns you find.

# Summary

In this chapter, we have tried our hand at a couple of different kinds of learner language analysis, targeting verb morphology and pronunciation. We did an error analysis to determine whether language differences revealed by CA predicted learner error. We also did some error analyses focusing on learner phonology, or pronunciation. Next, we looked for both incorrect and correct instances of the target morpheme.

In Chapter 4, we will turn to an exploration of developmental stages of some key structures in these learners' language. We will consider the way sequences and stages of development can be identified in the learner language produced when learners are focused on meaning rather than accuracy. We will focus on the sequence in which possessive determiners, negation, and questions develop in ESL.

## *Further Reading*

**Chang, J.** 2001. 'Chinese speakers' in M. Swan and B. Smith (eds.). *Learner English: A Teacher's Guide to Interference and Other Problems.* Cambridge: Cambridge University Press.

**Coe, N.** 2001. 'Speakers of Spanish and Catalan' in M. Swan and B. Smith (eds.). *Learner English: A Teacher's Guide to Interference and Other Problems.* Cambridge: Cambridge University Press.

**Ellis, R.** 1994. Chapter 2 'Learner errors and error analysis'. *The Study of Second Language Acquisition.* Oxford: Oxford University Press.

**Ellis, R.** and **G. Barkhuizen**. 2005. Chapter 3 'Error analysis', Chapter 4 'Obligatory occasion analysis'. *Analysing Learner Language.* Oxford: Oxford University Press.

**Gass, S. M.** and **L. Selinker.** 2008. Chapter 4 'The role of the native language: An historical overview', Chapter 5 'Recent perspectives on the role of previously known languages'. *Second Language Acquisition: An Introductory Course* (3rd edn.). New York: Routledge.

**Walther, C.** 2001. 'French speakers' in M. Swan and B. Smith (eds.). *Learner English: A Teacher's Guide to Interference and Other Problems.* Cambridge: Cambridge University Press.

# 4 EXPLORING DEVELOPMENTAL SEQUENCES

## Introduction

In Chapter 3, we began our exploration of the linguistic forms that make up learner language by doing error analyses: describing errors made by the learners at the level of phonology, morphology, syntax, and lexicon. We used contrastive analysis (CA) to identify possible native language (NL) sources of these errors, and we described learners' use of phonemes and morphemes using both error analysis and target-like use analysis. In this chapter, we turn to an exploration of some linguistic structures that are known to develop in established sequences regardless of the learner's NL or the way they were taught. In this chapter we will:

- discuss learner language structures that are acquired in developmental sequences, and the way those sequences may overlap with each other
- consider the methodology for identifying stages of development of particular linguistic structures
- review the stages of development of two learner language structures, examine samples of learner language for evidence of developmental stages of each one, and consider pedagogical implications. The two structures we will examine are negation and questions.

## The Importance of Developmental Sequences in Learner Language

We began this book with Corder's insight that when it comes to linguistic structures, input does not equal intake. Corder meant that no matter what order teachers present target language (TL) structures in, those structures always seem to emerge in the same order over time. The linguistic forms that express negation, ask questions, mark possession, or signal past time in meaningful communication all seem to develop in predictable sequences or stages quite independently of the teacher's syllabus. Research has now shown conclusively that regardless of the way learners are taught, and regardless of their NL, these structures can be seen to develop in the same orders in meaning-focused learner language. We need to understand the nature of this 'built-in syllabus' (Corder 1967) – this strong tendency that learners have to produce the same simple linguistic structures initially, and then over time to gradually change those structures in stages to become more like the ones the teacher had in mind.

Developmental stages can be studied longitudinally (for example, one individual over time) or cross-sectionally (for example, a group of learners at a single point in time). Longitudinally, we sample an individual learner's production of linguistic forms such as questions or negation over a period of time – even over years (for example, Schumann 1979; Liu 1991, 2000). Cross-sectionally, we sample the production of groups of learners who are at different ability levels (for example, first-year, second-year, third-year classes), and then infer that group differences reflect individual longitudinal changes (for example, see White 1998).

Both types of study show that instruction does not seem to strongly or permanently influence the developmental sequences of learner language as it is used in communication. At best, instruction can speed up the rate at which learners go through those sequences, but it cannot make learners skip stages, or alter the order of the stages. So, for example, Lightbown (1983a, b) showed that audio-lingual instruction (pattern practice) only temporarily improved the morpheme accuracy of ESL learners compared to learners who were uninstructed; after the drilling stopped, instructed learners reverted to the same accuracy order as uninstructed learners. Similarly, Pavesi (1984, 1986) showed instruction had no impact on the acquisition order of EFL relative clauses, and Pienemann (1987, 1989) showed that while instruction could speed the rate of acquisition of 'easy' word-order rules of German as a second language, instruction did not change the natural order by which rules were acquired. Even when NL structures are similar to TL structures, learner language follows the built-in syllabus.

Can we see evidence of developmental sequences in the language of our six learners? Obviously, we see these learners at only one point in time, so we cannot watch their learner language evolve longitudinally over time. Nor do we have proficiency scores for these learners, so we cannot do a precise cross-sectional study. But because some of the six learners have studied English longer than others, we might expect, in very general terms, to see them produce different developmental stages of learner language structures. Antonio and Rodrigo, who have had the least exposure to English input, might be expected to produce lower-level stages of these structures while Catrine and Jeanne, who have had more exposure to the language, might produce higher-level stages.

## Identifying Developmental Stages

Let's begin by looking at the learners' use of possessive **determiners** 'his' and 'her' in English. In English, these determiners take the gender of the possessor. A male possessor requires use of 'his', and a female possessor requires use of 'her'. This is not the case in languages like French or Spanish where determiners take the gender of the possessed item. According to White (1998) and Lightbown and Spada (2006: 88–90), the basic sequence that speakers of French and Spanish follow when learning English is:

1 Use 'the' or 'your' for all persons, genders, and numbers

2 Overgeneralize either 'his' or 'her' to most contexts

3 Use 'his' or 'her' correctly in all contexts.

Movement from one stage to another is gradual, not 'all or nothing'. Developmental stages do not turn on and off like old-fashioned light switches; rather each developmental stage seems to operate more like a dimmer switch, each one gradually fading out as another fades in. The acquisition of Stage 2 forms may not mean the replacement of all Stage 1 forms, and there is a period of transition in the movement from one developmental stage to the next. At such times we may see a learner shift back and forth in his or her usage of a feature. Sometimes even within a single sentence we can see a learner start out with a Stage 1 form, and then self-correct and begin again with a Stage 2 form. In his Narrative Task, line 10, Antonio runs through all three stages of possessive determiners before he settles on the final form: '… your, his, her her her mom …' This **variation** is something we can come to expect as an inherent feature of learner language; learner language is always in the process of development and formation.

As a result of this variation, different measures have been used to indicate when a learner language structure has developed to a higher stage. Schumann (1979), in studying negation, said 80 per cent of the negatives produced in three data collection sessions in a row had to be at Stage 2 in order to say that acquisition had reached Stage 2. Pienemann and Johnston (1987), in studying questions, took just ONE single instance of an independently produced Stage 2 form (i.e. not an imitation) to be evidence that questions had reached Stage 2. The choice of one or the other criterion is probably somewhat arbitrary, but once you have chosen to use either criterion (or any other criterion) you should be consistent, particularly if your goal is to compare one learner's developmental stage to another's.

# Developmental Stages: Negation and Questions in English

In the next sections, we will look at the language of the six learners to find examples of developmental sequences of negation and questions. At the end of the chapter, we refer you to studies documenting developmental sequences in other interlanguage (IL) structures: possessive determiners, relative clause types, and tense, in case you want to explore the development of those structures as well.

## *English Negation*

There is wide agreement on the developmental stages that L2 learners go through in acquiring English negation; both longitudinal and cross-sectional studies have identified the same stages. Though there are more elaborated descriptions of these stages in the research literature (Schumann 1979; Clahsen 1988; Berdan 1996), the basic stages of English negation are:

**Stage 1:** *No + X.* The negative markers *no* or *not* immediately precede the thing being negated (word, phrase, or sentence).
*No is happy. Not my friend.*

**Stage 2:** *No/Not/Don't + Verb.* Negative markers are placed before verb, but are never marked for person, number, or tense.
*He don't have job. They not working.*

**Stage 3:** *Aux. + Neg.* Auxiliary verbs like *are*, *is*, and *can* can now be followed by a negative marker. The negative element still precedes all other verbs.
*I can't play. They aren't there. He don't have job.*

**Stage 4:** Analyzed *do* (*doesn't, didn't*). *Do* is marked for person, number, and tense. Tense may mark both *do* and the main verb.
*He doesn't work here. And we don't. I didn't see her. He didn't went.*

As negation develops, the rule that underlies each of these stages is replaced by another rule in the next stage. So we do not expect native speakers (NSs) or Stage 4 learners to say 'No is happy', or 'He don't play'. It is tricky because a form like *don't* in Stage 3 may look 'correct' to you and indistinguishable in some contexts from a *don't* that appears in Stage 4, but the Stage 3 *don't* is produced by a different rule (it is a single lexical item) from that which produces the *don't* in Stage 4 (it is two lexical items: *do+ not*). In Exercise 4.1, we will look for examples of these four stages of negation in all the learners' language.

---

**EXERCISE 4.1**

*Rodrigo*    *Antonio*

*Xue*      *Chun*

*Catrine*      *Jeanne*

**Negation: All Learners**

DVD SEGMENTS 1–6

In Table 4.1 we list all the negative constructions each learner produced, in all tasks combined. Referring to Table 4.1, answer the following questions; remember that your answers may legitimately vary depending on the criteria you decide to use in identifying stages.

1 Are there any clear examples of Stage 1 (*No + X*) negation produced by any of the learners? If you find such cases, list them with speaker name, segment, and line numbers. Describe any pattern you see in this list.

2 Stage 3 negation (**unanalyzed don't**) is typically recognizable because of what is NOT there: we usually infer that the negation system is in Stage 3 if we only see *don't* and never see examples of *doesn't* or *didn't*. Which speakers in Table 4.1 use *don't*, but NEVER use the words *doesn't* or *didn't* in expressing negation? Do you think that you can conclude that their system of negation is at a Stage 3 developmental level?

3 A negation pattern that always occurs with the same verb and the same subject may be a memorized chunk, and not the result of application of developmental 'rules' of negation. (Such 'chunks' are produced relatively fluently, with unusually target-like blendings of consonants and vowels or syntactic features, and can be used relatively frequently.) Are there cases where a learner in Table 4.1 seems to have memorized and used over and over again an entire 'chunk' that contains a negative element? List examples of possible negation chunks with speaker name, segment, and line numbers. Explain why you think they might be memorized chunks.

4 Are there examples of Stage 4 negative constructions where the learner marks past

tense on both 'do' and the main verb? List them, with speaker name, segment, and line numbers. Why do you think this pattern of double tense marking, on both *do* and the main verb, occurs?

5 Antonio and Rodrigo produce a negation pattern that does not fit any of the developmental sequences for learner language negation. What are possible reasons for the negation structures of Antonio in DVD 1.2 (Interview), lines 36 and 75, and Rodrigo in DVD 6.1 (Comparison Task), lines 6–7? How would you account for the fact that the developmental sequences do not predict this pattern?

6 Which of the six learner languages seem to be at the lowest stage of development in negation? Why do you think so? Which learner language seems to be at the highest? Why? What pedagogical treatment, if any, is called for in response to each of these two learners, based on your analysis of the negation forms they produce?

| *Antonio* | |
|---|---|
| **Segment 1: Interview (DVD 1.2)** | |
| 7 | And I, I I can't do it. |
| 29 | Yeah uh the the teacher, um, don't use, the, the the tools? |
| 34 | with tools, that, eh that, um that the student can't, learn the more, easy. |
| 36 | Mm, games, mm, and the and the other, other things. In in Mexico no. |
| 55 | I need speak, eh because, the people, throughout, my office, and, don't, |
| 56 | eh eh, in, I, how you say in, m, don't use Spanish |
| 63 | I don't know |
| 75 | Yeah, the other way first noun and and second an adjective. Here no. |
| **Segment 3: Retell Task (DVD 3.2)** | |
| 4 | And, I don't know I can't I can't see. |
| 10 | to go the the school and, uh he, don't, don't find. |
| 17–18 | his his friend, clean, the the window, um, because, the snow, no allow the see? |
| **Segment 4: Narrative Task (DVD 4.2)** | |
| 2 | I don't know |
| 4 | I don't know |
| 6 | I don't know |
| 10 | I don't know |
| 10–11 | her mom, mm, tell, eh, "You, don't do that." |
| **Narrative Task Written (WR 4.2)** | |
| 3 | Her mom doesn't |
| 4 | didn't know the fact. Obviosly, wasn't pay it. |
| 5 | "don't do that." |
| **Segment 5: Jigsaw Task (DVD 5.1)** | |
| 9 | I don't know. |

| **Segment 6: Comparison Task (DVD 6.1)** | |
|---|---|
| 4 | it's no clean |

| ***Rodrigo*** | |
|---|---|
| **Segment 1: Interview (DVD 1.1)** | |
| 2 | Um, no, sorry, I |
| 15 | The teacher he are, not interact in, speak, or, with, eh eh students. |
| 25 | I don't know |
| 27 | But, no is good, in Mexico no is good. |
| 30–1 | I I I I can't, eh, talk when American people difficult, I I I can't, eh, take, the food … |
| 43 | I think my English is is, no is, is not good but … |
| 44 | I don't know |
| 46 | If if I don't speak English, I never never, I I don't learn English. |
| 48 | I don't know |
| 49 | I I I start learn English, but, never speak English in Mexico. |
| **Segment 2: Question Task (DVD 2.1)** | |
| 13 | Yeah no, level. What lev- |
| 50 | I don't know. |
| **Segment 3: Retell Task (DVD 3.1)** | |
| 10 | And and, he, eh, eh, don't, he don't, don't take, your class … |
| **Segment 4: Narrative Task (DVD 4.1)** | |
| 2 | I don't know |
| 2 | I don't know |
| 3 | I don't know |
| 6 | I don't know |
| 9 | I don't know |
| 13 | I don't know |
| 14 | I don't know |
| 15 | I don't know |
| 18 | I don't know |
| 20 | she can, she can't, eh, and the child, and, she can't, see, your bag. |
| 25 | I don't know |
| **Narrative Task Written (WR 4.1)** | |
| 5 | because she don't know that in your bag is a bottle milk |
| **Segment 5: Jigsaw Task (DVD 5.1)** | |
| 5 | I don't know what is |
| 5–6 | I don't know. |

| Segment 6: Comparison Task (DVD 6.1) | |
|---|---|
| 6–7 | and this house no. |

| Chun | |
|---|---|
| **Segment 1: Interview (DVD 1.4)** | |
| 29 | Um we will do um examination not the not very mm it's it's just uh the practice |
| 54 | I have a lot of words I don't know. |
| 64 | We don't have host brother and sisters. |
| 68 | we just say something that not very important yeah |
| **Segment 2: Question Task (DVD 2.4)** | |
| 7 | And so I have no question about this picture. |
| 49 | So, when the the driver get off the car he didn't found the the boy? |
| 68 | So he isn't [lake]. |
| **Segment 3: Retell Task (DVD 3.4)** | |
| 11 | because the driver mm didn't saw, don't saw him |
| **Narrative Task Written (WR 4.4)** | |
| 5 | But the old lady just doesn't realize it. |
| **Segment 5: Jigsaw Task (DVD 5.2)** | |
| 18 | No, No. I don't have a garage. |
| 36 | Uh, no. I just have I just have two windows. |

| Xue | |
|---|---|
| **Segment 1: Interview (DVD 1.3)** | |
| 17 | most of our classmates, they didn't like to learn English |
| 20 | many of them are, they don't really to, listen to that teacher |
| 27–8 | And actually I don't like grammars at all. |
| 55–6 | but I don't like that |
| 57–8 | a lot of questions and about those something I don't really understand mm |
| **Segment 3: Retell Task (DVD 3.3)** | |
| 5 | but he can't he can't find his car keys |
| 9 | so he can't catch the bus. |
| **Segment 4: Narrative Task (DVD 4.3)** | |
| 13 | but she, she can't find anything to play |
| 17–18 | so they didn't find that girl was doing that kind of naughty things |
| 18 | they didn't notice, notice that that girl |
| 20 | and nothing's going to happen. |
| 21–2 | they didn't notice that she has a vinegar |
| 27 | She didn't want that |

| **Narrative Task Written (WR 4.3)** | |
|---|---|
| 11 | and pretended that there was nothing happened. |
| 12 | Both of the adults didn't notice that |
| 14 | She didn't pay much attention to it. |
| 15–16 | there is a bottle of veniger that she didn't buy at all |
| **Segment 5: Jigsaw Task (DVD 5.2)** | |
| 41 | No because the the sky was covered |
| **Segment 6: Comparison Task (DVD 6.2)** | |
| 13 | But a lot of house they don't have fence around them. |
| 23 | mm they don't have, they didn't want to live in that apartment |
| 23–4 | so they, they don't want to share um the garage with others, other peoples |

| ***Catrine*** | |
|---|---|
| **Segment 1: Interview (DVD 1.5)** | |
| 23 | No. |
| 37 | I don't speak English with my brothers and sister but sometimes, um, like, I |
| 38 | can say like a word in English to them but not it's like speaking for long time. Yes. |
| 39 | I don't speak, really English with my brothers. |
| **Segment 2: Question Task (DVD 2.5)** | |
| 7 | Why didn't he, put his alarm? Like, why didn't he set, his alarm? |
| 10 | Why can't he stay and, look for a ride right now? |
| 26 | Why, the, bus driver can't, stop for him? |
| 46 | Why can't he help, his friend clean, the, remove the snow on the car? |
| **Segment 3: Retell Task (DVD 3.5)** | |
| 3–4 | he didn't set he just realized that he didn't set his alarm. |
| 5 | he can't find the keys |
| 7–8 | the bus driver can't, hear, or see him. |
| **Segment 4: Narrative Task (DVD 4.5)** | |
| 4 | because they didn't see each other for a long time ago |
| 6 | I can't really see. |
| 7 | And sh, she can't see. She can't see if in her bag, like she can't see if there's |
| **Segment 5: Jigsaw Task (DVD 5.3)** | |
| 8–9 | I can't see the whole house |
| 21 | No, my house, doesn't have a, doesn't have woods. |
| 25–6 | I, cannot see the other part of the house. |

| **Segment 6: Comparison Task (DVD 6.3)** | |
|---|---|
| I | Don't know if you understand what I say. |
| 11 | maybe there is, not much people living in, the house. |
| 19 | Maybe there's nobody living in that house. Um doesn't really mean that the other |
| 20 | house has more money, doesn't really but, maybe, there's no one living in the other |
| 21 | house. No one to take care of the house. |

| *Jeanne* | |
|---|---|
| **Segment 1: Interview (DVD 1.6)** | |
| 21 | No, just grammar. Writing let me see uh no, I never write in in English. |
| 23 | No, never wrote in English. |
| 24 | We had like some speaking too but not every day. |
| 27 | "No way, we're not going to do it," because we did not know a lot of word" |
| 31 | It wasn't every day. |
| 35 | we don't usually speak English |
| 40 | Mm, uh, not really |
| 41 | but, there's nothing, nothing. |
| 45–6 | I don't know |
| 48 | I don't know |
| **Segment 2: Question Task (DVD 2.6)** | |
| 55 | Oh. Mohammed didn't see him. |
| **Segment 3: Retell Task (DVD 3.6)** | |
| I | you did not tell me the name of this guy. |
| 3 | He did not set the alarm. |
| 4 | he wasn't really late for school. |
| 7 | he did not find it. |
| 9 | Mohammed did not see him. |
| 10–11 | he couldn't see where he was going |
| 13 | They did no- did not get late. |
| **Segment 4: Narrative Task (DVD 4.6)** | |
| 1–2 | her friend I don't know the name |
| 4 | But she did not know about it |
| 4–5 | I don't know how they call that. |
| 7 | I don't know |
| 10–11 | Oh, I did not know. It's maybe, maybe the baby, I don't know how it's got there. |
| 11 | she's not going to know that |
| 14–15 | she won't know about it. She won't know who put it there |
| **Narrative Task Written (WR 4.6)** | |
| 6 | They were astonished because they don't know what happened. |

| Segment 5: Jigsaw Task (DVD 5.3) | |
|---|---|
| 13 | No. There is no car. There is no access to the car |
| 16 | I cannot see, the tree, the, branch, or I can see. I cannot see the, |
| 28 | never mind. |
| **Segment 6: Comparison Task (DVD 6.3)** | |
| 13 | I don't know, they got a good life and, in this one it seems thats people |
| 14 | don't really, care about, how, about the out. |

*Table 4.1 Negation in Learner Language*

## Questions in English

Researchers are also in wide agreement about the order in which speakers of a wide range of other languages acquire questions in English, German, and other TLs. Pienemann, Johnston, and Brindley (1988) described this sequence based on large-scale studies of the acquisition of both German as a second language and English as a second language. Since that time, this sequence of development of English questions has been used in a large number of research studies, as well as in high-stakes testing as a means of identifying learners' proficiency level in acquiring English as a second language (see Pienemann 2005 for a more current presentation of the theory that underlies this work). Table 4.2 shows each stage of question development, with supporting examples.

As question stages develop, Stage 1 and Stage 2 question forms continue to appear in the speech of highly proficient learners (and native speakers too). Not all early stage questions persist in this way; Table 4.2 has several examples of ungrammatical questions that should not appear at higher levels, but it is striking how many early questions are not ungrammatical, and so should turn up even in the speech of native speakers. In Exercise 4.2, we ask you to look at the developmental stages of the questions that three learners ask in DVD Segment 2: Question Task. As in previous exercises, you will need to make some arbitrary decisions about how to classify the stages of some of these questions. We will tell you how we decided to classify them, but ours is by no means the only possible way to look at these learner language samples.

---

**EXERCISE 4.2**

**Developmental Sequence in Question Formation: Antonio, Chun, and Catrine**

 DVD Segment 2: Question Task

In the Question Task (DVD Segment 2), all the English language learners look at six pictures and ask questions about them. The instructions to the activity indicate that they will have to remember the interviewer's answers to their questions in order to work out what happens, because next they will have to retell the depicted story in the Retell Task (DVD Segment 3). For an interesting point of comparison, look at the way two native speakers of English (Olivia and Victoria) do the Question Task (DVD 2.7 and 2.8).

*Antonio    Chun*

*Catrine*

*Olivia*      *Victoria*

1   Watch Antonio, Chun, and Catrine doing the Question Task (DVD 2.2, 2.4, and 2.5). Then watch them again while following along on the transcripts for this task (see pages 136–7, 144–6, 150–51 for Transcripts and Written Narratives). On a separate piece of paper, list the questions asked by each learner, headed by the line number in which that question began. After each question, indicate whether the question is a 'yes/no' or 'wh-' question, and indicate the stage of development of that question. As always in analyzing learner language, there will be examples where things are not clear, or you are not sure. Mark those cases and list the possible options for each one. (Do not worry about or comment on errors that are not related to question formation; for example, if a learner leaves the third person singular –s off the verb, do not comment, because that error has nothing to do with question formation.) If you are doing this exercise in a class, you can divide up the work by having each person in the class describe just one of the learners. Then you can meet as a group to discuss and compare your descriptions with each other. If you are doing this exercise alone, you may want to pick out one or two learners to focus on in answering the exercise questions. (Of course, if you have lots of time, and really get interested in this exercise, you can explore the question formation of all six learners as well as that of the NSs who provide baseline data.)

2   Compare your list with lists your classmates may have made for the same learner, and also with the list we provide in Table 4.3. Like you, we were not sure about several cases. Were those the same cases you had problems with? Why were your cases hard to categorize? Does it help you make up your mind if you watch the video while you read the transcript? You may end up totally disagreeing with the way we categorized certain questions below. In fact, the two of us do not agree on every classification below. Chun's question in line 66: Is it a Stage 2 question with a false start 'would?' or a Stage 3c? All researchers know that they have this kind of difficulty categorizing learner language, although in their published research papers and presentations they almost always follow the convention of acting as if the categories they used, counted, and ran statistical analyses on were clear-cut. Never hesitate to ask a researcher how they categorized their data in any given study, and what difficulties they had doing so. You can learn a lot that way.

3   Consult Table 4.3 to answer the following questions. For each learner, roughly how many 'yes/no' questions and 'wh-' questions were asked? What question stages did you find for each learner? Discuss why learners at all levels of proficiency still might be producing Stage 1 and 2 questions.

4   Compare the sorts of questions asked by Antonio with those asked by Chun, and those asked by Catrine. What differences and similarities do you see? Explain possible reasons for these similarities and differences. Consult a contrastive analysis source such as Swan and Smith (2001) for possible native language transfer explanations.

5   Now look at the questions asked by Victoria in DVD 2.8: Question Task. How many of each stage of question type did you find for her? Compare the question types she used with those the learners used. Discuss and explain the patterns in the kinds of questions asked by the learners and the native speaker of English.

6   Given that 'yes/no' questions are structurally less complex than 'wh-' questions, why do you think the native speaker asked more 'yes/no' questions, while the

learners generally asked more 'wh-' questions? (HINT: We thought about it in terms of whether the native speaker might already think she knows the answers to the questions she was asking, and then which type of question elicits new information, and which type elicits confirmation of information one already knows.)

| Stage | | Examples* |
|---|---|---|
| 1a | Single words | Why? This? Scissors? Red? |
| 1b | Single units | A boy? To who? What else? What color? |
| 2 | SVO word order | *This is picture? *They stay oceans? |
| 3a | Fronting *wh-* | *What he is doing? *Why he is stopped the car? |
| 3b | Fronting *do* in *yes/no* questions | Do you have flowers? *Does he going home? |
| 3c | Fronting other followed by uninverted sentence | *Is he is mad? *Is he have neighbor? |
| 4a | Inversion: *yes/no* questions with auxiliary or copula | Is she mad about that? So is he going to drive the car? *Has he answering the phone? |
| 4b | Inversion: *yes/no* questions with modal | Can you draw the whole world? |
| 4c | Inversion: *wh-* questions with copula (not aux) | What is this lady? *Where are this place? Why is he surprised? Which color is yours? |
| 5a | Inversion: auxiliary (e.g. *is*) in 2nd position | *Who is the woman who talk to the girl? Who's buying it? What's he doing? Why's she going outside? |
| 5b | Inversion: *do* operator (e.g. *does/do*) in 2nd position | What does she hold in her hand? *What does she asking for, this girl? How do you call it? *Why did he crying? |
| 5c | Inversion: Modal (e.g. *may*) in 2nd position | Who may be calling? Where will she take this? |
| 6a | Tag question | You can't, can you? *You don't like green, are you? |
| 6b | Negative question | Can't she come in? (hypothetical) |
| 6c | Embedded question | Can you tell me who he is? (hypothetical) |

Table 4.2: Stages of Question Formation in English (Pienemann, Johnston & Brindley, 1988)

*Except where indicated as '(hypothetical)', examples are from the database for Bigelow et al (2006) and from Tarone and Liu (1995).

| *Antonio* | Total: 18 | Y/N: 5 | Wh-: 11 | Unclear: 2 | |
|---|---|---|---|---|---|
| Line | | | | | *Dev. stage* |
| 1 | Who is he? | | | | 4c |
| 3 | Ah, your friend? | | | Unclear | 1b? |
| 5 | Where is he from? | | | | 4c |
| 7 | What is, what is he? | | | | 4c |
| 9 | What is he? | | | | 4c |
| 11 | Where, uh, is, is, is in the bed? He sit in the bed? (2 questions) | | | Unclear | 2, 2? |
| 13 | Is, is, Ah, Ahmed? | | | | 4a |
| 15 | Oh, eh, What is he, he doing? | | | | 5a |

| 17 | What is, what is that? | | 4c |
|---|---|---|---|
| 27 | What is he, in the, in the, in the sta, bus station, or …? | | 4c |
| 31 | Is, is your friend? or… | | 4a |
| 35 | It's, it's your, uh your car? … the Ahmed, Ahmed's friend? | | 2 |
| 37 | What are they doing? | | 5a |
| 39 | What are, what are they, what is he doing? This guy. | | 5a |
| 46 | Why, he, say stop? | | 3a |
| 48 | Why, this guy, say, the, uh s-stop? | | 3a |

| Stage | 1a | 1b | 2 | 3a | 3b | 3c | 4a | 4b | 4c | 5a | 5b | 5c | 6 | Total |
|---|---|---|---|---|---|---|---|---|---|---|---|---|---|---|
| Antonio | – | 1 5.9% | 3 17.6% | 2 11.8% | – | – | 2 11.8% | – | 6 35.3% | 3 17.6% | – | – | – | 17 |

| **Chun** | **Total: 14** | | **Y/N: 6** | **Wh-: 4** | | **Unclear: 4** | |
|---|---|---|---|---|---|---|---|
| *Line* | | | | | | | *Dev. stage* |
| 1 | Is the man is a student? | | | | | | 3c |
| 5 | Oh. Yeah and … it's in the morning? | | | | | | 2 |
| 9 | Who's who's that man? | | | | | | 4c |
| 11 | Oh. It's so it's in the winter? | | | | | | 2 |
| 13 | Yeah and what's what's he doing? | | | | | | 5a |
| 18 | Car key? (Clarification question) | | | | | Unclear | 1b? |
| 28 | Does he want to take the taxi? | | | | | | 3b |
| 30 | Hitchhike? (Clarification question) | | | | | Unclear | 1a? |
| 32 | And is that way work? Is that way work?     (1 question) | | | | | | 3c |
| 36 | What's what's that man doing? | | | | | | 5a |
| 38 | The driver? | | | | | Unclear | 1b? |
| 49 | So, when the the driver get off the the car he didn't found the the boy? | | | | | | 2 |
| 54 | Yeah and what what's what is he's thinking? | | | | | | 5a |
| 66 | So would would his friend will uh take him to the school? | | | | | Unclear | 2? 3c? |

| Stage | 1a | 1b | 2 | 3a | 3b | 3c | 4a | 4b | 4c | 5a | 5b | 5c | 6 | Total |
|---|---|---|---|---|---|---|---|---|---|---|---|---|---|---|
| Chun | 1 7.1% | 2 14.3% | 3 21.4% | – | 1 7.1% | 3 21.4% | – | – | 1 7.1% | 3 21.4% | – | – | – | 14 |

| Catrine | Total: 21 | | Y/N: 7 | Wh-: 14 | | Unclear: 0 | |
|---|---|---|---|---|---|---|---|
| Line | | | | | | | Dev. stage |
| 1 | Why, who's the boy, in the bed? | | | | | | 4c |
| 3 | Why he looks so sad? | | | | | | 3a |
| 5 | Why is he holding, some … what is he holding in his hand? (1 question) | | | | | | 5a |
| 7 | What, Why didn't he, put his alarm? Like, why didn't he set, his alarm? (2 questions) | | | | | | 6a, 6b |
| 10 | Why can't he stay and, look for a ride right now? | | | | | | 6b |
| 12 | What is he looking for? | | | | | | 5a |
| 14 | Is he mad? | | | | | | 4a |
| 16 | OK. Why is he wearing a jacket? | | | | | | 5a |
| 19 | What is he, is he running? (1 question) | | | | | | 4a |
| 26 | Why, the, bus, driver can't, stop for him? | | | | | | 3a |
| 30 | Who's the person in the, blue car? | | | | | | 4c |
| 32 | OK. Is he going to give him a ride? | | | | | | 4a |
| 34–5 | OK. Is he going to, go? Is he, going to be OK? His friend give him a ride or, is he still mad because, wake up late? (3 questions) | | | | | | 4a, 4a, 4c |
| 37 | What's happen to the car right now? What is happening? (2 questions) | | | | | | 5a, 5a |
| 39 | OK. Is he helping, ah, his friend? | | | | | | 4a |
| 42 | Why are they happy now? | | | | | | 4c |
| 46 | Why can't he help, his friend clean, the, remove the snow on the car? | | | | | | 6b |

| Stage | 1a | 1b | 2 | 3a | 3b | 3c | 4a | 4b | 4c | 5a | 5b | 5c | 6 | Total |
|---|---|---|---|---|---|---|---|---|---|---|---|---|---|---|
| Catrine | – | – | – | 2 9.5% | – | – | 6 28.5% | – | 4 19.0% | 5 23.8% | – | – | 4 (6b) 19.0% | 21 |

| Victoria | Total: 7 | | Y/N: 6 | Wh-: 1 | | Unclear: 0 | |
|---|---|---|---|---|---|---|---|
| Line | | | | | | | Dev. stage |
| 1 | Um so does he have an alternative plan if he misses the bus? | | | | | | 3b |
| 3 | OK. Does he think that's a good plan? OK, um … | | | | | | 3b |
| 7–8 | OK, but he didn't, he … Did he know this person was coming or is he was he just randomly going to hitchhike? (2 questions) | | | | | | 3b, 4a |
| 12 | OK. Does this friend go to school with him? | | | | | | 3b |
| 16 | OK. So his friend was also late for whatever reason? | | | | | | 2 |
| 24 | Are they stopping to brush the snow off the car? | | | | | | 4a |
| 26 | What is in his hand? | | | | | | 4c |

| Stage | 1a | 1b | 2 | 3a | 3b | 3c | 4a | 4b | 4c | 5a | 5b | 5c | 6 | Total |
|---|---|---|---|---|---|---|---|---|---|---|---|---|---|---|
| Victoria | – | – | 1 14.2% | – | 3 43% | – | 2 28.6% | – | 1 14.2% | – | – | – | – | 7 |

*Table 4.3 Developmental Stages of Antonio's, Chun's, Catrine's, and Victoria's Questions*

# Summary

In this chapter, we have identified developmental stages in two areas of our learners' grammar: negative constructions, and questions. You may be interested in looking at stages in the development of other linguistic elements of learner language, such as relative clauses or grammatical tense. If you are interested in reading published research studies on developmental sequences in learner language, to get some ideas for your own explorations in the classroom, here is a list of basic descriptive studies, organized by linguistic structure:

- Negation: Schumann (1979); Clahsen (1988); Berdan (1996)
- Questions: Ravem (1978); Ellis (1984); Pienemann and Johnston (1987); Pienemann and Mackey (1993); Spada and Lightbown (1993)
- Possessive determiners: White (1998)
- Tense and time expressions: Bardovi-Harlig (1992a, b, 2000); Bayley (1994); Salaberry (2000)
- Relative clauses: Eckman, Bell, and Nelson (1988); Doughty (1991).

In this chapter, we have explored some of the choices that can be made in studying developmental sequences in learner language, and considered the implications of developmental sequencing for teaching. In the next chapter, we will turn to another kind of IL analysis, this kind focused on the learner language produced when the learner interacts with others. We will focus especially on the corrective feedback provided to learners in interaction, and what learners do when communication breaks down.

# *Further Reading*

**Ellis, R.** 1994. Chapter 3 'Developmental patterns: Order and sequence in second language acquisition'. *The Study of Second Language Acquisition*. Oxford: Oxford University Press.

**Ellis, R.** and **G. Barkhuizen.** 2005. Chapter 5 'Frequency analysis'. *Analysing Learner Language*. Oxford: Oxford University Press.

**Gass, S. M.** and **L. Selinker.** 2008. Chapter 7 'Typological and functional approaches'. *Second Language Acquisition: An Introductory Course* (3rd edn.). New York: Routledge.

**Larsen-Freeman, D.** and **M. Long.** 1991. Chapter 7 'Theories in second language acquisition'. *An Introduction to Second Language Acquisition Research*. New York: Longman.

**Lightbown, P.** and **N. Spada.** 2006. Chapter 4 'Learner language'. *How Languages Are Learned* (3rd edn.). Oxford: Oxford University Press.

# 5 LEARNING IN INTERACTION

## Introduction

In Chapters 3 and 4, we looked at learners' use of both correct and incorrect forms of phonemes and morphemes, and at some developmental sequences in their learner language. As we saw in Chapter 2, recent research in second language acquisition (SLA) recommends that language classrooms should provide an ongoing balance between a focus on accurate form and a focus on meaning (for example, see Norris and Ortega 2000; Doughty 2001; Lyster 2007; Mackey 2007). This balance is felt to be most effective in promoting SLA when it occurs in interaction, where learners negotiate meaning and receive corrective feedback. Up to this point, we have mainly explored our learners' interlanguage forms with little consideration of the fact that they were interacting with someone else. In this chapter we will:

- look at the way the learners use their language in interaction when they do not understand
- examine corrective feedback provided to the learners in the midst of interaction: how hard it is to determine whether such feedback focuses on meaning or form, the kinds of corrective feedback on form that the learners are given, and what learners seem to notice when this feedback is given
- find out how learners co-construct or scaffold one another's utterances in pairwork interactions.

## What Learners Do When They Do Not Understand

When speakers have difficulty understanding each other, they can choose either to pretend they understand and wait to see if things become clear later in the interaction, or they can negotiate the meaning of the unclear input. Teachers know that learners often pretend to understand; for example, they nod and say 'yes' to what they have been asked or told when, in truth, they have not understood. At the beginning, when learners understand very little in interaction, they cannot possibly negotiate everything. Even when they are fluent, there are certain situations when some learners are simply less able or less willing than others to alter the flow of interaction so they can negotiate meaning. But most learners are willing to interrupt the flow of interaction to clarify things when they really need to understand.

We can see an example of this **negotiation of meaning** at the very beginning of Rodrigo's interview in (1) below.

**1**

| | | |
|---|---|---|
| 1 | **I** | So let's start by saying, ah, what your native language is. |
| 2 | **R** | Um, no, sorry, I |
| 3 | **I** | What is your native language? |
| 4 | **R** | Ah, wha, my, first language? |
| 5 | **I** | Your first language. |
| 6 | **R** | Eh, Spanish. |

Since Rodrigo does not understand the interviewer's initial question, he first gains time by using fillers ('um, no') then he seeks help ('sorry'); this leads to a repetition of the input, and finally he makes a clarification request in line 4 ('first language?') as he successfully negotiates to make the problem phrase in the input, 'native language', comprehensible so he can answer the question. Using fillers, seeking help, and asking for clarification are all types of **interactional modification** – conversational moves that speakers make when a communication breakdown occurs or is anticipated.

Most of these moves to negotiate meaning in oral interaction provide opportunities for acquisition that would not otherwise occur. First, they provide learners with more comprehensible input (Long 1996; Pica 1996); in the example above, Rodrigo's negotiation caused the interviewer to give him a second chance to hear the problem phrase, and to provide confirmation when he guessed its meaning. Second, negotiation is felt to facilitate 'noticing', which Schmidt (1990) maintains is required for acquisition. In this view, Rodrigo is likely to have noticed the difference between 'first language' and 'native language' when these two terms were produced together in the negotiation sequence. Third, being forced to produce modified output in the midst of negotiation of meaning is thought to push learners to process the new language more deeply and so to remember it (Swain 1995, 2000). And, finally, in some contexts, negotiation of meaning may contribute to language acquisition by creating opportunities for learners to receive **corrective feedback** and modify their output in response (Long 1996).

To provide our learners an opportunity to negotiate for meaning in response to something incomprehensible in the input, in the interviews we tried to put the learners in a situation where, to answer a question, they needed to understand a word that they were not likely to know already: 'siblings'. In Exercise 5.1 we take a look at how they responded in interaction when the interviewer produced this word.

**EXERCISE 5.1**

### Siblings

DVD SEGMENT 1: INTERVIEWS

To see what these learners do when required to respond to a question about an English word they do not understand, look at the excerpts below from the learners' interviews. You may find it helpful to watch these sections of interviews as you read since intonation and hesitations may contribute to the meaning. For each learner, indicate:

1  whether you think the learner knew the word 'siblings' before the interview
2  whether and how the learner negotiated for meaning
3  whether you think the learner might have learned the word as a result of the negotiation.

*Rodrigo*

### Rodrigo

| | | |
|---|---|---|
| 47 | **I** | So, when do you speak English with your siblings? |
| 48 | **R** | When. Hm, all time, in in in, I don't know in maybe, in in in Mexico, In |
| 49 | | Mexico, maybe in high school I I I start learn English, but, never speak English |
| 50 | | in Mexico. |

*Antonio*

### Antonio

| | | |
|---|---|---|
| 39 | **I** | And do you speak English with your siblings? |
| 40 | **A** | Ehh. |
| 41 | **I** | Do you speak English with your siblings? |
| 42 | **A** | Siblings. |
| 43 | **I** | Siblings. Brothers and sisters. |
| 44 | **A** | Ah! oh, okay! Yeah! Yeah, I try it. Yeah. I try it. |

*Catrine*

### Catrine

| | | |
|---|---|---|
| 32 | **I** | And when do you speak English with your siblings? |
| 33 | **C** | My family? |
| 34 | **I** | Your siblings? |
| 35 | **C** | Like ... what do you mean by my siblings? |
| 36 | **I** | Your brothers and sisters. |
| 37 | **C** | Mm I don't speak English with my brothers and sister but sometimes, um, like, I |
| 38 | | can say like a word in English to them but it's not like speaking for long time. Yes. |
| 39 | | I don't speak, really English with my brothers. |

*Chun*

### Chun

| | | |
|---|---|---|
| 59 | **I** | When do you speak English with your host siblings? |
| 60 | **C** | Host what? |
| 61 | **I** | Siblings. |
| 62 | **C** | What that mean? |
| 63 | **I** | That means brothers and sisters. |
| 64 | **C** | Oh. We don't have host brother and sisters. |

### Jeanne

| | | |
|---|---|---|
| 32 | **I** | When do you speak English with your siblings? |
| 33 | **J** | Where? |

*Jeanne*

| 34 | **I** | When do you speak English with your siblings? |
|----|----|----|
| 35 | **J** | Mm, we don't usually speak English; we speak French. |
| 36 | **I** | Oh, OK. |
| 37 | **J** | Yeah, we don't, really, I speak English in school with my friends at school, and, people |
| 38 | | that I don't know so, I don't usually speak English with my siblings. Yeah. |

**Xue**

| 42 | **I** | And when do you speak English with your host siblings? |
|----|----|----|
| 43 | **X** | Host siblings, what's that? |
| 44 | **I** | Siblings means brothers and sisters. |
| 45 | **X** | Oh, uh, when? |
| 46 | **I** | Yeah, do you speak English with your host brothers and sisters? |
| 47 | **X** | Mm, yup, of, of course. |
| 48 | **I** | OK. |
| 49 | **X** | So, when. Actually our host blings? |
| 50 | **I** | Siblings. |
| 51 | **X** | Siblings, host siblings they are adults right now and they all get married and |
| 52 | | so they didn't really um live in our house right now so |

*Xue*

# Corrective Feedback

As we noted in the last section, negotiation for meaning is claimed to sometimes lead to the provision of corrective feedback in response to learner errors (Long 1996). In negotiation, someone may provide the learner with a signal that something he or she has just said is incorrect. There is at present considerable research interest in the way corrective feedback occurs, and the impact it has on learner language when it is provided in the midst of interaction focused on meaning. Corrective feedback is given to learners most frequently in language classrooms, and much of it occurs in the midst of interactive activities focused on meaning. In traditional language classrooms as well as content-based language classrooms, it is not always clear whether an interactional move focuses on meaning, or provides corrective feedback.

As we shall see below, there are many different forms of corrective feedback, but the most common type provided by teachers in the classroom (Lyster and Ranta 1997) is the **recast**, where the teacher correctly paraphrases a learner's error. In (2), the interviewer recasts Jeanne's error in verb tense as she speaks about her language learning experience in high school.

2

| 18 | **I** | Were they speaking exercises |
|----|----|----|
| 19 | **J** | Mm mm. |
| 20 | **I** | or written exercises or |
| 21 | **J** | No, just grammar. Writing let me see uh no, I never write in English. I just |
| 22 | **I** | You never wrote in English. |
| 23 | **J** | No, never wrote in English. |

Although the sequence above does not take place in a classroom, it is typical of a three-part exchange that occurs when a teacher corrects a student's error:

1 There is a **trigger** (an utterance with an error) in line 21

2 a recast is provided in line 22

3 there is learner uptake (immediate **repair** of the error) in line 23.

Some researchers (for example, Lyster and Ranta 1997; Lyster and Mori 2006; Ellis and Sheen 2006) have pointed out that the recast as a form of corrective feedback is ambiguous when it occurs in a classroom exchange that is otherwise focused on meaning. This occurs for several reasons. Sometimes, in a meaningful interaction, an empathetic listener repeats what a speaker says just to show they are listening. This commonly occurs in classroom routines where teachers repeat what students say to confirm it and make sure that the entire class can hear it. This seems to be what happens in the classroom example below (from Lyster and Ranta 1997). In (3), the teacher recasts S1's question by providing the correct word order but S1 is not able to correct the mistake or acknowledge hearing the correction (there is no **uptake**) because S2 immediately responds to the meaning of the teacher's question.

**3**   S1   Why you don't like Marc?
　　　T　　Why don't you like Marc?
　　　S2   I don't know, I don't like him.

It is not always easy to discern the teacher's intent when he or she provides repetitions like the one in (3). Is it a confirmation, a recast providing corrective feedback that needs to be repeated, or a question seeking more information? In Exercise 5.2, we will explore some instances where the interviewer responded to the learners' utterances with either repetitions or questions. Let's see if you can tell if she was focused on meaning, or focused on form.

---

**EXERCISE 5.2**   **Interviewer's Intent: Focus on Meaning or Form?**

DVD 1.4, DVD 1.2, DVD 1.1: INTERVIEWS

Look at the excerpts below from Chun's, Antonio's, and Rodrigo's interviews. You may find it helpful to watch these sections of interviews as you read since intonation and hesitations may contribute to the meaning. For each utterance with an asterisk (*), what do you think the interviewer's intent was: Was she focused on meaning (for example, trying to get more information or confirming her understanding), or was she focused on form, trying to correct the learner? In each case, do you think the interviewer's move was effective in achieving its goal?

**Chun**

16   *I   Can you describe a typical class in China when you were 12?

17   C   Uh it's the English English teacher on the stage and the way it's just they uh

18       they told us the the pronunciation the words the vocabulary the words and the

19       pronunciation and we repeat his his pronunciation. And then it's we do a lot [pratɛks]

20   *I   A lot, a lot of what?

21   C   Mm [pratɛk] um what's that uh, practice.

*Chun*

| 22 | **I** | Practice. |
|----|----|----|
| 23 | **C** | Yeah yeah [practice] |
| 24 | **I** | [You did a lot] of practice. |
| 25 | **C** | Yeah. |

### Antonio

*Rodrigo*

| 13 | **A** | Yeah, eh, in in high school, I I study English, very ea-, it's English, uh, very |
| 14 | | easy. |
| 15 | ***I** | It was easy. |
| 16 | **A** | Yeah, its, el-elemental. |
| 17 | ***I** | I'm sorry, it's what? |
| 18 | **A** | Elemental? It's it's it's easy for example, eh, "My name", eh, "He is", it's |
| 19 | | it's it's easy. |
| 20 | **I** | Oh, elementary. |
| 21 | **A** | Elementary, [ok, it' all right,] yeah, elementary. |

### Rodrigo

*Antonio*

| 33 | **R** | But now, in the fourth, s, s, s, week, is |
| 34 | | more easy. I I I I I feel, to learn, more English vocabulary, eh, grammar, eh |
| 35 | | compo, eh speak. So I think, the the most important, is, eh, think, in English. |
| 36 | ***I** | Think in English. |
| 37 | **R** | Yes. |
| 38 | ***I** | So you said it's easier now. |
| 39 | **R** | More easy, yes. |
| 40 | **I** | More easy. |
| 41 | **R** | Yeah, yeah, I I I I |
| 42 | **I** | It's easier now. |
| 43 | **R** | Yes (laughs) yes uh I I think my English is is, no is, is not good but I, I, feel, I |
| 44 | | feel that, 'n maybe, I don't know c four, c, four, four months or six months I I, |
| 45 | | my English is is, ve, is, I don't know I I I will, feel very very good. |

## Types of Corrective Feedback

We have seen, both in Exercise 5.2 and in reading the research literature, that in the midst of oral interaction, a native speaker's (NS's) responses to learner errors and unclear utterances can be hard to interpret. A teacher would certainly like to make it clear when he or she is correcting a learner's error, so that the learner will notice the correction and have a chance to repair. How can teachers give clear corrections?

Based on Lyster's research, Lyster and Mori (2006: 271) have identified three basic kinds of corrective feedback moves, which differ in terms of their clarity to learners: **explicit correction**, **recasts**, and several different kinds of **prompts**. Recasts and prompts are both considered **implicit** corrective feedback, and contrast with **explicit** corrective feedback. Let's illustrate these corrective feedback moves using some of the errors learners made.

In **explicit correction**, the learner is clearly told what was incorrect, and given the correct form. The example below is adapted from Rodrigo's interview (DVD 1.2) to show how the interviewer could have provided an explicit correction following a recast. In this case, she could have directly indicated the error and given the correct reformulation (shown in italic below as a made-up example).

**4**

15  **R**  The teacher he are, not interact in, speak, or, with, eh eh students.
16  **I**  *He doesn't interact. You should say 'he doesn't'.*

In **recast**, the teacher reformulates all or part of the learner's utterance, providing a correct alternative, without explicitly signaling that it is a correction. In (5) below, the interviewer uses a recast in response to Rodrigo's error in line 34 of the Interview.

**5**

34  **R**  more easy. I I I feel, to learn …
38  **I**  So you said it's easier now.

**Prompts** differ from both explicit correction and recasts in that they do not provide a repair, offering instead a variety of signals to push the learner to self-repair. Lyster argues that prompts are more effective ways to provide corrective feedback than explicit correction and recasts, because they put the burden of self-repair on the learner, forcing more depth of processing (Lyster and Mori 2006). Types of prompts include **clarification requests**, **elicitations**, **metalinguistic feedback**, and **repetition**.

We have already seen an example of **clarification requests** in Exercise 5.2, when the interviewer says, 'I'm sorry, it's what?' to Antonio. Clarification requests may be used to negotiate meaning or to provide feedback, but in either case, they indicate that the interlocutor's utterance was misunderstood or incorrect. We see another clarification request in line 10 of Jeanne's Question Task (DVD 2.6), where the interviewer is trying to indicate that Jeanne's question included a pronunciation error.

**6**

9  **J**  Does, his head hurt?
10  **I**  I'm sorry, what?

In **elicitation**, the teacher invites the learner to reformulate a specific form. One way is by asking a question. In (7), adapted from Jeanne's interview as shown in italic below, the interviewer could have used elicitation by directly asking Jeanne to repair the form of the verb.

**7**

**J**  It was like require in my school …
**I**  *Require. How do we say that?*

Asking a question of a learner like this is one of three types of elicitation (Lyster and Ranta 1997). The other types the interviewer could have used are (1) eliciting completion of the teacher's utterance ('It was like …') and (2) asking about the correct form ('What is the passive form of "require"?').

The last type of prompt is a **metalinguistic** clue, a comment or question about the form used in the error. This may be as simple as saying, 'We don't say it like that in English'. Or it could invoke metalanguage, as, for example, 'You need to put an –*ER* on the end of "easy" to make the comparative form'. Metalinguistic clues may help learners not only correct a mistake they just made but also generalize the correct form to other words (Lyster and Ranta 1997; Ellis, Loewen, and Erlam 2006). A summary of the types of corrective feedback is shown in Table 5.1 with examples directly taken from or adapted from interaction with our learners.

In Exercise 5.3, we will look at the interviewer's corrective feedback to another learner. Use the information in Table 5.1 to categorize and evaluate the effectiveness of that feedback.

| Type | Example (made-up examples in italic) |
|---|---|
| Explicit correction | R  The teacher he are, not interact in, speak or, with, eh eh students.<br>I  *You should say, 'he doesn't'.* |
| Recast | R  The teacher he are, not interact in, speak or, with, eh eh students.<br>I  He doesn't interact. |
| Prompts: Clarification request | J  Does his head hurt?<br>I  I'm sorry, what? |
|     Elicitation | J  It was like require in my school …<br>I  *Require. How do we say that?* |
|     Metalinguistic feedback | R  But now, in the fourth, s, s, s, week, is more easy.<br>I  *You need -ER on the end of 'easy' to make the comparative form.* |
|     Repetition | J  It was like require in my school …<br>I  *It was like require?* |

*Table 5.1 Types of Corrective Feedback (examples in italic are adapted by the authors)*

**EXERCISE 5.3**  **'Grammars'**

DVD 1.3: INTERVIEW WITH XUE

Look at Xue's interview, lines 25–41, as she talks about how she learned English in China. Answer the following questions about Xue's use of the word 'grammar(s)' and the feedback she receives from the interviewer in the interaction. Refer to the transcript, providing line numbers where relevant (see pages 139–40).

1  Is Xue focused on meaning in this interaction, or on grammatical accuracy (form)?
2  List all the instances of her use of the word 'grammars'. Is her usage correct or incorrect? What seems to be her rule for this lexical item?

3  Identify lines in which there is error correction. Using Table 5.1, categorize the feedback the learner gets from the interviewer in response to this error. Do you think the learner notices the error correction provided? What evidence suggests, or would suggest, that she notices it?

4  If you were Xue's teacher and this interaction occurred in your classroom, how would you respond to Xue's use of 'grammars' in line 27? Would you put into practice any classroom activities based on this error? Explain.

5  Now read (8), which occurred in the interview almost five minutes after the exchange we've been looking at in lines 25–41. During those five minutes before (8), there was no further reference to grammar by either Xue or the interviewer.

**8**

55  **X**  Yeah, um, when I learn grammar, I will focus on those uh hard parts and, but I
56         don't like that, but I have to learn that …

In line 55, Xue produces the correct word 'grammar'. Why do you think she got it right in line 55, when earlier in the conversation (in lines 25–41) she consistently got it wrong? Did the fact that she used it correctly here change your opinion about the effectiveness of the feedback?

6  How do you think the Noticing Hypothesis would explain Xue's correct production of 'grammar' in (8), line 55? How would the Monitor model explain it? Which explanation fits best, in your opinion? Can you think of any other possible explanation?

## *What Do Learners Think Is Being Corrected?*

It is considered important for learners to notice discrepancies between forms in their own linguistic systems and those in the input (Schmidt 1990) if they are to acquire the input forms. Corrective feedback contains important information about those discrepancies. But it turns out that second language (L2) learners tend to notice corrections to some types of their linguistic errors more than others. In a research study with learners like ours, the learners were most accurate in identifying phonological, lexical, and semantic feedback, but they often failed to notice corrections to their morphology or syntax (Mackey, Gass, and McDonough 2000). They noticed when their pronunciation or their vocabulary was corrected, but they did not notice when the correction added a morpheme, as in (9), or changed the word order. They mistook such moves either as confirmations of meaning, or as focused on pronunciation or vocabulary.

**9**

| NNS | It have mixed colors. |
| NS | It has mixed colors. |
| NNS | Mixed colors aha. |

(Mackey, Gass, and McDonough 2000: 486)

Review your responses to Exercises 5.2 and 5.3 to see whether the learners seem to follow this same pattern. Do they too seem to misinterpret feedback on morphology or syntax more than feedback on pronunciation or vocabulary?

# Scaffolding

In many of the interactions we have examined so far in this chapter, the interviewer provided assistance to the learners who asked for it. In Exercise 5.1, for example, they were able to comprehend and in some cases use the word 'siblings' with her help, something they could not do on their own. This is an example of **scaffolding**, a phenomenon that is very important in sociocultural theory, as we saw in Chapter 2.

Scaffolding occurs in collaborative dialogue with learners as they jointly try to construct utterances containing linguistic forms they are in the process of acquiring; such forms are said to be in the learner's Zone of Proximal Development (ZPD). Cazden (1992) defines a language scaffold as 'a temporary framework for construction in progress' (page 103). Just as when a building under construction cannot stand alone, but requires scaffolding, so the learner's language requires support until the process of acquisition is complete. In sociocultural theory, it is important that the learner do as much as possible independently with forms in the ZPD, before the partner steps in to provide scaffolding for those forms. This is because the goal is for the learner to achieve self-regulation over language production, in a process that moves away from dependence on social regulation by others.

L2 learners' language can be scaffolded not only by NSs, but also by their peers in collaborative tasks. With scaffolding, two learners can build together a language structure in their ZPDs that neither one would be able to build alone. In fact, sociocultural theorists claim that in such tasks learners co-construct a context in which 'expertise emerges as a feature of the group' (Lantolf 2000: 17).

In Exercise 5.4, we look at the way two relatively proficient learners, Catrine and Jeanne, build their language expertise in collaborative interactions in DVD 6.3: Comparison Task. In Exercise 5.5, we look in detail at an example of student scaffolding between two beginning learners, when Antonio and Rodrigo help each other in DVD 6.1: Comparison Task. This task, requiring comparison of such abstract concepts as social class, would have been very difficult, perhaps impossible, for either of these beginning learners to perform alone. But when they help each other by providing scaffolding, together they are able to produce comparative statements that neither could have produced alone.

---

**EXERCISE 5.4**

*Catrine    Jeanne*

**Collaborative Interaction: Catrine and Jeanne**

DVD 6.3: COMPARISON TASK

Watch Catrine and Jeanne as they interact in DVD 6.3: Comparison Task. Identify two places where one of them has difficulty expressing her ideas. What words or grammatical structures is the speaker having difficulty with? What scaffolding does her partner provide in each case? Do they end up with an appropriate expression or correct structure?

**EXERCISE 5.5**

*Rodrigo*    *Antonio*

### Collaborative Interaction: Rodrigo and Antonio

DVD 6.1: COMPARISON TASK

In DVD 6.1, the learners are asked to find differences between two pictures of houses and make inferences about who lives in each house, their social class, and what the differences in houses say about American culture. The task requires that they make comparisons. English has many structures that can be used for comparison including:

| | |
|---|---|
| Adjective | 'This house is *bigger* than that one'. |
| Adverb | 'Those people must work *harder* than these'. |
| Noun | 'That house has *more space* than this one'. |
| Verb | 'The houses *contrast* in three ways'. |
| Conjunction | 'My house is big *but* your house is not'. |
| Connector | 'My house is big; *however*, your house is not'. |

1 Using the list above, categorize the words and structures that Antonio and Rodrigo used to express similarities and differences (underlined below). How did they scaffold each other's efforts to express similarities and differences?

2 If Antonio and Rodrigo were completing this task in your classroom, given the words and structures they are currently using, what structures would you scaffold for them and how would you provide that scaffolding at the moment that they need it in a way that accelerates their movement toward self-regulation with the language?

3   **A**   It's it's it's big, it's it's clean, eh, there is a car, and and, this eh house it's it's it's
4       small, it's no clean, em I I I think I think so.
5   **R**   Yes, is correct, I think so, too. Eh, this house eh eh eh, show, eh, the the the,
6       poor, poorer money, I don't know, I I, this house, show, there are very money and
7       this house no. This house is, is, it's a good house but, eh, is better this house and
8       and and, and the and are worth in Mexico, in United States, in other countries, yes
9       I I I eh, um, I am, m, is is, em, show, eh, different ...
10   **A**   Different classes, different ...
11   **R**   Different classes, social classes ...
12   **A**   Yeah.
13   **R**   Is in United States, is the same in in other countries.

## Scaffolding in the Classroom

In Exercises 5.4 and 5.5, the learners provided scaffolding for each other naturally in conversation. If these interactions had taken place in the classroom, the teacher could have supplied scaffolding in several ways to give the learners temporary assistance as they built new language structures and deeper understanding of their second language. Jeanne and Catrine could have been given written sentence stems ('It depends on ...') or vocabulary words ('salary', 'earnings') that are at the outer edges of their ZPD but not beyond it. The teacher must be sensitive to the students' current abilities within the ZPD to provide the assistance that is needed when it is needed. This sensitivity is seen in classroom example (10) in which a student, Wang, is telling his teacher about a movie (example provided in Ellis 1999: 217). Notice how Wang's utterances become longer and more target-like as a result of the teacher's scaffolding in this interaction which is both communicative and instructional.

**10**

| | |
|---|---|
| W | Kung Fu. |
| T | Kung Fu? You like the movie Kung Fu? |
| W | Yeah ... fight. |
| T | That was about a great fighter? A man who knows how to fight with his hands. |
| W | I fight ... my hand. |
| T | You know how to fight with your hands? |
| W | I fight with my hand. |
| T | Watch out guys, Wang knows karate. |

Within the ZPD for the student, scaffolding must be both timely and appropriate in helping the student move from other-regulation (dependence on another's input) to self-regulation. Development of the student's language forms in the ZPD will not occur if too much help is given, or the task is too hard, requiring forms and activities that the learner is not yet ready to learn in the ZPD.

To facilitate scaffolding among groups of students, the teacher can create opportunities for the students to use stretches of discourse in situations where they have to focus not only on what they mean but also on how they say it. The teacher can also provide opportunities for the students to give each other metalinguistic feedback. For example, pairs of students may be asked to do a **dictogloss** task, in which they recreate in writing a short science text they have just heard read aloud, a text containing language structures that fall within the learners' ZPD: just challenging enough. As they recreate the text, they discuss the language choices they make, which creates opportunities for them to notice gaps in their knowledge of the second language. Students can also be taught to plan, predict, and evaluate their language use and to think aloud as they do so (Swain 2000). For example, if students are working in pairs to write a report on a science experiment they have done, they might plan to use the past tense, predict that they will have difficulty remembering to add *-ed* to certain regular verbs, and evaluate their report with an editing checklist provided by the teacher. As they think aloud while writing the report, they focus not only on what they are writing, but how they are writing it.

# Summary

In Chapter 5 we explored the way learners use language in interaction to negotiate for meaning, how they process corrective feedback received while the interaction is focused on meaning, and how they construct both meaning and linguistic form in interaction with other learners. In the next chapter we continue exploring learner language in interaction as we look at the ways in which learners exchange information about people, things, and events.

## *Further Reading*

**Doughty, C.** and **M. Long.** 2005. Chapter 9 'Input and Interaction', Chapter 10 'Instructed SLA'. *Handbook of Second Language Acquisition*. Oxford: Blackwell.

**Ellis, R.** and **G. Barkhuizen.** 2005. Chapter 8 'Interactional analysis', Chapter 10 'Sociocultural methods of analysis'. *Analysing Learner Language*. Oxford: Oxford University Press.

**Gass, S. M.** and **L. Selinker.** 2008. Chapter 9 'Interlanguage in context', Chapter 10 'Input, interaction and output', and Chapter 11 'Instructed second language learning'. *Second Language Acquisition: An Introductory Course* (3rd edn.). New York: Routledge.

**Lightbown, P.** and **N. Spada.** 2006. Chapter 5 'Observing classrooms'. *How Languages are Learned* (3rd edn.). Oxford: Oxford University Press.

**Lyster, R.** and **H. Mori.** 2006. 'Interactional feedback and instructional counterbalance'. *Studies in Second Language Acquisition* 28: 269–300.

**Lyster, R.** and **L. Ranta.** 1997. 'Corrective feedback and learner update: Negotiation of form in communicative classrooms'. *Studies in Second Language Acquisition* 19: 37–66.

**Mackey, A., S. M. Gass** and **K. McDonough.** 2000. 'How do learners perceive corrective feedback?' *Studies in Second Language Acquisition* 22: 471–97.

**Swain, M.** and **S. Lapkin.** 1998. 'Interaction and second language learning: Two adolescent French immersion students working together'. *Modern Language Journal* 82: 320–37.

# 6 EXPLORING REFERENCE

## Introduction

In Chapter 5, we explored some of the ways learner language functions in interaction. We looked at the way learners use their language in interaction when they do not understand something, how they process corrective feedback given in the midst of interaction, and how they co-construct or scaffold one another's utterances. Chapter 6 examines another aspect of learner language in interaction: the way it is used in **referential communication**, as speakers use language to exchange information about people, things, and events. (Referential communication is distinct from **interpersonal communication**, which aims primarily to maintain social relationships rather than to exchange information (Brown and Yule 1983: 1–3; Yule 1997; Paul 1999).)

In this chapter, we will:

- describe referential communication and its importance in the lives of learners
- consider the referential expressions learners use in their efforts to make sure the listener knows who and what they are talking about
- examine the communication strategies learners use when they do not have the referential expressions they need to refer to an entity or event.

## Referential Communication

In referential communication, information is exchanged between two speakers. In an act of **reference**, a speaker identifies entities (people and things) by naming or description; he or she must do so clearly enough for a listener to know which entity is being referred to. This involves establishing common ground, as speaker and listener come to agree on what is being referred to. Acts of reference are evaluated in terms of their communicative effectiveness, not their grammatical correctness. In addition to identifying entities, acts of reference also locate or move entities relative to other entities, as in instructions or directions; they also follow entities through sequences of events and locations, as in narratives (Yule 1997; Paul 1999).

In referential communication, the focus of speaker and listener are primarily on meaning, not linguistic form. But in every language, certain linguistic forms function as tools that enable speakers to refer to entities clearly so that listeners can identify them. In English, noun modifiers like adjectives (the <u>red</u> book), prepositional phrases (the book <u>on the table</u>), and relative clauses (the book <u>that I gave you yesterday</u>) all serve as tools the speaker can use to help a listener understand which book the speaker has in mind.

Effective referential communication is inherently interactive. In order to be communicatively effective in referential communication, speakers must take into account any information the listener already has, and any information the listener needs to know in order to identify the entity being referred to. So, for example, it is not communicatively effective for a speaker to say to a listener who has just walked into a room: 'Give me the book', when there are five books on the table between them. Without any prior shared knowledge between the two people, the listener cannot identify which one is meant. However, if the two have been talking about a history book, and there is only one history book on that table, the speaker may be justified in assuming that the listener knows which one is meant, and 'Give me the book' may be effective. Thus, the communicative effectiveness of an act of reference crucially depends on the speaker's success in accurately assessing what relevant information the listener has in that particular situation. An effective act of reference requires placing oneself in the role of listener, to understand what that listener needs to know to identify the entity.

In effective referential communication, the speaker needs to send a signal to indicate to the listener whether the entity referred to is **given information** (information the speaker assumes the listener already knows about or can identify from what was said), or if the entity is **new information** (information that the speaker assumes the listener does not already know about). In English, speakers typically use 'the' to signal given information, as, when referring to a book they have just been talking about, they say 'Give me the book'. In colloquial speech, they may also use 'that' for given information, as in 'You know that book?' In English, the indefinite **article** 'a' or 'an' is used to signal new information, as in 'I saw an interesting guy today'; new information can also be signaled colloquially by 'this,' as in 'Carolyn met this guy in her physics class'. Yule (1999) provides a thorough discussion of the uses of 'a' versus 'the' in referring to old versus new information.

Second language (L2) learners need many opportunities to engage in referential communication activities using the target language (TL) in order to build their communicative effectiveness. In those activities they will need linguistic forms like those described above: noun and verb modifiers that function to answer questions like 'which one?' 'where?', 'in what order?', and 'which direction?' They will need core vocabulary for describing entities that they, or their listeners, do not know the name for. They will need to know how to signal their listeners about what they assume is given information or new information. Some learners will also need to improve their ability to accurately assess their listeners' world knowledge in order to figure out what information their listeners need to know to identify the entity being referred to. These skills, developed with practice, improve the learner's communicative effectiveness in using learner language in referential communication.

## A Referential Communication Activity

The Jigsaw Task in DVD Segment 5 is a referential communication task; it offers speakers an opportunity to exchange information by referring to concrete entities. Constructed according to the guidelines for referential communication tasks (Yule 1997), the Jigsaw Task sets up a situation in which each speaker has information that the other speaker needs in order to complete the task. Each speaker must convey that information through language to his or her partner clearly enough for the pair to establish common ground and collaboratively accomplish their goal. In this case, each speaker can see a photo of a house that the other speaker cannot see. The speakers must describe their houses to each other clearly enough for them to identify three similarities and three differences between the photos of the houses (their goal). In Exercise 6.1 you will explore the way Chun and Xue work together to complete this referential communication task. Remember: neither speaker can see the other's photo.

---

**EXERCISE 6.1**

*Chun*      *Xue*

**Are they Communicating Effectively?**

DVD SEGMENT 5: JIGSAW TASK

1  Watch Chun and Xue in DVD 5.2: Jigsaw Task, and answer the following questions:
   a  Do they succeed in reaching their goal: effectively identifying three similar things and three different things in their photos?
   b  What, in Chun and Xue's interaction patterns, helps them succeed in effectively exchanging information? Is the length or function of their speaking turns a factor?

2  Now look at the transcript of DVD 5.2, Xue and Chun's interaction while doing the Jigsaw Task (see pages 147–8). What does the transcript help you see, that you might have missed in first watching the video?

3  In lines 30–31 of the transcript, Xue asks whether Chun's house has a tiny window by the door. In the subsequent lines, how clearly do you think each one refers to the windows in her photo, and where they are located? What seems to cause each one trouble clarifying what is being referred to? Are Xue and Chun taking each other's perspective into account in the exchange? In line 32, Chun asks: 'Which house?' Why does she ask this question? Does Xue's answer clarify what is being referred to? If not, what is the problem?

4  Even though the goal of the Jigsaw Task is to promote clear information exchange, in line 4, Xue gives Chun a piece of corrective feedback. What do you think Chun notices in this feedback? Is Xue consistent in her use of the correct form?

*Catrine*      *Jeanne*

5  Now watch Catrine and Jeanne's and Rodrigo and Antonio's Jigsaw Task activity (DVD 5.3 and DVD 5.1). Do they reach their communicative goal of identifying three things that are the same and three that are different, without intervention from the interviewer? Compare their patterns of interaction with the interactive patterns used by Chun and Xue in DVD 5.2; consider eye contact and turn length. Explain how

these patterns might be related to whether the partners establish common ground or reach their communicative goal.

## *Keeping Track of Characters in Narratives*

One of the more challenging problems for referential communication occurs in narratives when a speaker has to refer clearly to several different people, things, and their actions over a period of time. When, as in the Narrative Task (DVD Segment 4) there are three female characters in the story, and a rather complicated event occurs involving transfer of an object into a container, how does the narrator provide enough linguistic cues to enable a listener to keep track of who did what? Let's see how our learners did.

**EXERCISE 6.2**

### Who Did What?

DVD SEGMENT 4: NARRATIVE TASK

In the Narrative Task, the narrator has to distinguish among three different female characters, and so has to use **linguistic expressions** that help the listener keep them separate. Just saying 'she' will not work because there are three female characters, and just saying 'the woman' is inadequate because there are two women. Remember that in this task, unlike the Jigsaw Task, the speaker and the interviewer can both see the pictures being referred to.

1　How did all the speakers refer to the child in the story, in a sequence where typically they had to first introduce the child, then refer to the two women conversing in the aisle, and then refer again to the child as she transferred a bottle into an old woman's purse? Watch DVD Segment 4: Narrative Task and if needed, read the transcripts of this segment on pages 133–155. Write in Table 6.1 the linguistic expressions used by each speaker to refer to the child, the women, and then the child again; we have helped by writing in what the NSs said. Some may not mention the women a second time. Where more than one expression is used to refer to the child the second time, list them all, in order. Note that Xue recounts this series of events twice; the table has space for you to write in the referential expressions she used in each version of the story.

2　Rodrigo does not mention the child in his narrative until the bottle event occurs, and then he uses the expression 'the child'. This is a referential problem; why?

3　What are some linguistic expressions (other than use of the articles 'a/an' and 'the') that the learners use to maintain clear reference to the female characters in their narratives? How effective are they in helping you keep track of who the narrator is referring to?

4　Why do you think Xue uses so many linguistic expressions to refer to the child in her narrative, even retelling the part of the narrative where the bottle transfer occurs? What explains the relative abundance of referring expressions in her narrative?

|  | **First mention of child** | **Second mention of women** | **Second mention of child** |
|---|---|---|---|
| *Olivia* | a small child | they | the small child |
| *Victoria* | her young daughter | the two women | the little girl, she |
| *Rodrigo* |  |  |  |
| *Antonio* |  |  |  |
| *Xue* |  |  |  |
| *Chun* |  |  |  |
| *Catrine* |  |  |  |
| *Jeanne* |  |  |  |

Table 6.1 Characters in the Narrative Task

Photocopiable © Oxford University Press

## *Keeping Track of Events in Narratives*

Just as it can be difficult for a narrator to clearly refer to the characters in a story so that listeners can keep track of them, so also it can be difficult to describe complex events so that the listener can understand exactly what happened. In Exercise 6.3, we explore the way the learners as well as the NSs gave accounts of a complex event: a child's transfer of a bottle from a shelf to a purse.

**EXERCISE 6.3**

**What Did the Child Do with the Bottle?**

 DVD SEGMENT 4: NARRATIVE TASK

We have laid out for you in Table 6.2 the way each of our six learners and two NSs referred to the same event in DVD Segment 4: Narrative Task.

1 Compare the learner versions to the way the NSs, Olivia and Victoria, describe this event. What differences do you notice between the native-speaker and the learner versions of this event? What are some possible reasons for those differences?

2 Based on their versions of this event, do you think that Antonio and Rodrigo know the English word 'put'? What verb does Rodrigo use instead? Why do you think he uses this word? How does Antonio solve the problem of not knowing, or being able to retrieve, the word 'put'? What do you think of this solution?

3 The verb 'put' is a two-place verb; that is, it must be followed by both a thing and a place (if you use the verb 'put' you have to say WHAT was put: a direct object, and WHERE: an adverb or prepositional phrase). Learners sometimes omit one or the other. Does this omission of an object, adverb, or prepositional phrase occur following the verb 'put' with any of the learners? Describe it.

4 Discuss Catrine's use of the verb 'take'. What do you think is the problem with her account? Is she using the wrong lexical verb 'take', intending to use 'put'? Or does she misunderstand what is happening in the picture (she does say she cannot really see the picture). How can you decide?

5   Compare the noun phrases the learners use to refer to the place the child put the
    bottle, in both their oral versions and their written versions. Does native language
    (NL) transfer affect the way they construct these noun phrases in either version?
    What problems do the learners have indicating whose purse it is? Do you think it
    helps learners to do the same task twice – first orally, and then again in writing, or
    vice versa? Why? Do you give students a chance to repeat activities in this way in
    your classroom?

| | |
|---|---|
| **Rodrigo** | the child, eh, is a, th take, she take, eh [wa] one, maybe red, eh, red w-, bottle wine. I don't know, is is is (laughs) dangerous, because … the child, eh, in, introduce the, the, I don't know, introduce in in the bag, in the nother person, in the in the friend your mom |
| **Antonio** | the kid, the little, little girl, eh, take the the bottle, and, eh uh, OK in this picture, eh, the bottle, is in, is in the bag, the bag, the, this, this person. |
| **Chun** | she grab, one one bottle of wine and put it in the in the old lady's bag. |
| **Catrine** | here there is the, her friend's daughter, trying, to take something, I can't really see. She trying to take something, in the, bag, in her bag. |
| **Xue** | he put out a bottle of vinegar and put into Mrs. Anderson's basket. |
| **Jeanne** | the baby put, um, something in her bag that she took from, the grocery, and she put it in her, bag, in the, in her mom friend's bag. |
| **Olivia** | the child picks up a bottle of what looks like probably wine and um puts it in the other, older woman's purse. |
| **Victoria** | she takes the bottle and drops it in the elderly woman's purse um without the woman noticing |

*Table 6.2 Eight Speakers Refer to Transfer of a Bottle Into a Purse (DVD Segment 4: Narrative Task)*

# Communication Strategies

In the process of carrying out all the communicative activities, the learners
periodically encounter roadblocks to effective communication; many of these
appear to be caused by gaps in their own linguistic knowledge. From time to
time we can see a learner start to refer to an entity or action and then hesitate,
searching for the right word or phrase to convey an intended meaning. Their word
and phrase search sometimes ends abruptly, with abandonment of the attempt to
continue. You probably saw an example of this in Exercise 6.1 when Rodrigo said:

I, many, I don't know what is, three or four er four er street, and two, two, I don't know

 (DVD 5.1: Jigsaw Task, lines 5–6)

But often, the learner persists in trying to make a clear act of reference, even
without knowing the appropriate vocabulary word, as when Antonio refers to
teaching techniques as 'tools'. In such cases, the learners are using **communication
strategies**.

Communication strategies are mutual attempts of two communicators to agree
on a meaning in situations where they do not share the required language forms

(Tarone 1980). To do this, they may use words that are paraphrases, or that describe the characteristics or function of the entity or action they want to refer to. They may use gesture, or they may use a word that is a literal translation from their NL. In the next section, we will explore the learners' use of communication strategies to refer to entities and actions.

## *Communication Strategies to Refer to Entities*

We will begin by looking at how the learners refer to things when they do not know, or cannot remember, the 'right' words. There are many different taxonomies listing different types of communication strategy (such as Faerch and Kasper 1983; see Yule and Tarone 1997 for a review). Here we will give you examples of some to help you get started, but be aware that some of these are more common than others, and that you may also find other types of communication strategy as well. An appeal for assistance occurs when a learner asks someone to supply a word, as when Xue says, '… he wants to hike, hi-, hi-, hi-. What, what he is doing?' (Question task: DVD 2.3, line 16). Mime is used when the learner uses a gesture or facial expression, as when pantomiming an action or pointing at an object in the room. Approximation is using a word that is close to the one needed, but not exactly the one desired; in Retall Task DVD 3.2, line 17, Antonio says 'window' instead of 'windshield'. **Circumlocution** can be seen when a learner who lacks the name for a referent describes it in terms of its elements, function, or purpose; an example is when Catrine refers to a 'trellis' as 'something that can help me climb' (Jigsaw Task:DVD 5.3, line 4). **Word coinage** occurs when the learner makes up a word, as when a learner who does not know the word 'balloon' makes up the word 'airball'. In NL borrowing, a learner may use either a literal translation of a NL word or the word itself; a French-speaking learner might say 'grammaire' instead of 'grammar'. **Avoidance** occurs when learners do not refer to an entity or action because they do not know or cannot access the relevant lexical item

It is not clear whether communication strategy use helps or hinders L2 acquisition. In Exercise 6.4 below, we have a case where using a communication strategy might lead a learner to get some valuable language input from the interviewer: the vocabulary item she is looking for. In this way, communication strategy use can lead to an opportunity for second language acquisition. In Exercise 6.5, we will look at a number of different examples of learner use of communication strategies to refer to entities, and consider whether each use is likely to lead to acquisition, and if so, what is likely to get acquired through use of that strategy.

**EXERCISE 6.4**

### The Shopping Cart

DVD SEGMENT 4: NARRATIVE TASK

In every picture in the Narrative Task there is at least one shopping cart. The native speakers (NSs) both mention this entity, and refer to it as either 'a grocery cart' or 'a shopping cart'. However, the English name of this entity may not be familiar to all the L2 learners; four of them are very recent arrivals to the US, and the living situations of these four (two with family friends, and two with a host family) may not require them to visit the grocery store. Do they know this vocabulary item? This is how the learners refer to it in telling the Narrative Task.

| | |
|---|---|
| **Rodrigo** | the this, c car, eh market car or eh I I don't know |
| **Antonio** | [does not mention it] |
| **Xue** | who is sitting in his car, is that? Car? No. |
| **Chun** | a car |
| **Catrine** | [does not mention it] |
| **Jeanne** | [does not mention it] |

1  How many learners avoid mentioning the cart? Avoidance is a communication strategy of last resort, since it reduces the informational value of the speaker's message. Do the learners who avoid mentioning the cart in their oral grocery story also avoid mentioning it in their written versions? What does this tell you?

2  What is Rodrigo's communication strategy? Do you think a listener would be able to tell what he is referring to?

3  How do Chun and Xue refer to the shopping cart? Do you think a listener would be able to tell what they are referring to?

4  In line 11 of Xue's Narrative Task (DVD 4.3), the interviewer provides her with a recast: 'Cart'. Do you think Xue's communication strategy in this interactive exchange might lead to her acquisition of a new term? Explain.

---

**EXERCISE 6.5**

### Communication Strategies Referring to Entities

DVD SEGMENTS 1–6

In Table 6.3, you will find ten linguistic expressions that were used by the learners to refer to objects and relationships they did not know a word for. In each case, one or more types of communication strategy were being used.

1  For each object or relationship, (a) indicate what the intended meaning was, based on the context. You will find it helpful to view the relevant video segments so you can look at the learners' facial expressions and gestures. Then, (b) indicate what communication strategy, or strategies, the learner used to get that intended meaning across and whether the learner signaled that they knew that the expression they were producing was not quite the one they wanted; and (c) indicate whether you think the learner might have acquired some aspect of English through using that strategy, and if so, what that was.

2 Do certain types of communication strategy lend themselves to certain kinds of potential learning outcomes? Discuss what is likely to be acquired through the use of those types of communication strategy.

| Name | Task | Communication strategy |
|---|---|---|
| 1 Rodrigo | DVD 4.1: line 6 | market car |
| **R** and eh put on the the this, c car, eh market car or eh I I don't know | | |
| 2 Antonio | DVD 1.2: lines 71–2 | first there are adjective and after noun |
| **A** It it's difficult because eh in in in my language, for example, eh first, in in the structure in the sentence, first eh there are uh uh adjective, and, eh after, noun. | | |
| 3 Antonio | DVD 1.2: lines 72–6 | Gesture |
| **A** Uh No. It's it's (gestures)<br>**I** The other way around?<br>**A** Yeah, the other way first noun and and second an adjective. Here no. Here it's first adjective, it's difficult. | | |
| 4 Antonio | DVD 2.2: lines 17–19 | What is that? |
| **A** What is, what is that?<br>**I** That's a scarf.<br>**A** A scarf. | | |
| 5 Xue | DVD 3.3: lines 16–19 | what's that thing? |
| **X** that man was just stand up and pull outside uh what's that thing?<br>**I** A scraper?<br>**X** Scraper. And he begin to clean the windshield. | | |
| 6 Xue | DVD 4.3: lines 14–15 | basket |
| **X** she saw that Mrs. Anderson's um blank, basket and so he put out a bottle of vinegar and put into Mrs. Anderson's basket. | | |
| 7 Catrine | DVD 1.5: line 15 | secretarary, secretaire |
| **C** If you want to be a secretarary, I don't know, secretaire | | |
| 8 Jeanne | DVD 4.6: lines 4–5 | /yalon/ |
| **J** But she did not know about it, when they went out, the /yalon/, I don't know how they call that. | | |
| 9 Catrine | DVD 6.3: lines 1–2 | woods |
| **C** because the woods in front of the house it's, kind of old, old | | |
| 10 Jeanne | DVD 6.3: lines 13–14 | out |
| **J** in this one it seems thats people don't really, care about, how, about the out. | | |

*Table 6.3 Communication Strategies Referring to Entities and Relationships*

## *Communication Strategies to Refer to Actions*

The narratives the learners produce in retelling the story in DVD 3: Retell Task contain descriptions of three actions that require the use of linguistic expressions in **verb phrases** that the learners do not seem to know: 'to miss the bus', 'to hitch hike', and 'to scrape/brush off snow'. In the next exercise we will explore the learners' use of communication strategies to refer to these actions when most of them either do not know, or cannot remember, the appropriate English phrases to use.

---

**EXERCISE 6.6**      **Communication Strategies Referring to Actions and Events**

 DVD SEGMENT 3: RETELL TASK

In Table 6.4, we have listed three actions from the Retell Task story in DVD Segment 3, in which the two NSs of English appear to be in agreement about the appropriate linguistic expressions to use to refer to the action. In general, we think it is a good idea to have NSs do the same tasks the learners do in order to see what linguistic expressions they use, for purposes of comparison. In Table 6.4, we provide the NS responses in italics for purposes of comparison. In referring to each action, the learners usually do not use the linguistic expressions that the NSs do. In most cases, the learners do not avoid mentioning the three actions; they try to use communication strategies to refer to them. Using the information in Table 6.4 answer the following questions:

1   Only one learner uses the same expression as the NSs for 'miss the bus'. Describe the communication strategies used by Antonio and Rodrigo, the two learners with beginning-level knowledge of English; do they refer directly to the action of 'missing the bus'? Consider the communication strategy used by Xue and Catrine. Do their descriptions make clear what happens? What syntactic structures do they use when they use this strategy? Do you think either Antonio or Rodrigo could have produced these syntactic structures at their proficiency level?

2   The NSs use two different linguistic expressions to refer to the next action: 'flag him down' and 'hitchhike'. Describe the communication strategies each learner uses. Which of these strategies do you think is the most conducive to acquiring new vocabulary? Why?

3   The NSs refer to the third action as 'brushing off' or 'scraping off'; the recipient of this action is either 'snow' or 'the car' in which case a reason must be given: 'because there's snow all over the car'. These linguistic expressions are likely to be unfamiliar to the learners, either because this action does not occur in the countries they are from, or because they have not yet heard it referred to in English.

  a  What linguistic expressions do the learners use instead of the expressions 'brush off' or 'scrape off'? Do you think these words are acceptable substitutes? If not, explain what is wrong with them.

  b  Which learners provide a reason for the action, similar to the NS's 'because there's snow all over the car'? Evaluate the way in which the reason is given, in each case: Is it communicatively effective? When the learners give reasons for the action, what syntactic structures do they use?

| What Ahmed does at the bus stop: | |
|---|---|
| *Olivia* | *just misses the bus* |
| *Victoria* | *misses the bus* |
| *Rodrigo* | don't take, your class |
| *Antonio* | the bus, it's uh, it's far. |
| *Xue* | the bus just went up and go go and keep going so can't catch the bus |
| *Chun* | missed the bus |
| *Catrine* | he miss the bus, and he's trying to catch the bus but it's too late |
| *Jeanne* | was late for the bus |

| What Ahmed does after missing the bus: | |
|---|---|
| *Olivia* | *he sees his friend, who is driving down the street and tries to flag him down um so that he can get a ride.* |
| *Victoria* | *he's still looking for a way to get to school, decides to stand on the side of the road and hitchhike* |
| *Rodrigo* | (does not refer to this action) |
| *Antonio* | He, Ahmed, he, eh, he say the, a, a ride? |
| *Xue* | he stand beside the road and wait for hike ... (Interviewer: Hitchhike.) Hitchhike, thank you, and then he found a car which is blue and he found that car coming toward him so he just um thumb up his hand and waiting for there |
| *Chun* | and then he want to he want to uh take a take a ride? (looks at Interviewer) Ride? Right? Uh yeah take a ride but and he just do this (gestures with thumb) then uh (gesture) and then he found he found there is a car |
| *Catrine* | he see his friend in the car, and he think his friend can give me a ri-, can give him a ride. |
| *Jeanne* | good luck his friend Mohammed came up |

| What the friend does after stopping the car: | |
|---|---|
| *Olivia* | *his friend stops to brush off his car because there's snow all over the car* |
| *Victoria* | *the driver had just pulled over to scrape the snow off of his windshield.* |
| *Rodrigo* | He, clean, cleanest, eh up the window, and, the winter and cold |
| *Antonio* | his friend, clean, the window, um, because, the snow, no allow the see? |
| *Xue* | he begin to clean the windshield. |
| *Chun* | he just want to clean the windshield. |
| *Catrine* | His friend stop to clean, the snow, from the car |
| *Jeanne* | He was washing the windshield because of the snow. |

*Table 6.4 Communication Strategies Referring to Actions in DVD Segment 3: Retell Task*

## Communication Strategies and Language Form

In reviewing what we have seen in exploring the learners' use of communication strategies, we might conclude that there are ways that communication strategy use can affect learner language. Sometimes, learners get creative in using word coinage. They devise their own words to serve their purposes, and they may retain those words for a period of time. Sometimes in interaction, an interlocutor responds to a learner's communication strategy by supplying them with the word they lacked; in this way, communication strategy use produces the language input the learner lacks, just when they need it. And we see that when the learners do not know a vocabulary word that they need, they sometimes use circumlocution – they describe the characteristics or the function of the entity or action. When our learners used this particular strategy, you may have noticed that some of them used more causal conjunctions and even some relative clauses. So, using that communication strategy required learners to use more complex syntax. Maybe these were structures they already knew, and were practicing. But they may also have been structures the learners had only partial mastery of. Using partially mastered structures in interaction with supportive interlocutors may have provided them with opportunities for acquisition.

# Summary

In Chapter 6, we have explored the way learner language is used in referential communication, to exchange information about people, things, and events. Our exploration has led us to look at learners' use of referential expressions to ensure that listeners know who and what is being referred to, and at the communication strategies learners use when a desired referential expression is lacking. We noticed that the effort to make themselves clear in using these referential expressions sometimes led them to use more complex syntax.

In Chapter 7, we will explore the learners' use of complex syntactic structures and vocabulary in using learner language for higher-level cognitive functions such as making inferences about causes and effects, or supporting hypotheses by relating observable facts to abstractions.

## *Further Reading*

**Ellis, R.** 1994. 'Communication strategies'. *The Study of Second Language Acquisition*. Oxford: Oxford University Press, pp. 396-403.

**Tarone, E.** and **G. Yule.** 1989. Chapter 9 'Strategic competence'. *Focus on the Language Learner*. Oxford: Oxford University Press.

**Yule, G.** 1996. Chapter 3 'Reference and inference'. *Pragmatics*. Oxford: Oxford University Press.

**Yule, G.** 1997. Chapter 1 'Overview'. *Referential Communication Tasks*. Mahwah, NJ: Lawrence Erlbaum Associates.

**Yule, G.** 1999. Chapter 2 'Articles'. *Explaining English Grammar*. Oxford: Oxford University Press.

**Yule, G.** and **D. Macdonald.** 1990. 'Resolving referential conflicts in L2 interaction: The effect of proficiency and interactive role'. *Language Learning* 40: 539–56.

# 7 EXPLORING COMPLEXITY IN LANGUAGE

## Introduction

In the last chapter, we examined learner language as it is used in referential communication, exchanging information about people, things, and events. We noted that in the effort to make themselves clearer, learners sometimes repeated the same vocabulary item, but they also sometimes used increasingly complex syntax and a variety of vocabulary items. In this chapter, we continue our exploration of complex syntax and vocabulary development in learner language and consider the way in which academic and professional discourse may both require and elicit the use of more complex linguistic forms. In this chapter we:

- review research showing how use of a language for academic purposes, rather than just for social purposes, elicits the use of complex syntax and vocabulary development
- use two analytical measures to explore the way sentence complexity in learner language is affected when the six learners are asked to move beyond describing concrete entities, to making inferences about underlying abstract concepts
- explore complexity in vocabulary in learner language using type-token ratios (TTRs)
- examine the way the learners express the academic language functions of inference and justification
- consider the relationship between language complexity and current pedagogical models of content-based instruction (CBI), which balance instruction in academic content and language.

## Social and Academic Language

Up to this point in the book, we have focused on what Cummins (1981, 2000) refers to as social language proficiency: the ability to use contextually supported language in everyday communication with reference to concrete entities and actions. But in order to use the language for academic tasks, Cummins points out that second language (L2) learners need academic language proficiency: the ability to use cognitively demanding language with considerably less contextual support. In academic language, the student moves from using language to refer to concrete, observable entities to using it to refer to abstract concepts as a tool for critical thinking. Academic language includes mastery of discipline-specific vocabulary, and use of Language for **academic language functions** such as comparison, classification, synthesis, evaluation, and inference. Though there is a continuum between social and academic language, scholars like Biber (1988, 2006) and Schleppegrell (2004) have shown that language used for academic purposes usually becomes more syntactically complex, with more nominalizations, noun clauses, relative clauses, adverbial clauses, and other complex sentence constructions, and a wider range of vocabulary. These are the core structural features of written registers in academic language. Ravid and Tolchinsky (2002) point out that native-speaking children do not acquire these complex sentence constructions or vocabulary items until the upper-elementary grades, when they begin to encounter more complex, dense written language.

> Written text conventions promote metalinguistic thinking in various linguistic domains such as sound/letter correspondence, word and sentence boundaries, and appropriate grammatical constructions (e.g., past perfect in English, passé simple in French, or optional bound morphology in Hebrew). … the reciprocal character of speech and writing in a literate community makes it a synergistic system where certain features (e.g., basic syntax) originate in the spoken input, while others, such as complex syntax and advanced and domain-specific lexical items, originate in the written input.

(Ravid and Tolchinsky 2002: 430)

Second language (L2) learners learn the complex syntax and vocabulary of academic language in school contexts. Whether they are in K-12 or post-secondary school settings, L2 learners must not only know what grammatical features to draw on, but they also need to know when and how to use them to complete academic tasks (Schleppegrell 2004, Zwiers 2008). For example, to compose a successful historical account, a common academic history genre which retells events and explains why they happened, students must be able to express both temporal and causal links through adverbs, prepositional phrases, and conjunctions; additionally, they must be able to nominalize events (for example, compete → competition, rebel → rebellion) to explain how one event led to another; and finally, they must be able to organize their writing to highlight these explanations (Coffin 1997). Adamson (1993) shows in detail how academic language develops in several case studies of English language learners. Language learners in primary grades learn to perform academic language functions such as predicting and inferring at the same time that they learn the language structures to do so. Older language learners who have had limited formal schooling in their native language (NL) need to develop new language resources to demonstrate their abilities as they engage in unfamiliar academic tasks. Those learners who have had experience with academic discourse in their native language find this task easier, but still must become familiar with the features of academic tasks in their new language. With all the cognitive demands of vocabulary, academic tasks, background knowledge, and language structures, it is no wonder that academic language takes much longer for a second language learner to acquire than social language. Where social language may be acquired in just two years, Thomas and Collier (1997) estimate that it can take a learner anywhere from five to ten years to become proficient in using a second language for academic purposes. Hakuta (2000), in a controlled study of schools with reputations for excellence in English language learner instruction, finds that academic language proficiency takes four to seven years to develop, in comparison to only three to five years for social language.

# Language Complexity

The complexity of learner language can be seen in the variety of structures and the breadth of vocabulary that a learner uses. One type of complexity is grammatical, which we will examine next as we look at the relationship between sentence complexity and the cognitive demands of a task.

## Sentence Complexity

The photos that we used in the Jigsaw Task (DVD Segment 5) to elicit comparisons of the physical characteristics of two houses are also used in the Comparison Task (DVD Segment 6) for a task that probes the learners' ability to use learner language for more decontextualized, abstract functions. In the Jigsaw Task, we asked the learners to compare visible characteristics of two houses such as exterior color and number of windows; these are concrete observable entities. However, in the comparison task, we ask the learners to view the photos as 'cultural documents' (Barnes-Karol and Broner 2008b), and tell us what those photos reveal about such abstract concepts as the culture in which the photos were taken. Here we are asking the learners to use the information in the photos as evidence in articulating through their learner language some inferences about abstract cultural constructs such as the social class and economic status of the occupants, their lifestyles, their family structures, and their cultural values. Implicit in such a task is an 'academic' comparison between the learners' native cultures and those cultures represented in the photos. This task is more cognitively demanding than the tasks in DVD Segments 2 through 5, though the use of the photographs provides contextual support in springboarding to a discussion of abstract, non-concrete concepts. In this way, the task provides support for the expression and development of language that is typically used in academic tasks.

There are many possible ways to measure sentence complexity (see Ellis and Barkhuizen 2005: 147–56). For our first window into sentence complexity, let's look for learners' production of sentences that contain more than one verb, as in the following examples.

- 'He's late because his alarm clock *is* broken'.
- 'He's frantically *looking* for his car keys, which he can't *find*'.
- 'There *is* no one *living* in the house' or 'She ... *gets* ... very confused about *finding* it in her purse'.
- 'The two women ... don't really *notice* what the little girl *is doing*'.

- 'He's *trying to find* ... ' or 'I *would like* you *to make* me *practice*' or 'There *is* no one *to take* care of the house'.

---

**EXERCISE 7.1**        **Sentence Complexity and Task Demand**

DVD SEGMENT 5: JIGSAW TASK AND DVD SEGMENT 6: COMPARISON TASK

In Tables 7.1 and 7.2 below we list all the complex sentences each pair of learners produced in DVD Segment 5 and in DVD Segment 6. (In some cases, the complexity of the sentence is co-constructed across more than one utterance.) Referring to these sentences, answer these questions:

1  How is the cognitive demand of each task related to the complex sentences that the learners produced?
2  Below are the directions read to the learners before the Jigsaw and Comparison Tasks. Read the directions, then look at the transcripts of Jeanne and Catrine's Jigsaw and Comparison Tasks (see pages 155–6), and classify nouns that they use as concrete or abstract. How do the directions affect the learners' use of concrete or abstract terms?

*Directions for Jigsaw Task:*
Each of you has a photograph of a house in Minnesota. I would like you to compare the houses by giving each other information about your photograph or by asking questions, but don't show the other person your photograph. For example, you could say, 'This house has 4 windows', or you could ask, 'Is that house in a city?'

*Directions for Comparison Task:*
I would like you to talk about who might live in each house. For example, how many people do you think live in this house? What do you think their social class is? Are these typical houses in Minnesota? What do these kinds of houses tell you about American culture?

*Rodrigo*   *Antonio*

*Xue*   *Chun*

*Catrine*   *Jeanne*

| **Rodrigo and Antonio (DVD 5.1)** | | |
|---|---|---|
| None | | |
| **Xue and Chun (DVD 5.2)** | | |
| None | | |
| **Catrine and Jeanne (DVD 5.3)** | | |
| line 3: | **C** | mine has something that could help me go to another place |
| line 4: | **C** | and something that can help me climb |
| line 25–6: | **C** | I can only see four windows but I cannot see the other part of the house. |

*Table 7.1 Complex Sentences in the Jigsaw Task (DVD Segment 5)*

| **Rodrigo and Antonio (DVD 6.1)** | | |
|---|---|---|
| Lines 1–2: | **A** | This house show me that the people had a good job because the house show it. |
| Lines 6–7: | **R** | This house show there are very money and this house no. |
| **Xue and Chun (DVD 6.2)** | | |
| Line 1: | **C** | this house will have four people to live in |
| Lines 9–10: | **C** | when we go back home on the bus, we saw a lot of this kind of houses. |
| Line 23: | **X** | they didn't want to live in that apartment |
| Lines 23–4: | **X** | they don't want to share the garage with other peoples |
| Line 25: | **X** | they have lawns belongs to them. |
| **Catrine and Jeanne (DVD 6.3)** | | |
| Line 3: | **C** | I can understand that by the culture of the American, there's classes |
| Lines 4–5: | **C** | different people, depend on how they job are, to have the kind of house they have. |
| Line 6: | **J** | its depend on how much they earn. |
| Lines 8–9: | **C** | the person earn more than the people living in the other house. |
| Lines 12–13: | **J** | there may be people who got enough. |
| Lines 13–14: | **J** | it seems that people don't really care about the out. |
| Line 19: | **C** | there's nobody living in that house. |
| Lines 19–20: | **C** | doesn't really mean that the other house has more money |
| Lines 20–21: | **C** | maybe there's no one living in the other house. No one to take care of the house. |
| Lines 22–23: | **J** | they are tired to wash and clean up and kind of putting everything clean. |

*Table 7.2 Complex Sentences in the Comparison Task (DVD Segment 6)*

In Exercise 7.1, we segmented the learners' utterances into units for you, based on our relatively loose definition of sentence complexity. As you explore learner language on your own and delve more deeply into syntactic complexity, a more precise way of segmenting language into units is needed. One commonly used unit is the **AS-unit**, which is defined as: 'a single speaker's utterance consisting of an **independent clause** or **subclausal unit**, together with any **subordinate clause**(s) associated with it' (Foster, Tonkyn, and Wigglesworth 2000: 365). An independent clause has a subject and a tensed verb, and can stand alone as a sentence, for example, 'he's late', 'he's frantically looking for his car keys', 'she gets very confused'. A subclausal unit is a segment of speech or writing that can be expanded into a full clause by recovering elements that were omitted (such as 'Want to go?' when the subject is clear from the context and 'Just grammar' in answer to a question such as 'What did you study?') or it is a minor utterance such as 'Thank you' or 'OK' (Ellis and Barkhuizen 2005: 148). A subordinate clause would be considered a sentence fragment if it were used alone, such as, 'which he can't find', 'to take care of the house', and 'because the house show it'. It includes a verb (either tensed or not tensed) and at least one other element such as a subject or object. To illustrate this, part of the discussion of Olivia and Victoria during the Jigsaw Task is shown below, divided into AS-units which are marked by ||.

1  **V**  || So the three similarities between our houses, I suppose, if we were to list them, would
2        be they're both two-story houses, ...||
3  **O**  || They both have white siding. ||
4  **V**  || Right. ||
5  **O**  || Um. ||
6  **V**  || And they're both in residential areas. ||
7  **O**  || That works. || Or they both have green lawns, depending ... ||
8  **V**  || Right, more than three similarities. ||

In the next exercise, we ask you to use this measure to take a more precise look at the impact of task on the grammatical complexity of the language of a learner of your choice. We recommend that you start by comparing DVD Segments 5 and 6 again, this time in terms of AS-units. We will supply answers to Exercise 7.2 based only on the learners' performance in DVD Segments 5 and 6; you will be on your own as you branch out to other tasks!

---

**EXERCISE 7.2**          **Impact of Task on AS-Units**

DVD SEGMENTS 1–6

1  Focusing on just one learner and two tasks (we recommend starting with DVD Segments 5 and 6), choose a language segment from each task with the same number of words. Compare the number of AS-units in the two segments. How many of the units contain subordinate clauses?

2  Discuss the difficulties that arose as you analyzed the language segments. For example, how did you deal with false starts and repetitions? If you compared spoken and written language, did you have to make any changes in your analysis for the different modalities?

There are many other ways of exploring syntactic complexity in learner language. Depending on your question or puzzle, and your comfort with linguistic analysis, you might find it useful to look for examples of specific grammatical constructions that are characteristic of academic language proficiency, such as:

• relative clauses
  (classify people or things, as in 'the woman *who built the house*' or 'the house *that Jack built*')
• adverbial clauses
  (usually begin with conjunctions like 'although', 'because', 'when', 'if', as in '*Although the sun's shining*, it's freezing outside'.)
• noun clauses
  (can be used as object of a verb, as in 'I hope *that it gets warmer*'.)
• passives
  (focus on the recipient of some action, as in 'The car *was damaged (by hail)*'.)
• compound nouns
  (as in '*high-risk borrowers*' or '*multiply-embedded relative clauses*')

There are excellent descriptions and more examples of these syntactic constructions in Yule (1999, 2006). While we are not going to structure this exploration for you with another exercise, we know that there are interesting patterns to be found in the learner language of our six learners.

## *Lexical Complexity*

Some learners may use relatively simple sentence structure with a wide range of vocabulary words while for other learners the reverse may be true. Breadth of vocabulary is also a type of complexity. We saw in Chapter 6 that referential communication tasks could affect vocabulary range, as some learners used the same vocabulary item over and over to make sure the listener could keep track of a referent. We noted in the Answers to Exercise 6.2 that a native speaker's (NS's) use of two different lexical items to refer to the same character provided stylistic variety but might reduce referential effectiveness for a less-proficient listener. In this section, we look at the range of vocabulary words that our learners employed as a way of assessing complexity in their language.

One way to measure lexical complexity is to count the number of different words that occur in a segment of written or spoken text: a **type-token ratio** (TTR). To illustrate this, we work through an example from Jeanne's Narrative Task (DVD 4.6) As our segment to analyze, we choose the first 50 fluent words, which are shown below. To count the first 50 fluent words, we omit hesitations (um), false starts (in the), and repetitions; for example, we omit the second instance of 'her friend'. The omitted words are underlined below.

1 **J** This is a lady; she went to the grocery, and then she met her friend, <u>her friend</u>, I don't
2 know the name, with her baby. And then the baby put, <u>um</u>, something in her bag that she
3 took from, the grocery, and she put it in her, bag, <u>in the</u>, in her mom friend's bag.

The TTR is the total number of different words used (types) divided by the total number of words in the segment (tokens), in this case, 50 (Robinson 1995). In the 50 fluent words, we count the number of different words used, which is 29 in Jeanne's oral narrative, so the TTR is 29/50. The closer this number is to one, the greater the learner's lexical richness in this segment. Biber (1988) found that native-speaker written language had more lexical richness (that is, higher TTRs) than native-speaker spoken language; other comparisons of written versus oral task performance have supported this finding. Let's see if learner language follows this same pattern.

---

**EXERCISE 7.3** **Lexical Complexity**

DVD SEGMENT 4: NARRATIVE TASKS: ORAL AND WRITTEN

*Jeanne*

We computed the TTR for Jeanne's oral narrative in DVD 4.6, but one number by itself doesn't tell us very much, so in this exercise, we ask you to compare Jeanne's oral narrative to her written narrative (WR 4.6 Narrative Task (Jeanne), page 155) and to compare her performance to that of other learners.

1 Compute the TTR for the first 50-word segment of Jeanne's written narrative. Compare this to the TTR for her oral narrative in DVD 4.6. What does this comparison tell you about Jeanne's vocabulary?

2 Compute the TTR for the initial 50-word segment of one other learner's oral and written narratives, and one of the NSs' oral and written narratives. Different students should choose different speakers and share their results. How can you account for differences or similarities that you see between speakers and between the two tasks?

3	Choose a 50-word segment of Jeanne's speech from her Question Task in DVD 2.6 and compute the TTR. Compare it to the TTR from her oral narrative in DVD 4.6. Does the difference in tasks affect the richness of her vocabulary? Explain.

4	Look again at a Narrative Task from one of the other learners in DVD Segment 4. How does omitting or including formulaic language ('chunks') in the word count affect the TTR?

## Academic Language Functions

In order to succeed in the classroom, 'students not only must know the content of academic subjects, they must learn the appropriate form in which to cast their academic knowledge' (Mehan 1979: 133). They must learn how to express academic language functions such as inferring, predicting, and synthesizing in appropriate grammatical forms and precise vocabulary. In this section, we explore how our learners expressed the academic language functions of inference and justification in DVD Segment 6: Comparison Task. We look at the range of expressions they used for these functions because using a wide range of different structures is another type of language complexity. In the Comparison Task, the learners were asked to go beyond what they could see in pictures and make inferences about who might live in the houses and what their social class might be. We begin by first looking at what the NSs said in this task:

| | | |
|---|---|---|
| 1 | **V** | Well, I think that these are both family homes, so I would assume that |
| 2 | | there's a family living in both of these houses um but your house strikes me as a m-, like |
| 3 | | a upper-middle class family whereas my house is more of a lower-middle class um home |
| 4 | | just based on, it just doesn't look quite as kept up, um and also just not quite as big, so, |
| 5 | | that's my impression. |
| 6 | **O** | I get the same impression. Um, my thoughts also um just from looking at these that |
| 7 | | it's possible that the house that I, that my house has one or two children but if you saw |
| 8 | | the other house, even though they're the same size, you would expect them to have more |
| 9 | | children. |
| 10 | **V** | Yeah. |
| 11 | **O** | Because people in lower-class families can't afford large houses. |

Victoria infers that one house is upper-middle class and the other is lower-middle class, introducing her inference with the phrase 'strikes me as'. She brings in the evidence for her inference using the phrase 'just based on' and ends it with the clause 'that's my impression'. The justification for her inference is 'it just doesn't look quite as kept up, um and also just not quite as big'. We have written these expressions in Table 7.3 along with Olivia's for comparison.

| Speaker | Inference | Signals for inference | Justification | Signals for justification |
|---------|-----------|----------------------|---------------|---------------------------|
| *Victoria* | your house ... a upper-middle class family whereas my house is more of a lower-middle class um home | strikes me as | it just doesn't look quite as kept up, um and also not as big | just based on, that's my impression |
| *Olivia* | my house has one or two children but if you saw the other house, even though they're the same size, you would expect them to have more children. | my thoughts | people in lower-class families can't afford large houses | from looking at these, because |

*Table 7.3 Inference and Justification – Native Speakers*

**EXERCISE 7.4**     **The Language of Inference and Justification**

 DVD SEGMENT 6: COMPARISON TASK

In the same way that we looked at the NSs' expressions for inference and justification above, analyze the expressions of one pair of learners in the Comparison Task (DVD Segment 6). Read the transcripts (see pages 138, 148, 156) and watch the video as you do so since opinions may also be expressed nonverbally. Use Table 7.4 to fill in your answers. Discuss your answers with a partner in class.

1  What expressions are used by the pair of learners to infer?
2  Do the learners give evidence for their inferences? What expressions do the learners use to justify their inferences?
3  What expressions, if any, do they use to signal that they are making an inference or giving a justification?
4  Given the answers to 1 and 2 above, what are some ways you, as these learners' teacher, could provide scaffolding for their development of expressions used for inference and justification?

| Speaker | Inference | Signals for inference | Justification | Signals for justification |
|---|---|---|---|---|
|  |  |  |  |  |
|  |  |  |  |  |

*Table 7.4 Inference and Justification – Learners*

Photocopiable © Oxford University Press

# Academic Language and Content-Based Instruction

Through examples and exercises in this book, we have seen some of the relationships between the form and complexity of language and language function. In particular, academic discourse includes language features that correspond to the knowledge structures that students are learning. Thus a focus on language itself is crucial for helping students learn academic material. One very successful pedagogical model for promoting academic language is **Content-Based Language Instruction** (commonly referred to simply as CBI). CBI is a flexible curricular approach that can include a variety of teaching styles and programmatic purposes. It can be used across a range of program models from, for example, foreign language immersion in elementary school to university-level intensive English as a Second Language (ESL) programs (see Snow 2001 for a description of this continuum). CBI can be particularly powerful because it merges students' goals of language learning with learning new academic, workplace, or cultural information and thought processes. It also encourages access to and use of a range of genres (for example, writing personal narratives, expository text, email, leaving a voice mail), contextualized by highly meaningful content.

Public schools can provide CBI for mainstreamed ESL students (Mohan, Leung and Davison 2001), and colleges and universities provide CBI for international students. In such programs, academic content is delivered through the medium of the L2, with ancillary instruction for language learners who need support in developing the requisite academic language skills. Examples of such CBI programs include adjunct ESL courses attached to disciplinary courses, International Teaching Assistant (ITA) courses, and writing support centers. Colleges and universities also use CBI as a model in Foreign Language Across the Curriculum (FLAC) programs for NSs of English, where academic courses are delivered through the foreign language, again with ancillary language support (Klee and Barnes-Karol 2006). The content of CBI courses for L2 instruction can vary from sociology to political science to history. In one of the most successful world language CBI models in the country, at St. Olaf College, Barnes-Karol and Broner (2008a) make culture the content of their CBI program, and use it to promote critical thinking in the L2.

CBI presents challenges to teachers. Sometimes language teachers fail to prioritize and assess the content learning, which minimizes the relevance of the content. Other times, the teacher may find it difficult to remember to scaffold and assess the language objectives. Bigelow, Ranney, and Dahlman (2006) write:

> … just as it is difficult for language learners to attend to language and content simultaneously (VanPatten 1990), it seems difficult for teachers to explicitly focus on content and language simultaneously in instruction. To lessen the cognitive load of this work … teachers sometimes devise parallel tracks where traditional grammar is taught alongside thematic content, as in dividing the lesson between the present perfect tense and the content theme. While the addition of a content component will make the ESL class more engaging, this parallel track approach fails to bring content and language together because the chosen grammar points do not reflect content-related language, making it difficult for students to apply their study of language to actual uses outside of class (Larsen-Freeman 2001) or to capitalize on connections that may exist with other classes.
> (p. 41)

These authors propose a CBI curriculum planning model for teachers that serves to keep the balance between language and content, as well as better connect the two. A research-based model for counterbalanced CBI instruction with similar goals is presented in Lyster (2007), with several examples. The further readings at the end of this chapter provide valuable information about CBI. In addition, free online information about content-based language learning – everything from a discussion of underlying principles to sample lesson plans and units – can be downloaded at: Content-Based Language Teaching with Technology (2009), and information on K-6 language immersion curricula, programs, and research is available at: Language Immersion Education and Research (2009).

## Summary

In Chapter 7, the complexities of language have been the target of our explorations. We looked into ways to measure the complexity of syntax and vocabulary that are characteristic of school language, as opposed to social language. We investigated the range of expressions that may be used to articulate some academic language functions in academic and professional contexts. As we have moved through Chapters 3–7, we examined the language of six learners in multiple ways: through error and target-like use analysis, developmental sequences, interactional analysis, referential effectiveness, and the complexity of language needed for academic purposes. In Chapter 8, we will use the framework of Exploratory Practice to suggest a process for you to use as you go to work on puzzles and problems in your own classroom.

## *Further Reading*

**Bernach, C., K. Galinat**, and **S. Jimenez.** 2005. Chapter 5 'Co-teaching in a sheltered model: Maximizing content and language acquisition for beginning-level English language learners' in D. Kaufman and J. Crandall (eds.). *Content-Based Instruction in Primary and Secondary School Settings*. Alexandria, VA: TESOL.

**Brinton, D., M. Snow**, and **M. Wesche.** 2003. Chapter 7 'Suggestions for content-based materials development and adaptation'. *Content-Based Second Language Instruction*. Ann Arbor, MI: University of Michigan Press.

**Bunch, G., R. Lotan, G. Valdés**, and **E. Cohen.** 2005. Chapter 2 'Keeping content at the heart of content-based instruction: Access and support for transitional English learners' in D. Kaufman and J. Crandall (eds.). *Content-Based Instruction in Primary and Secondary School Settings*. Alexandria, VA: TESOL.

**Ellis, R.** and **G. Barkhuizen.** 2005. Chapter 7 'Analysing accuracy, complexity, and fluency'. *Analysing Learner Language*. Oxford: Oxford University Press.

**Lyster, R**. 2007. *Learning and Teaching Language through Content: A Counterbalanced Approach*. Amsterdam: John Benjamins, pp. 71–8, and 133–6.

**Schleppegrell, M.** 2004. Chapter 3 'Linguistic features of academic registers'. *The Language of Schooling: A Functional Linguistics Perspective*. Mahwah, NJ: Lawrence Erlbaum Associates.

**Zwiers, J.** 2008. *Building Academic Language: Essential Practices for Content Classrooms, Grades 5–12*. San Francisco, CA: Jossey-Bass.

# 8 EXPLORING LEARNER LANGUAGE IN THE CLASSROOM

## Introduction

In Chapter 7, we looked at the vocabulary and complex language produced by the six learners, and considered its function in academic and professional discourse. We have now analyzed the language of these learners from five different points of view: error and target-like use (TLU) analysis, developmental sequence, interactional analysis, referential effectiveness, and complexity of language needed for academic purposes. In the process, we hope you have acquired skills and tools, and gained confidence in your ability to use these different approaches, to analyze learner language. Chapter 8 is intended to serve as a guide as you move on to study puzzles and problems related to learner language in your own local context, whether this be in your classroom or your particular community. We structure this guide using the framework of Exploratory Practice (Allwright 2001, 2005; Allwright and Hanks 2009), as we:

- review in detail the framework provided by Exploratory Practice
- walk you through a step-by-step process of carrying out a study of learner language in your own classroom, showing how to identify a puzzle or question, protect learners' rights, collect language learner data
- analyze it using techniques practiced in this book
- consider pedagogical responses.

## The Exploratory Practice Framework

The central goal of Exploratory Practice is to improve the quality of life in the language classroom for both teachers and learners by expanding their understanding of their learning and teaching processes, and, where needed, by acting to improve those processes. The processes of Exploratory Practice, which start with Reflective Practice and may lead to Action Research, are illustrated in Figure 8.1.

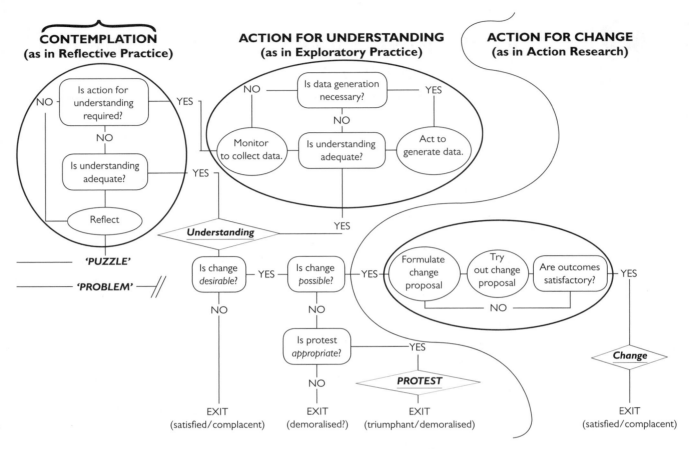

*Figure 8.1    A Flow Chart Illustrating Choices Made in Exploratory Practice (Allwright 2001)*

Within the framework of the three-part process that is shown in the flow chart in Figure 8.1, we might begin with a teacher who has a desire for better understanding of a local puzzle or problem about language learning. In part one of the process, Contemplation, the teacher simply reflects; the teacher thinks about the puzzle in light of what he or she knows. So, for example, what you have learned about the process of second language acquisition (SLA) may improve your understanding of learner language in your classroom, if you just stop and think about it a bit. For example, you may have noticed that the learners in your advanced English as a second language (ESL) class, after several years of English study, are still leaving the final *–s* off third person singular verbs, and you may have wondered if this was due to some problem in your pedagogy. After a little reflection, you may remember that SLA research on morpheme orders (see page 17) consistently ranks third person singular *–s* as one of the last morphemes to be acquired by English language learners, no matter what the teaching approach. Having reached this understanding through contemplation, you can decide whether to move on to part three in Figure 8.1, Action Research. Is curricular change either desirable or possible? If it is, you may decide to take action to see if a change in your curriculum can speed up the acquisition process. For example, you may decide to implement an intensive program of corrective feedback in which you provide a barrage of prompts in response to third person singular errors, coupled with a reward system for successful repairs, to see if learner performance can be improved.

Simple reflection is not always enough to achieve understanding; we often need more information. In such a case, the teacher moves on in the flow chart in Figure 8.1 to part two, Exploratory Practice proper, and Action for Understanding, to gather information about what is going on with the learner languages in this particular context. For example, suppose you are wondering whether your students are able to scaffold one another's production of learner language forms in classroom pairwork. Perhaps they are not accustomed to doing groupwork, or perhaps they lack confidence in their peers' ability to help them. You even wonder if they will lapse into the native language (NL) in interactions where you are not watching. What you know about SLA theory will not help you understand this puzzle or problem; you need more data – more information about the way your particular students interact in pairwork and small group interactions, and whether they help each other produce learner language forms in interactions when you are not watching. Figure 8.1 shows two ways you can gather that information (or collect your data) in taking Action for Understanding.

The first way is simply to monitor more systematically, to gather data on the nature and extent of the puzzle you have identified. In this first approach to collecting data, you are looking for what Ellis and Barkhuizen (2005: 23) call 'naturally-occurring samples' of learner language in interaction – the way your students use the language in normal classroom activities. For example, you may assign a pairwork activity from your textbook, and find ways to unobtrusively observe their interactions. You may listen from afar while you work at your desk, or ask your students to audio-record their interaction while they are engaged in the pairwork activity. If you work with a co-teacher, paraprofessional or volunteer in your classroom, you may be able to observe while your partner is teaching, or vice versa. Based on these observations, or a relatively quick listen to the recordings, you should be able to identify instances of NL use, and assess the degree to which your students do try to help each other in producing learner language. Depending on your question, you may or may not want to transcribe some or all of the learner language on the recordings so you can analyze what is going on more precisely; we will discuss some issues to consider in undertaking such transcriptions in 'Collecting Learner Language Data' below.

The second way to collect data as part of Action for Understanding is to generate it, as shown in the flow chart in Figure 8.1. There are different kinds of data you can generate by using 'clinical elicitation', depending on your question or puzzle. If you want to learn what your students believe to be grammatical sentences in the target language (TL), you could use a written task that focuses learner attention on grammatical correctness, such as a grammaticality judgment test or a multiple choice test. If you want to learn about learner language forms your students produce unconsciously, you could use oral tasks that focus their attention on meaning while also encouraging the unconscious production of particular linguistic forms. Most of the learner language samples you have analyzed in this book were 'clinically elicited' in this way. For example, you might wonder what stage of questions your students unconsciously produce when they are engaged in meaningful interactions with each other and you are not present. You could assign an oral pairwork task (perhaps the one we used in this book) that specifically elicits questions, and ask students to audio-record themselves while doing the task together. Then you could analyze those recordings the same way you analyzed the data in Chapter 4 to achieve a better understanding of the puzzle – what stage of questions do your students unconsciously produce with each other when they are focused on meaning? Are some of your students producing higher-level questions in such interactions than others? Armed with this information, you may or may not decide to move on to part three, Action Research, to take action to change your pedagogical practice in light of what has been learned.

In pursuing the goal of a better understanding of learner language and learning processes in the classroom, Allwright and Hanks (2009) strongly suggest that teachers partner with learners in posing and answering puzzles about language learning and teaching. Allwright and Hanks argue convincingly that learners, like teachers, should be investigators in Exploratory Practice – that they too can benefit by reflecting, observing, and generating data as they work with teachers to try to solve language puzzles and learning problems. For example, in each of the examples we gave above, you could ask the students in your class to listen to the recordings they make of their own interactions, and ask them to answer the same questions you did. Did they use the NL? Why or why not? Did their partners help them produce learner language forms they were struggling with? How? What question forms were they and their partner producing in the interaction? Can they repair those questions to make them more native-like? You can also ask learners what puzzles and problems *they* have with regard to central issues like NL use in the classroom, or the value of peer assistance in groupwork. Their puzzles and problems may be of interest to you and help everyone to improve their understanding of learning processes in the classroom. (If this approach interests you, then we urge you to learn more by reading Allwright and Hanks 2009.)

Having outlined the general framework of Exploratory Practice, we will now turn to a step-by-step description of the typical process one goes through in a descriptive study of learner language in the classroom.

## *Identifying a Problem or Puzzle*

Your process of exploration begins with your identification of a puzzle, problem, or question: something that you want to understand that is related to learner language or the way it is used and learned in your classroom. Perhaps it seems to you that students from a particular NL background have unusual difficulty learning a particular TL form, and you want to find the exact extent and nature of the difficulty. For example, knowing that Spanish speakers typically have a hard time moving out of Stage 1 negation in English, you might ask, 'What Stage 2 negation forms do Spanish speakers in my class produce first, in what contexts and tasks?' Here are some other questions you might ask: 'What referential expressions do students in my class use to help listeners keep track of who did what in a narrative?' 'What linguistic forms do advanced learners in my content-based instruction (CBI) class use to define academic terms, express causality, or create classifications?' 'Does the presentation in our textbook of relative clause types match my students' built-in syllabus for acquisition of that feature?' There are many other interesting puzzles or problems related to learners and their language that could be the focus of Exploratory Practice. The main thing is to find a topic that is really interesting to you and helpful in your classroom – one that you really want to spend some time on. Follow your own interest and intuition.

Now, ask yourself if it is possible to get the information you need to answer your question. Not all questions about learner language are answerable in descriptive small-scale studies. For example, you cannot compare the behavior of learners in your class to that of all learners in all other classes; you do not have the time, access, or (possibly) the training in inferential statistics. As another example, you cannot definitively establish exactly what caused a particular type of learner error, because you do not have a direct window into the human brain. And of course, you cannot once and for all 'prove' that one SLA theory is right and another wrong; you do not have major grant funding or years to spend on that project. So ask questions about your learners that you can reasonably expect to answer with information you can easily get and analyze.

## *Protecting Learners' Rights*

If you are gathering data in your classroom entirely for your own purposes (and possibly also for the purposes of your students), with *minimal disruption* to the normal function of classroom processes focused on learning and teaching the language, and with the *sole purpose of improving those classroom processes*, then you do not need the approval of outside agencies (for example, the program director, principal, superintendent, or school system) to carry out your inquiry. However, if your data gathering will interfere with the normal processes of learning and teaching in your class, or if you plan to share the results of your inquiry with others outside the classroom, as for example at a local teachers' meeting or conference, then you will indeed need such approvals. You should check with those in charge locally to determine the procedures for gaining that approval before you gather any data for your study. (In addition, if you are a college or university student, you should check with your institution about the approval process for research plans.) In all these cases, you must give careful thought to protecting the rights of the students in your classroom you will be studying.

If you are a college or university student or teacher, you should know that in all post-secondary institutions, the rights of what are referred to as 'human subjects' (in our case, language learners) in research are carefully protected by Institutional Review Boards (IRBs). University-based researchers, who usually plan to present their research publicly at the university and write it up in the form of a thesis or other publication, must submit their research plans to such boards and have them approved before they can begin to gather data from their participants. The primary concern of such Boards in studies of learner language is to make sure ahead of time that the rights of the learners being studied will be protected. Those rights include:

- freedom from coercion: the right not to participate in the study and to withdraw from it at any time
- general purpose: the right to know the general purpose of the study and how the data will be used
- understanding of risks and benefits: the right to know possible risks and benefits, including what they will be asked to do and how long it will take
- confidentiality: the right to keep their identities secret from outside audiences, unless they give explicit permission
- recourse: the right to know who to contact if they have complaints about the study.

When the researcher is a teacher who wants to study his or her own students, whether or not outside approval is an issue, avoidance of coercion is one of the most important priorities. It is difficult for students to refuse to participate in a study when the researcher is also the teacher who controls their grades and decides whether they pass the class. Instructors who plan to move beyond observation of natural learning in their classrooms, to assign tasks to elicit data for study that go beyond normal class requirements, need to bend over backward to make sure that their students know why those tasks are being assigned, how task results will be used to improve classroom processes, and that they have the right to agree or disagree to participate.

The rights of the learners are typically specified in a consent form written in language they can understand – in their NL, if necessary. The learners (or their parents or guardians if the learners are not adults) must read the form and, if they choose to participate, sign it before the study begins; the researcher also signs the form; and both keep a copy. We provide the outline of such a consent form on page 161.

Finally, we stress again that this kind of official approval process is typically not required when teachers do exploratory studies in their own classrooms for the sole purpose of improving internal processes of learning and teaching. Generally, as long as they do not intend to present the results of their study to audiences outside their own classrooms, teachers are allowed to gather and analyze data there without outside permission. Of course, if teachers partner with their own students in investigating puzzles and problems (Allwright and Hanks 2009), then many problems related to infringements of learners' rights can be avoided. The teacher should be sensitive to power imbalances and make sure that their student co-investigators are actively involved, and that they (or their parents or guardians) consent to all phases of the project.

## *Collecting Learner Language Data*

As we outlined in our discussion of Exploratory Practice at the beginning of this chapter, there are two ways to collect learner language data in your classroom: by systematically observing learner language as it is produced naturally in your classroom, and by administering tasks – either tasks designed to focus learners' attention on target linguistic forms, or tasks designed to elicit targeted linguistic forms of learner language while maintaining a primary focus on meaning.

### Systematically Observe Naturally-Occurring Learner Language

It is very important that you be systematic in your observations of learner language use as it occurs naturally in your classroom. Learner language production has been shown to be very sensitive to small changes in social context – including the presence of the teacher – so it is important for you to keep a record of as many features of the social context as possible, even as you try to keep a low profile to avoid unduly influencing your students' naturally occurring speech production. Ellis and Barkhuizen (2005: 25) provide a useful list and discussion of some of the most important of these factors. For oral data, these factors include the name of the speaker, who the speaker was addressing and who was within hearing range, the topic of the interaction, and the location.

Because spoken language is ephemeral, you will need to find some way to keep a record of it so you can analyze it later. There are three primary recording options: note-taking, audio-recording, and video-recording (Ellis and Barkhuizen 2005). Audio- and video-recordings will need to be transcribed if you want to analyze the language carefully. Transcription usually takes far longer than you might think. Ellis and Barkhuizen estimate that it takes about seven hours to transcribe one hour of oral data in 'broad' transcription (broad transcription usually uses standard spelling, with pauses marked). Using that as a rule of thumb, a five-minute stretch of oral interaction between two speakers might take you 35 minutes to transcribe. 'Narrow' transcription, such as that conventionally used for conversation analysis, or a phonetic transcription using the **International Phonetic Alphabet** (IPA), takes much longer. So you should only transcribe those parts of the oral data that you intend to analyze (for example, only the questions, or only the references to past time). One of the drawbacks of naturally occurring language data is that it is not focused on the linguistic feature you want to study, so you may need to listen to long stretches of the recording before you find examples of the feature you are interested in and want to transcribe. That is a good reason to assign tasks to generate more targeted data, in ways we discuss in the next section.

### Experimentally Elicit Learner Language Samples

The type of task you use to generate targeted data depends on what it is you are trying to learn about learner language. Experimental elicitation tasks are form-focused, and designed to get learners to produce specific, predetermined linguistic features. Here you want to know whether the learners have studied the form, and can use it consciously when focused on accuracy. Form-focused classroom tests are typically of this type. They provide highly constrained linguistic contexts in which learners only need to produce relatively short responses. If you want to know what your students believe is the correct rule for a particular linguistic form, then you can give a **discrete-point test** that asks them to identify correct and incorrect versions of that form, possibly in a multiple choice or true/false format. Ellis and Barkhuizen (2005: 36–40) give examples of other discrete-point test formats, and also describe tests that elicit slightly longer, but still form-focused, responses, using formats like sentence completion, discourse completion, question-and-answer tasks, and stimulated recall tasks. Just remember that a learner's noticing or production of a linguistic form on an experimental elicitation task does not mean that learner will unconsciously produce that same form in interactions when he or she is focused on meaning.

## Clinically Elicit Learner Language Samples

Clinical elicitation tasks are needed if you want to identify linguistic features that are automatic in your learners' language, the ones that are produced unconsciously when learners are focused on meaning, not accuracy. The clinical elicitation tasks used in this book keep learners focused on meaning while eliciting targeted linguistic features. In earlier chapters in this book, you analyzed learner language that was elicited by several different kinds of tasks. We did error analysis and TLU analysis with language produced in interviews; these types of analysis can be done with data from many types of task. Developmental sequence analysis is best done with data from tasks eliciting such targeted linguistic features as questions, negation, or relative clauses. Interactionist perspectives require data from tasks where learners must interact with other interlocutors. Analyses of the referential effectiveness of noun phrase or verb phrase expressions require data elicited by referential communication tasks. All of these tasks require a focus by the learner on both meaning and form. To illustrate how this can be achieved, consider the communicative requirements of a common type of clinical elicitation task: the referential communication task.

At its most basic level, a referential communication task must provide a speaker with three things: some information to convey, a listener who requires that information in order to complete some task, and an awareness that an information gap exists (Tarone and Yule 1989: 104). Other characteristics of referential communication tasks follow:

1 They elicit speaker-focused, extended discourse. In carrying out the speaking task, the speaker controls the floor and must produce extended discourse in order to convey the required information. There is no intervention from the teacher or researcher to take the floor from the speaker. And the speaker cannot accomplish the task with short utterances or responses.

2 They elicit controlled, structured discourse. The task materials control what has to be talked about (for example, certain people and actions are essential to the narrative), and provide a basic structural organization with a completion point. The completion point can be defined as the listener's completion of the listener's

task. The task does NOT, however, specify the use of any particular linguistic forms by the speaker. The speaker is free to use whatever linguistic forms he or she wants to in referring to the people and actions who are essential to the narrative. (In this way, SLA interaction theory would say that the speaker is focused on meaning, not form.)

3 They can elicit a range of discourses. Different task types should be used, whether in a classroom or a research study, to elicit such discourse types as descriptions, comparisons, instructions, directions, narratives, and inferential reasoning to get a more complete profile of the speaker's ability (see Yule 1997: 30–32).

Absence of any of these characteristics in a task or activity makes the task less effective in eliciting referential communication, and more likely to be viewed by the learner as an invitation to display linguistic knowledge. In other words, when asked to do a speaking task that has no obvious communicative purpose or goal, a language learner is likely to assume that that task has some other purpose – the most likely one being to assess the accuracy of their language knowledge.

Among the tasks the six learners completed, the Comparison Task (DVD Segment 6) is the best example of a referential communication task. There is an information gap, in that both speakers are required to provide information (their inferences) that their listeners cannot know in advance. The listeners need to listen to each other's hypotheses about the house residents because they need to evaluate the evidence for those inferences based on what they can see in the photos of the houses. There is a defined completion point, in that agreement must be reached about an answer to the questions regarding who lives there and what the house reveals about American culture. The task elicits extended discourse, and the speakers have control of the topic. In carrying out the task requirements, the speakers will need relatively complex linguistic forms, but the task does not dictate what those forms must be.

In the Retell Task (DVD Segment 3), which is a **clinical elicitation task** according to Ellis and Barkhuizen (2005), there is no real information exchange because of the way the task was administered, with the addressee being an interviewer who has already answered questions about the story. There is thus no information gap and no addressee with a need to listen to the narrative for any defined purpose. In this way, DVD Segment 3 is similar to an oral book report or historical recount that a student must give to a teacher who already knows the material. In a classroom task, an information gap and reason for listening can be created by the teacher. For example, each student in a small group could read a different excerpt from the autobiography of a famous statesperson and then, as they share their information, the group could construct a timeline of his or her life. To emphasize language that focuses on entities and processes in authentic referential communication, a group of students could analyze diagrams and pictures of printing presses from the 1500s, make a physical model of the machine, and describe the model and how it works to their classmates, who need the information to write a report on the press' impact on the Reformation. (You can read more about this task in Bunch, Lotan, Valdés, and Cohen 2005.)

In theory, those video segments involving learners in more authentic referential communication (for example, DVD Segments 5 and 6) contain more meaning-focused learner language. Other segments (for example, DVD Segments 2 and 3) may have produced more form-focused and less fluent learner language due to learner monitoring and self-correction. As you structure your classroom tasks to gather data, you will want to keep in mind whether the learners are likely to focus on meaning or form in their interactions.

# Analyzing Learner Language

Most of this book has been devoted to teaching you how to analyze learner language, by means of five different analytical frameworks and techniques. We hope that you now feel that you have some good tools for learner language analysis at your disposal. Here we will focus on the construct of essential task structure, made possible by the careful design of elicitation tasks, as an extremely useful approach to analyzing learner language and comparing it to the language produced by speakers of the TL.

Many tasks contain a basic structural organization where reference to given entities and actions is essential to task completion. This organization of a task has been called its essential structure (Tarone and Yule 1989). **Essential task structure** can be used as a framework in comparing linguistic forms used by different speakers – learners and native speakers alike – to perform the same functions in a task. The essential structure of a task is the set of actions, characters, objects, and locations, and their connections that must be referred to for the successful completion of the task.

The elements of the essential structure of the task in the Narrative Task (DVD Segment 4) were worked out in Tarone and Yule (1989: 55–7), based on written narratives by 50 native speakers of English. As part of the essential structure of that task, the referents are listed in order of appearance, beginning with Character 1, Action 1, Location 1. It may be tempting to try to use your intuition to decide what linguistic expressions ought to be used to refer to each of the referents in the grocery store narrative, and to evaluate the learners' performance in light of your intuition. But referential communication is best evaluated by comparison to actual native-speaker performance – not intuition. Tarone and Yule show what linguistic expressions were used by a group of 50 native speakers of English to refer in writing to each referent in order of mention. For example, Character 1 was referred to as: 'a woman', 'a lady', and Name ('Mrs. Smith'). For Action 1, the linguistic expressions were: 'was shopping', 'went', 'was', and 'was walking'. Location 1 was 'in the grocery store', or 'in the deli' and the second time Character 1 is referred to in the narrative, the linguistic expressions are either 'she' or zero pronoun. (Zero pronoun occurred in coordinate constructions, as in: 'Mrs. Smith was walking in the grocery store and 0 saw a friend.') Their analysis shows that there is not one uniquely correct version of the story that is preferred by native speakers; there is a range of versions. In fact, actions (i.e. verbs) are referred to using a wider range of linguistic expressions than when characters and objects are mentioned (i.e. noun phrases). But in spite of this variation in linguistic expressions, we can also see that there is a kind of functional equivalence across stories in terms of what is referred to. That set of functional equivalences constitutes the task's essential structure, and makes it possible for us to more systematically analyze the linguistic expressions used by several speakers – learners as well as native speakers – to refer to exactly the same entities and actions in telling the same story. In this way, the essential structure provides a needed control on speaker production of linguistic features of interest to the investigator, while still keeping the speakers focused on meaning rather than form.

## Action Research and Pedagogical Responses

In Exploratory Practice, teachers engage in a process leading to understanding, which in turn may lead to initiation of a program of action to change pedagogical approaches (Allwright 2003; Allwright and Hanks 2009). In terms of Figure 8.1, in this section, we move from 'Action for Understanding' to 'Action for Change'. Now we decide whether and how you can use your improved understanding of learner language to test out some possible changes in your pedagogy. In terms of Figure 8.1, does your improved understanding suggest that a change in your pedagogical practice is both *desirable* and *possible* in your context? If so, the next step is to formulate a proposal for change in pedagogy and try it out with your students to see if it results in a satisfactory outcome.

This Action for Change phase is sometimes referred to in the literature as Action Research. You try to see whether a change in your pedagogy has the kind of outcome you want. Perhaps a real example will help here. One of our students, a teacher of French, learned about contrastive analysis and NL transfer. Based on this principle, he wondered why his textbook first taught English-speaking students of French to ask questions using the *Est-ce que…?* form. In French, a statement like *Elle peut dormir* ('She can sleep') can be turned into a question in two ways: *Est-ce qu'elle peut domir? ('Est-ce que* she can sleep?'), or with subject–auxiliary inversion, as in English (*Peut-elle dormir?* is exactly the same word order as 'Can she sleep?'). He wondered why the more English-like form was not taught first, to maximize positive transfer. He posed his puzzle this way: 'English and French questions can be formed exactly the same way with subject–auxiliary inversion, so why does the textbook teach English speakers to use a French question form that does not exist in English? Wouldn't they learn to ask questions in French faster if I taught them to ask questions using subject–auxiliary inversion first, since that is the way they do it in English?' The next semester, as he was teaching two sections of beginning French, he designed an Action Research project to find out. In one section he taught his students *Est-ce que …?* questions straight from the book, but in the other, he taught his students to ask questions in French using subject–auxiliary inversion. What he learned was that, in fact, his students mastered French questions best the way they were taught by his textbook: using *Est-ce que … ?*. And upon reflection, when he thought about question forms in terms of developmental stages (Chapter 4 in this book), he could see why his pedagogical experiment turned out the way it did. One of the earliest stages of question formation is a question marker plus declarative word order, such as *'Why* you can sleep?' Viewed from this perspective, *Est-ce que … ? + SVO* is an early stage question, with *Est-ce que … ?* serving as a question marker. That is why presenting *Est-ce que* questions first produced the best learning outcomes in his class. This teacher completed his puzzle-solving with a better understanding of his students' language learning process, and renewed confidence in his textbook … at least in this area of French grammar.

As part of your own process of Exploratory Practice, consider what you have learned from your in-class study of learner language, and what kinds of pedagogical changes you might want to try out – keeping in mind that these changes in pedagogy are themselves part of your learning process. You will need to keep an eye on learner outcomes in evaluating the real impact of the pedagogical changes you make. And here again, as Allwright and Hanks (2009) point out, it is always a good idea when trying out a new pedagogical approach to involve the students themselves in the exploratory process of research.

## Summary

In this chapter, we have used Exploratory Practice as a framework to help you set up your own exploration of learner language in your own locale. We considered a process to use in involving learners for study. We provided principles to help you design and administer tasks and activities to elicit the learner language you want to look at, and our whole book has provided practice and suggestions to help you analyze the linguistic features of that language. Finally, we considered ways in which your exploration of learner language might inform your understanding as a reflective practitioner, lead to Action Research, and influence your pedagogical choices.

Now it is up to you. We hope you will find practical ways to use some of the analytical frameworks and techniques you have studied in this book – and that you will design and carry out your own explorations of the language produced by learners in your classroom. We hope that these explorations will inform and enrich your teaching by helping you to better understand your students' language learning processes and needs, and, where needed, to take action to improve your pedagogy.

## *Further Reading*

**Allwright, D.** 2005. 'Developing principles for practitioner research: The case of Exploratory Practice'. *The Modern Language Journal* 89: 353–66.

**Allwright, D.** and **J. Hanks.** 2009. Chapter 1 'Learners and what we think of them', Chapter 10 'The research we now need'. *The Developing Language Learner. An Introduction to Exploratory Practice.* Basingstoke: Palgrave Macmillan.

**Ellis, R.** and **G. Barkhuizen.** 2005. Chapter 2 'Collecting samples of learner language'. *Analysing Learner Language.* Oxford: Oxford University Press.

**Gass, S. M.** and **L. Selinker.** 2008. Chapter 3 'Second and foreign language data'. *Second Language Acquisition: An Introductory Course* (3rd edn.). New York: Routledge.

# ANSWER DISCUSSION SECTION

*Chapter 1*

**Individual Characteristics of the Six Learners**

## ANTONIO AND RODRIGO

1 Although Antonio and Rodrigo struggle to express themselves as beginners in the language, they are confident risk-takers. They are effective in using gesture and facial expression to communicate information that perhaps cannot yet be conveyed through their learner language. It may be difficult for a listener to process the long pauses and false starts that characterize their discourse in English. Antonio seems to be more fluent in English than Rodrigo, who tends to speak in much shorter chunks and seems to have more difficulty understanding the interviewer.

2 a They studied English in high school for two or three years in formal classrooms that had an accuracy orientation. They have been in the US for about three weeks.

  b Both Antonio and Rodrigo have strong Spanish accents, and were probably past the critical period for language acquisition when they learned English in high school. They did not study English after leaving high school.

  c Rodrigo and Antonio are well-educated young professionals with five-year bachelor's degrees in law from Mexico. Rodrigo wants to earn a master's degree in the US. Antonio needs to be able to speak English as a lingua franca in his law office in communicating with international clients about human rights issues.

  d Both say they are working on speaking, pronunciation, and grammar.

  e They both appear confident and seem to be risk-takers.

  f They are motivated by their need to use English in their professions.

  g Antonio's contrastive analysis of the word orders of nouns and adjectives in English and Spanish could indicate an analytical learning style.

  h They are both male, and Antonio is Rodrigo's older brother.

## XUE AND CHUN

1 Xue's and Chun's English is fluent and easy to understand. They seem to have only a few pronunciation problems in speaking English. Sometimes their English rhythm sounds choppy.

2 a They learned English in China in formal classrooms that had an accuracy orientation. They have been in the US less than one month.

b Xue was nine years old when she began learning English, most likely before the end of the critical period for language acquisition, and she has studied English for ten years. Chun began learning English at age 12, closer to the end of the critical period; she has also been studying English for a shorter time, six years.

c Xue and Chun are lower division undergraduates.

d They are quite confident, and good conversationalists. Xue says that she has to study 'boring grammars'.

e Xue says she is outgoing and likes to communicate with others. She is clearly competitive: she says she liked the challenge of learning English in China, and was 'the greatest student' in her class. Chun may be more introverted than Xue; she talks more about her reading and vocabulary work than her interactions with others.

f Their motivation for English language learning seems not to be individual, but rather group-oriented – both say they are learning English for their country, and appear to take very seriously their roles as spokespersons and ambassadors for the People's Republic of China.

g Many of their language learning strategies focus on pop culture; both mention American films (sometimes watching them over and over), television, American songs (presumably pop songs?), and American magazines. Both also enjoy dinner conversations with their host family where they learn common slang.

h They are both female.

## CATRINE AND JEANNE

1 Both Catrine and Jeanne have slight accents in English. Their language is fluent and easy to understand.

2 a Their learning in Africa took place in formal classrooms that evidently had an accuracy orientation. They have lived in the US for 18 months.

b Catrine has studied English for nine years, starting at age ten, possibly before the end of the critical period. Jeanne has studied English six years, beginning at age 15, probably past the critical period. Even though Catrine began learning before the critical period, it is possible that input was provided in accented English because her teachers in their native country were not native speakers (NSs) of English.

c  Jeanne is in community college while Catrine is still in her last year of high school.

d  They seem to be more oriented to communication than accuracy, as they mention reading and writing in English.

e  Catrine and Jeanne are confident communicators with outgoing personalities.

f  They both need English for their education and daily lives in the US.

g  Catrine describes herself as having two kinds of language learning strategies – reading aloud to practice her pronunciation, and talking with friends on her sports teams. She does not like writing, and when asked what she likes about English, she says she's glad she does not have to worry about writing accents the way she does in writing French. Jeanne appears to be strongly focused on learning English vocabulary. She likes to look up words in the dictionary when she's reading. And in fact, Jeanne's vocabulary is very good; for example, of all the learners, she is the only one in the interviews who knows the meaning of the word 'sibling'.

h  They are both female, and Jeanne is Catrine's older sister. Catrine plays on sports teams with American friends.

3  All six learners have formal educations and are literate in their NL. They are typical of international students who take ESL classes on college and university campuses in the US. They are also typical of the types of English language learners whose language has been the focus of most SLA research to date.

## Chapter 2

### Transfer in Rodrigo's Speech

Throughout Rodrigo's Interview, he seems to rely heavily on his NL, Spanish. Examples deriving from Spanish transfer include:

- Line 33: Rodrigo starts to say s-s-s (*semana*) before producing 'week'
- Line 34: 'more easy' literally translates Spanish *más fácil*
- Line 35: 'the most important' literally translates Spanish *lo mas importante*, where *lo* means 'the thing'
- Lines 38–42: 'more easy' literally translates *más fácil*. Rodrigo wants to say it that way in spite of the interviewer's corrective feedback: 'easier'
- Line 43: 'no is, is not good' Rodrigo begins with 'no is good' a literal translation from Spanish *no es bueno*
- Line 44: Rodrigo starts to say '[k] four, [k] four'; the Spanish equivalent of four is *cuatro*

### Features in Antonio's Speech *Not* Due to Transfer

Examples in Antonio's interview that could not possibly be due to Spanish transfer are:

- Line 9: the placement of 'more' before the verb, in 'I more practice' cannot be due to transfer; the Spanish is *práctico más*. Perhaps Antonio is overgeneralizing word order rules for English noun phrases, where adjectives go before the noun, unlike Spanish.
- Line 16 and following: the placement of stress on the second syllable of 'elemental' cannot be due to transfer. Stress in Spanish would be on the final syllable of 'elemental'. Perhaps Antonio is over generalizing from a four-syllable English word he knows where stress is placed on the second syllable.

**EXERCISE 2.3**  **Overgeneralization of /h/ in Catrine's Speech**

In DVD 3.5, lines 1–4, Catrine deletes /h/ from 'he' and 'hi,', but erroneously inserts /h/ initially in the words 'Ahmed' and 'alarm'. Behaviorism can explain the /h/ deletion as transfer from French, but it is hard to see how it could account for the use of /h/ before /ɑ/ introducing the words 'Ahmed' and 'alarm'.

**EXERCISE 2.4**  **Monitoring, Learned Chunks, and Morphemes in Rodrigo's Speech**

In his interview, Rodrigo monitors his speech quite laboriously; he hesitates for long periods of time, produces words slowly one by one, and self-corrects multiple times. There are also several phrases he produces more fluidly, as chunks. These chunks are easy to identify by the ease with which they are produced as a phrase: 'I would like to', 'the Master's degree', 'with American people', 'in high school', 'in Mexico', 'I don't know'. The morphemes he produces are shown below. They are generally consistent with the 'natural order', except for the possessive *'s*. However, this morpheme seems to only appear inside a memorized chunk. Also, you might be surprised by the irregular past tense verb 'was' he produces correctly, but perhaps it is also in another memorized chunk. He does not produce a regular past tense *–ed*, or any other irregular past tense verb.

- Line 11: article 'the', possessive *'s*
- Line 15: article 'the', plural *–s*
- Line 19: article 'the'
- Line 24: copula
- Line 27: copula
- Line 29: copula, irregular past tense 'was'
- Line 31: article 'the'
- Line 33: copula, irregular past tense 'was', article 'the'
- Line 35: copula, article 'the'
- Line 43: copula
- Line 44: plural *–s*.

Morphemes missing:
- Line 29: irregular past tense 'went'
- Line 30: irregular past tense 'couldn't'
- Line 49: regular past tense 'started', irregular past tense 'spoke'.

**EXERCISE 2.5**

### Rodrigo and Antonio's Collaborative Interaction

Rodrigo starts a sentence about the different values of the two houses in the photos, and gets stuck when he tries to articulate what this illustrates: he says 'is, em, show, eh, different ... ' and he hesitates. Antonio supplies a word – 'classes' – but then he too gets stuck. Rodrigo produces the phrase 'different classes, social classes'. This example shows how the ZPD works – both learners help each other co-construct a phrase in English, and because each of them is able to recall different pieces of the puzzle, together they are able to produce more than either of them can produce separately.

## Chapter 3

**EXERCISE 3.1**

### First Impressions of Rodrigo's and Xue's Proficiency and Learner Language

1 Xue probably seems more proficient than Rodrigo. Rodrigo seems to have more difficulty understanding the interviewer's questions, asking periodically for her to repeat her questions. He hesitates a good deal in framing his responses, seeming to need to stop and think more before responding. The interviewer asks him to repeat his responses several times.

2 You may recall Rodrigo's pronunciation of words you initially did not understand, like 'not book' instead of 'notebook', or his use of constructions such as 'no is good' that seem to derive directly from Spanish constructions. You may have noticed Xue's ability to produce longer sentences, but also that she does not always mark her verbs accurately for tense or person. You may have come away with a sense that her pronunciation is a little 'choppy', without as much blending of words as you might expect from a NS.

**EXERCISE 3.2**

### Error Analysis: Rodrigo and Xue

**1**

## RODRIGO

| | | |
|---|---|---|
| 11 | | to study the, master's degree. And for |
| 11a | | to work for a master's degree/ to study for a master's degree/ to earn a master's degree |
| 12 | **I** | You need English because why? |
| 13 | **R** | Because I I would like, to st, to study the master's degree. ... |
| 13a | | Because I would like to work for a master's degree/ to study for a master's degree/ to earn a master's degree |
| 14 | **I** | What does the teacher do? |
| 15 | **R** | The teacher he are, not interact in, speak, or, with, eh eh students. |
| 15a | | The teacher does not/ doesn't interact with, speak with, students |
| 19 | **R** | Uh write. They write in the [naybor] they write in the book in the notebook, |

| 19a | | They write in their notebooks |
|---|---|---|
| 20 | | write, only write |
| 20a | | write, just write |
| 21 | **I** | Only writing. |
| 24 | **R** | Mm, no. No, no, no, no, is, the the more the more the most important, is write, |
| 24a | | No, the most important thing is to write/ writing |
| 25 | | write and, I don't know, and, grammar, maybe |
| 25a | | writing/ to write, and I don't know, and grammar maybe |
| 26 | **I** | Grammar. |
| 27 | **R** | But, no is good, in Mexico no is good. … |
| 27a | | But it isn't good, in Mexico it isn't good/ but it's no good, in Mexico it's no good |

## XUE

| 1 | **I** | Why did you start learning English? |
|---|---|---|
| 2 | **X** | Mm, because our school force us to learn English because um it's, it's a trend |
| 2a | | Mm because our school forced us/ because it was/ a trend |
| 2b | | because it was a requirement at our school/ because it was/ popular |
| 2c | | because it was required at our school to learn English/, because it's the latest thing |
| 3 | | to learn English in China. |
| 4 | **I** | Your sch-, your school did what? |
| 5 | **X** | Force us. |
| 5a | | Forced us. |
| 6 | **I** | Forced you. |
| 9 | **X** | Um, because I think English is the biggest language in the world and of course |
| 9a | | because I think English is spoken by the most people in the world/ |
| 9b | | because I think English is the most popular language in the world |
| 9c | | because I think more people speak English than any other language in the world |
| 10 | | in, because Chinese, China enter the WTO organization so it's our duty to learn |
| 10a | | because China entered the WTO organization |
| 10b | | because China joined the WTO |
| 11 | | English and also because um Beijing 2008 Olympic Games and Chine-, China has |
| 11a | | English and also because of the 2008 Olympic Games in Beijing |
| 12 | | a lot of chance to, uh, to communicate with uh other countries from the, all over |
| 12a | | a good opportunity to |
| 12b | | many chances to/ a lot of chances to |
| 16 | **X** | Um, actually when I was in the elementary school, when I started to learn |
| 16a | | actually when I was in elementary school |
| 17 | | English and most of our classmates, they didn't like to learn English because um |
| 17a | | English and most of my classmates/ they didn't like learning English |
| 18 | | it's hard for them to learn language, another language, uh and also because |
| 18a | | it was hard for them to learn languages, a foreign/second language |
| 19 | | English is too different from Chinese and so when we troo- took English classes |
| 19a | | English is really different from Chinese |
| 20 | | and many of them are, they don't really to, listen to that teacher, but I just like to |
| 20a | | and many of them were, they didn't really listen to the teacher, but I just liked to |

| 21 | um adjust a language and I feel it's um a new experiment to learn English because |
| 21a | um play with language/ manipulate language/ and I feel it's / a new experiment/ an adventure/ |
| 22 | it's too different and I like to challenge this kind of difficult, so I am the, at that |
| 22a | it's so different and I like the challenge of this kind of difficulty, so I was the |
| 23 | time I am the, the um greatest student in the, in my class. And I li-, I like to learn |
| 23a | at that time I was the best student in the, in my class. And I like learning |
| 24 | English. Yeah. … |

## Selected errors from Rodrigo's transcript (entire interview)

| 11 | to study the, master's degree. And for |
| 13 | Because I I would like, to st, to study the master's degree. … |
| 15 | The teacher he are, not interact in, speak, or, with, eh eh students. |
| 19 | Uh write. They write in the [naybor] they write in the book in the notebook, |
| 24 | Mm, no. No, no, no, no, is, the the more the more the most important, is write, |
| 27 | But, no is good, in Mexico no is good. … |
| 29 | When I, I, go in Minnesota, I, I, for me, eh I was very difficult speak English. |
| 30 | I nerv, for, I I I I can't, eh, talk when American people difficult, I I I can't, eh, |
| 31 | take, the food, I I (laughs) the more language |
| 33 | Yes, no, it it it it's is ah it was, difficult. But now, in the fourth, s, s, s, week, is |
| 34 | more easy. I I I I I I feel, to learn, more English vocabulary, eh, grammar, eh |
| 35 | compo, eh speak. So I think, the the most important, is, eh, think, in English. |
| 39 | More ease, yes. |
| 46 | If if I don't speak English, I never never, I I don't learn English. |
| 49 | Mexico, maybe in high school I I I start learn English, but, never speak English |
| 50 | in Mexico. Now, in, in September 4 maybe I I I now start. … |

## Selected errors from Xue's transcript (entire interview)

| 2 | **X** | Mm, because our school force us to learn English because um it's, it's a trend |
| 4 | **I** | Your sch-, your school did what? |
| 5 | **X** | Force us. |
| 9 | **X** | Um, because I think English is the biggest language in the world and of course |
| 10 | | in, because Chinese, China enter the WTO organization so it's our duty to learn |
| 12 | | a lot of chance to, uh, to communicate with uh other countries from the, all over |
| 16 | | Um, actually when I was in the elementary school, when I started to learn |
| 18 | | it's hard for them to learn language, another language, uh and also because |
| 20 | | and many of them are, they don't really to, listen to that teacher, but I just like to |
| 21 | | um adjust a language and I feel it's um a new experiment to learn English because |
| 22 | | it's too different and I like to challenge this kind of difficult, so I am the, at that |
| 23 | | time I am the, the um greatest student in the, in my class. And I li-, I like to learn |
| 27 | | grammars because Chinese are always focus on grammars. And actually I don't |
| 28 | | like grammars at all. |
| 30 | | because we have took a lot of examinations |
| 32 | | middle school, and high school, the most important thing is to take a college |
| 33 | | entrance examinations, so there, there's a lot of pressures on us and so we have to |

34    learn those <u>grammars, boring grammars</u>, and uh we have to take a lot of
36    students who are um, you know, they <u>want to take a chance to go into the</u>
37    <u>university</u> and they will have um, have a bright future so we have to learn the
38    <u>grammars.</u>
40  **X**  Yeah, but when I enter the university, I don't usually learn <u>grammars</u> because I
41     don't like <u>them.</u> Yup.
51  **X**  Siblings, host siblings they are adults right now and <u>they all get married</u> and
52     so <u>they didn't really um live in our house right now</u> so

     **2**

| Name of learner: *Rodrigo* | | | |
|---|---|---|---|
| **Line number** | **Phrase with error (phonology, morphology, syntax, vocabulary)** | **Target language reformulation(s)** | **Cause of error?** |
| 4 | Ah, wha, my, *firs* language? (phonology: dropped final consonant) | first | NL |
| 10 | because yes (syntax) | just because<br>because I need to | NL |
| 11 | to *study the,* master's degree (syntax) | study *for a* master's<br>*earn a* master's | NL<br>? |
| 15 | not interact in, *espeak,* or (phonology: epenthesis w/C clusters) | speak | NL |
| 15 | The teacher, *he are* (syntax: S-V agreement) | he is | Not NL: overgen.? |
| Name of learner: *Xue* | | | |
| **Line number** | **Phrase with error (phonology, morphology, syntax, vocabulary)** | **Target language reformulation(s)** | **Cause of error?** |
| 2 | our school *force* us (phon. or morphology: no final *–d* on verb) (lexicon: word choice) | we *were required*<br>it *was required/a requirement* | NL pron<br>? lexical |
| 10 | China *enter* the WTO (phon. or morphology: no final *–d* on verb) | China *entered* the WTO | NL: past tense<br>NL pron…? |
| 12 | with uh *other* countries (/d/) (phonology: uses /d/ for /ð/) | uh *other* (/ð/) (voiced (th)) | NL pron… |
| 16 | when I was in *the* elementary school. (syntax: wrong article) | in elementary school | NL: no articles |
| 20 | many of them *are,* they *don't* … (morphology: no past tense marking) | many of them *were,* they *didn't* … | NL: no past mark |

*Table 3.1 Error Analysis/Contrastive Analysis (EA/CA Form)*

4  Xue's error in line 2 is very interesting. The first thing you might notice is that
   the verb 'force' has no final *–d*. This could be because Chinese does not mark

verbs for past tense (a morphological error), or because this is a final consonant cluster that does not occur in Chinese (a pronunciation error). But even if the final /d/ were there, this utterance would sound odd. The problem is that the lexical item 'force' is typically not used to refer to situations where institutions make us do things. We tend to use 'force' with persons, but 'require' with institutions, and even then typically we do not specify agency; a NS would probably use 'require' here only in passive voice ('are/is required') or nominalized ('a requirement').

4 a The learners both seem to make roughly the same number of errors. Xue makes a few more than Rodrigo but then she attempts more complex structures. Xue and Rodrigo make different kinds of errors (Rodrigo with negation; Xue with choppy rhythm and with more complex syntax) but it is interesting that both of them also tend to leave verbs unmarked for tense, and both of them make errors in choice of articles ('a', 'an', 'the'). Although we marked such errors as due to NL transfer above, the fact that both these learners make these errors despite having very different NLs suggests that there may be other factors at work as well.

 b Many differences in the errors they make could in theory be traced to NL transfer. Rodrigo's errors in lines 27 and 34, both due to transfer, do not seem to occur in Xue's learner language. On the other hand, many of the differences between them could also be due to the fact that Rodrigo is a beginner in English, and Xue is not; we do not know whether Xue's early error patterns would have looked more like Rodrigo's.

 c Your first impression may have been that Rodrigo makes more errors than Xue because he is a beginner. Your error analysis may have contradicted that impression. Xue is attempting harder constructions than Rodrigo is, so this also needs to be taken into account. Number of errors, by itself, is not a good measure of proficiency.

 d First, the error analysis might have helped you see certain errors that initially you did not notice, and that could benefit from some instructional input. Second, in doing this exercise, you may also have identified potential causes of these errors that you did not consider earlier. Finally, you may have noticed a certain imperviousness to correction on the part of both learners with regard to some features ('grammars' for Xue, or 'more easy' for Rodrigo). In this latter case, a teacher might decide to take a more explicit approach to teaching these structures.

**EXERCISE 3.3**      **Error Analysis: Xue's Pronunciation**

| | Name: *Xue* | | Name: *Xue* |
|---|---|---|---|
| | **Phonological error: Voiced (th) /ð/** | | **Phonological error: final cons. cluster** |
| 9 | in (the) world | 2 | (forced) us to (learn) English |
| 12 | to communicate with (other) countries | 2 | it's a (trend) |
| 23 | (the) greatest student | 10 | (entered) the WTO |
| 36 | (they) want to take a chance | 17 | (most) of our classmates |
| 36 | (the) university | 17 | they didn't like to (learn) English |
| 40 | I enter (the) university | 18 | it's (hard) for them to learn |
| 41 | I don't like (them) | 26 | in front of the (blackboard) |
| 51 | host siblings, (they) are | 31 | the (most) important thing |
| 51 | (they) all get married | 35 | it's (hard) for us, because |
| 52 | (they) didn't really live in our house | 55 | focus on those (hard) parts |
| 56 | I don't like (that), … to learn (that) | 57 | (ask) you a lot of questions |

*Table 3.2 Phonological Errors in Context: Xue*

Xue replaces (th) /ð/ in the words above with (d), and she tends to delete the last consonant in the final consonant clusters above. Also, you may have noticed that she does not always pronounce final consonants like /d/ and /t/. She omits these in words like 'trend' and also in past tense verbs like 'force' and 'enter'. Later when we look more closely at her use of past tense marking, keep in mind that her NL phonology may influence her to omit final /d/ and /t/.

**EXERCISE 3.4**      **Error Analysis: Jeanne's Pronunciation**

| | Name: *Jeanne* | | Name: *Jeanne* |
|---|---|---|---|
| | **Phonological error: Voiced (th) /ð/** | | **Phonological error: (h)** |
| 5 | French and (other) language | 10 | (how) to use the verb |
| 7 | a class like (that) | 12 | (how) to use the verb |
| 10 | all (that) stuff | 16 | know (how) to use them |
| 14 | use it in (the) sentence | 17 | (how) to use, kind of that |
| 16 | how to use (them) | 28 | it was (hard), so really (hard) |
| 17 | how to use, kind of (that) | 29 | (he) 's going to give us |
| 26 | if (the) teacher say | 49 | just (help) me out |
| 30 | say it in front of (the) student | 50 | still (have) to learn |
| 46 | I'm a fast learner (though) | | |
| 51 | it's gonna be welcome (though) | | |

*Table 3.2 Phonological Errors in Context: Jeanne*

Jeanne does delete the (h) sound at the beginning of each word identified above. Xue and Jeanne make very similar kinds of substitutions for the English (th)

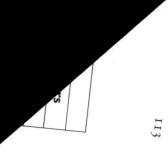

Both of them seem to replace the voiced (th) in words like 'the,' 'that', ...m' with the voiced stop (d). Jeanne does not use the stereotypical French ...place the voiced English (th) in 'this' and 'that'. Substitutions for English ...ve been shown to vary by geographical region; Canadian French speakers ...risian French speakers tend to opt for different substitutes. Maybe Jeanne's ...of /d/ as substitute is influenced by this kind of regional variation, or by her ...edge of Lingala and Swahili in addition to French. Or maybe this is just an ...dual preference.

**EXERCISE 3.5**    ...L— **Analysis of Xue's Pronunciation of Voiced (th) /ð/**

1 At least in our small sample, Xue seems to pronounce voiced (th) /ð/ correctly after the prepositions 'of' and 'for'. Maybe preceding consonants that are fricatives or glides help her produce the fricative /ð/: we need more examples to know for sure. In our small sample, she has most difficulty producing it correctly in medial position after vowels in a word like 'other', or word-initially after a pause. (One of our students who analyzed more of the interview thought that in cases where Xue repeats the (th) sound, she has a tendency to produce it correctly the first time and incorrectly the second; listen and see if you agree. If you agree, why do you think this is happening?)

2 You may not have noticed the contexts in which she got /ð/ right until you did a TLU analysis.

3 The equation for TLU is $3/(7 + X)$, where 3 is the number correct in obligatory context, 7 is the number of obligatory contexts, and X is the number of uses of voiced (th) /ð/ in incorrect contexts. To complete the equation, listen to the sample again to determine if Xue used voiced (th) where it should not have been used.

4 In teaching, you could draw Xue's attention to the contexts where she gets it right, and get her to compare her production there with contexts where she gets it wrong. Figure out if it is the preceding phonemes /v/ and /r/ that facilitate by testing with words like 'worthy' or 'love them'. Practice the easiest context first, and then gradually expand to harder and harder phonological contexts.

| Incorrect (th) in context | | Correct (th) in context | |
| --- | --- | --- | --- |
| 12 | with uh other /d/ | 18 | it's hard for them |
| 18 | language, another language /d/ | 20 | many of them are |
| 41 | don't like them. Yup. /d/ | 26 | front of the blackboard |
| 43 | Host siblings, what's that? /d/ | | |

Table 3.3 Correct and Incorrect Versions of Target Form

**EXERCISE 3.6**    **Third Person Singular –s on Present Tense Verbs**

1 In almost every case, the only verbs marked for third person singular by the six learners on this task are 'is' and 'has'. Rodrigo correctly uses all third person singular forms of 'is' and 'has'. All other verbs are unmarked for third person

singular: 'don't', 'smile', 'clean'. The only verb Antonio uses correctly in third person singular form is 'is'. In lines 11–12, he repeats 'it's' in three consecutive short sentences, in a sequence of 'fill-in-the blank' type utterances that seem like memorized chunks. Other verbs he produces are unmarked for third person singular: 'try', 'have to', 'don't', 'say' (2 ×), 'clean', 'allow'. Chun only marks third person singular in her four uses of 'is'; all other third person verbs are unmarked: 'hurry', 'want' (4 ×), 'do', 'don't', 'think', 'get' (2 ×), 'clean'. Xue uses third person 'is' in two-thirds of its obligatory contexts. She does not mark 'go' for third person singular, but does mark 'wants' (2 ×). Catrine uses the third person singular 'is' correctly nine times, and 'has' once. All other verbs are unmarked for third person singular: 'wake up', 'miss', 'find', 'see', 'think', 'stop', 'get'. Jeanne uses 'is' correctly in the one obligatory context she provides; all other verbs are unmarked for third person singular: 'wake up', 'find out', 'jump', 'ask', 'say'.

2 There does not seem to be any difference between third person singular marking on the copula 'is' as opposed to the auxiliary 'is'. Auxiliary 'has' seems to follow a pattern similar to 'is'.

3 Xue uses third person singular marking twice on the verb 'want'. Other than that, no one puts this morpheme on a main verb. Proficiency level of the learner does not seem to affect suppliance of this morpheme. The morpheme orders we reviewed on page 17 in Chapter 2 predict that third person singular –*s* is one of the last morphemes to be acquired; even relatively proficient speakers still have trouble with it. Our analysis is consistent with that prediction. (Morphemes acquired later tend to be less perceptually salient, or noticeable to the learner, than morphemes that are acquired earlier. For example, irregular past tense verbs have vowel changes that are usually more perceptually salient than the final endings of regular past tenses. In the same way, the forms of copula and auxiliary 'be' that accord with first, second, and third person are irregular and may be more perceptually salient than the third person singular –*s* on main verbs.)

4 In teaching these learners to mark third person singular on all verbs, it is important to know which verbs each learner is marking correctly. You can point this out to the learner, thereby giving them a place of confidence from which to start in extending the rule to new contexts.

## Chapter 4

**EXERCISE 4.1**    **Negation: All Learners**

1  Antonio uses a *no* + *X* form to negate verbs in Retell Task: DVD 3.2, line 17, and Comparison Task: DVD 6.1, line 4. Rodrigo uses *no* + *X* to negate verbs in Interview: DVD 1.1, line 27, and in line 43 where he self-corrects it. Antonio also uses a version of *no* + *X* negation to negate a proposition in Interview: DVD 1.2, lines 36 and 75, and Rodrigo uses this same form in Comparison Task: DVD 6.1, lines 6–7. None of the other learners uses the *no* + *X* form. Antonio and Rodrigo are NSs of Spanish, in which a *no* + *X* negation rule is grammatical so transfer is a likely source of this error. Also these two learners are at a lower level of proficiency in English than the other learners, and so more likely to be using Stage 1 negation.

2  Both Antonio and Rodrigo produce 'don't', with no examples of 'doesn't' or 'didn't'. They both also have examples of 'can't'. These facts would suggest that their oral language is at about Stage 3 negation. However, Antonio's Narrative Task Written: WR 4.2 does contain one instance of 'didn't', revised from an initial use of 'doesn't'. His ability to self-correct suggests that he may be on the verge of acquiring 'doesn't' and 'didn't' for oral use. At present he only produces them when writing, with time to monitor and focus on accuracy.

3  Possible examples of memorized chunks containing negation:

Antonio:   'I don't know' (Interview: DVD 1.2, line 63; Retell Task: DVD 3.2, line 4; Narrative Task Written: WR 4.2, lines 2, 4, 6, 10; DVD 5.1, line 9). This chunk is used frequently, with relative fluency, almost like a filler word.

Rodrigo:   'I don't know' (Interview: DVD 1.1, line 25, 45, 48; Question Task: DVD 2.1, line 50; Narrative Task DVD 4.1, lines 1, 2, 3, 9, 13, 14, 15, 18, 25; Jigsaw Task: DVD 5.1, lines 5, 6). This chunk is used frequently, with relative fluency, almost like a filler word.

Jeanne:   'I don't know' is used eight times. But Jeanne also varies this phrase in ways that Antonio and Rodrigo do not: Interview DVD 1.6 line 27: 'we did not know'; Narrative Task DVD 4.6 line 4: 'she did not know', line 10 'I did not know'. These uses suggest that she has analyzed the chunk 'I don't know' into its component parts and can use them productively.

4  In Question Task: DVD 2.4, line 49, Chun says 'he didn't found the boy'. In Retell Task: DVD 3.4, line 11, she says 'the driver didn't saw … don't saw him'. Chun has learned that she needs to mark past tense on the 'do' form in negated verbs, but she still marks the main verb as well.

5  Antonio and Rodrigo both produce an *X* + *no* form of negation that occurs in Spanish, where the *no* negator follows a word or phrase. Thus, we can find evidence for BOTH developmental sequences of negation and transfer of negation forms from Spanish.

6 Rodrigo's language seems to be at the lowest stage of negation (see answer to Question 2 above). Jeanne's language seems to be at the highest stage, because she produces the widest range of negative forms, including future negatives (Narrative Task: DVD 4.6, lines 11 and 14), and past tense negative modals (Retell Task: DVD 3.6, line 10). The notion of developmental stage means that pedagogy cannot get learners to skip stages or move ahead until they are ready. But teachers can help learners to move through these stages more quickly by exposing them to higher stage negation structures, and a wider range of negative structures in the input. Since many of these learners have said they like to learn by listening to songs and watching television, the teacher might try to look for songs or lines from movie dialogues that contain English negation structures. Rodrigo and Antonio might be asked to focus on hearing and producing 'do not' and later 'does not' instead of only 'don't'. Instruction on 'didn't' should come later, since it involves past tense as well as 'do' support.

**EXERCISE 4.2**

## Developmental Sequence in Question Formation: Antonio, Chun, and Catrine

3 All three learners produce questions Stage 1–5, but only one adds Stage 6 questions. The inclusion of higher-stage questions in the mix is evidence of higher proficiency.

4 Antonio produces several 5a questions ('wh-' questions with auxiliary 'be' inversion like 'What are they doing?'). He does not produce any question with inverted modal (4b, 5c) or 'do' (3b or 5b). Chun's highest level questions are 5a just like Antonio. Because she does have a level 3b question with 'do' ('yes/no': 'Does he want to take the taxi?'), she is using a wider range of question types than Antonio on this task. Catrine uses the highest level questions of the group on this task, several 6b ('wh-' questions with negation), that begin 'Why didn't he … ?' and 'Why can't he … ?'

5 Victoria asks far more 'yes/no' questions than 'wh-' questions, unlike most of the learners. 'Wh-' questions are used to seek completely new information, whereas 'yes/no' questions tend to confirm assumed (old) information. She may use 'yes/no' questions more because she is mostly verifying what she already believes, while the learners may be asking for genuinely new information. For example, these winter events may be new to them. Another possibility is that the learners treat the activity more like a testing context, and try to display their linguistic knowledge more. Victoria does not produce Stage 5 and 6 question types on this activity. We happen to know that Victoria does produce such question types in other contexts, so for some reason this activity did not elicit them. We must recognize that the six learners, like Victoria, may be capable of producing higher-level questions that this activity just did not elicit. Victoria's performance is a reminder of why it is important to ask NS to do the same communicative activities we give our learners, establishing an authentic baseline to use in evaluating learner performance.

## Chapter 5

**EXERCISE 5.1**   **Siblings**

1 Only Jeanne knows the word 'siblings' before it is supplied in the interview. (We confirmed this with her afterward.) Catrine seems to make a fairly accurate guess, based on her clarification request.

2 Rodrigo:  Does not negotiate for meaning.

   Antonio:  Gains time and indicates confusion ('ehh', line 40) and makes a clarification request ('siblings' with rising intonation, line 42).

   Catrine:  Makes clarification requests in lines 33 and 35.

   Chun:  Makes clarification requests in lines 60 and 62.

   Xue:  Makes clarification requests in line 43 and in line 49 when she attempts to use the word again.

3 All of the learners who negotiate appear to comprehend the meaning although it is not clear from Antonio's answer if he does actually speak English with his brother Rodrigo or if he intends to try that. Catrine may have acquired 'sibling' since her fairly accurate guess of the meaning may indicate she is ready to do so. However, she does not use the word again in this interaction. Xue does use the word again, practicing the pronunciation, so she may have learned the word but we do not know if she has acquired the ability to use it spontaneously.

**EXERCISE 5.2**   **Interviewer's Intent: Focus on Meaning or Form?**

1 In Chun's interview at line 16, the interviewer is focused on meaning; she is trying to get more information. At line 20, she asks for clarification of a word she does not understand. In both cases, her moves are effective in getting Chun to provide information or clarify her intended meaning.

2 In Antonio's interview at line 15, the interviewer confirms the meaning of what he just said. At line 17 she asks for clarification of a word she does not understand. Both moves are effective – the first in assuring Antonio she understands, and the second in getting him to clarify the word 'elemental'.

3 At line 36, the interviewer repeats what Rodrigo says in an attempt to get him to expand his previous utterance, but it is not effective. He seems to hear it as a confirmation check and does not say anything more. At line 38, the interviewer gives a partial recast in lines 33–4. This is not effective either; again Rodrigo appears to hear it as a confirmation, not a correction: There is no uptake.

**EXERCISE 5.3**   **'Grammars'**

1 Xue seems mainly focused on meaning in this exchange. She hesitates a few times, perhaps searching for the right word or structure but overall the focus is on meaning.

2 Xue uses the word 'grammars' seven times, listed below. They are all incorrect since 'grammar' is a non-count noun so it does not have a plural form. Her rule seems to be that 'grammar' is a count noun (perhaps like 'structure') and she always adds the plural –*s*. She also uses 'those' in line 34 to agree with the plural.

27  grammars because Chinese are always focus on <u>grammars</u>. And actually I don't
28  like <u>grammars</u> at all.
34  learn those <u>grammars</u>, boring <u>grammars</u>, and uh we have to take a lot of
38  <u>grammars</u>.
40  Yeah, but when I enter the university, I don't usually learn <u>grammars</u> because

3  There are two corrective moves. Line 29 is a clarification request that could possibly also function as a partial recast of 'Chinese are always focus on grammars'. We categorize it as a clarification request because it is a question and the original utterance is a statement. Line 39 is a recast of the prior utterance. Xue does not appear to notice either correction, as suggested by the absence of repair, or acknowledgement of the error, or any hesitation before using the word again.

4  Since this interaction is a meaning-focused exchange, a more evidently form-focused correction, such as a metalinguistic comment, would probably be more effective as correction. The teacher should also investigate why Xue thinks that a noun like 'grammar' should be plural. This would help predict in what other instances the student might add the plural –s morpheme to a noun that does not allow it in English. With this knowledge the teacher can design activities that would allow Xue to notice the form of non-count nouns. Any activity that requires her to focus not only on what she says, but also on how she is saying it, will help Xue modify her interlanguage.

5  Perhaps in line 55 Xue is focusing on form rather than meaning. She stops for a second before uttering this sentence ('Yeah, um, when I learn grammar'), so she might have had time during this hesitation to think about the correct form of her next utterance. Another possibility is that (despite the absence of any observable evidence of noticing) the previous corrective feedback did make her attend to the correct form and, after processing it, she is now using it correctly. A third possibility is that the lack of the plural morpheme is a result of the pronunciation problem with word-final consonant clusters that we noticed in her speech in Chapter 3. Xue's correct use of the word 'grammar' here might not be a real case of uptake and repair on the part of the learner, but rather a pronunciation problem consisting of final consonant cluster simplification. Finally, it is possible that Xue has two ways to use the word 'grammar', the first as a count noun meaning something like 'structure' or 'rule', and the second as a non-count noun meaning an area of study akin to 'chemistry' or 'mathematics'.

6  The Noticing Hypothesis would say that the interviewer's recasts act as the trigger to make Xue aware of her own error; that is, they help her notice the gap between her own hypothesis about the L2 (that 'grammar' is a count noun and takes the plural –s) and the NS's use of the word in the singular form. The Monitor model would say that this use of 'grammar' is a result of the learner's conscious linguistic knowledge about the L2 and that she has time (in the hesitation in line 55) to focus on form and monitor this utterance; this part of Xue's interview shows what is part of her learned knowledge about English whereas the previous one shows what is part of her acquired knowledge.

**EXERCISE 5.4**      **Collaborative Interaction: Catrine and Jeanne**

Catrine has trouble in lines 3–5 and makes a confirmation check.

3          ... I can understand that the culture by the culture of American there's classes like
4          different people depend on how um um how they job are to have a hou- like to have the
5          kind of house they have. Don't know if you understand what I say.

Jeanne provides the scaffolding in line 6;

6          You mean uh its depend on how much they earn?

Catrine responds with 'Yeah. It depend on how much they earn'. The form of 'depend' does not show correct subject–verb agreement, but 'how much they earn' has correct form and is appropriate to the discussion.

Jeanne has difficulty in line 14 expressing her opinion of the maintenance of the house's exterior:

14          really care about how, about the out.

They provide several paraphrases in lines 15–18.

15    C    About renewing like stuff,
16    J    Yeah.
17    C    And make it new.
18    J    Clean up.

Finally in line 21, Catrine expresses the idea fully with the correct and appropriate expression 'No one to take care of the house'.

**EXERCISE 5.5**      **Collaborative Interaction: Rodrigo and Antonio**

1    Antonio uses the adjectives 'big' and 'small', and negation with adjectives in 'clean' versus 'no clean'. Rodrigo uses a comparative adjective + noun 'poorer money', which he contrasts with adverb + noun 'very money'. He also uses the adjective 'good' to contrast with the comparative form 'better'. He uses negation: 'this house no', and the conjunction 'but' (line 7). Rodrigo has difficulty expressing himself in line 9 and Antonio provides scaffolding with the word 'classes' in line 10, then Rodrigo continues the construction by adding 'social' in line 11 and concludes by stating that class differences exist in other countries in line 13.

2    The goal of instruction, as of scaffolding, should be learners' improved ability to self-regulate: to produce forms on their own, without support. One possibility to help them use more adjectives would be to have them brainstorm their own list of adjectives and antonyms before the comparison task so they are prepared to use them. The teacher could provide words where gaps are apparent, such as 'dirty' to contrast with 'clean'. To scaffold their use of comparative adjectives while they are doing the comparison task, the teacher could give one student the job of checking the form of adjectives as they speak to help them internalize their regulation over use of the correct forms. Another possibility is for the

students to record themselves completing the task, then evaluate their own speech as they listen afterwards.

## Chapter 6

**EXERCISE 6.1**

### Are They Communicating Effectively?

1  a  Chun and Xue succeed in explicitly identifying three similar things and three different things in their photos. They do this by a very interactive process of questioning or making statements, and then requesting and getting confirmation on what is in each other's photo.

   b  What seems to help them succeed is their succession of very short turns, in which they repeat one another's words, in an attempt to establish common ground; that is, to agree about what is in each other's pictures. Xue at first seems to dominate the discussion. She leans forward, and she initiates almost every turn exchange.

2  The transcript makes clear how often they repeat each other's information from one turn to the next:

6  **X**  In my picture there's four windows in the house. How about you?
7  **C**  Um I just have two windows.

   The transcript also may let you see that although Chun does not ask as many questions as Xue does, the questions she does ask are targeted towards task completion and move the interaction towards its goal. Thus, she has more influence in the interaction than you might first have thought.

3  Here the learners' systematic asking and answering of questions as a way of establishing common ground breaks down. Neither speaker seems to be trying to find out exactly what is in the other's photo; each is just describing her own photo, and not attending to what her partner says about her own photo. When Xue asks if Chun has a tiny window by the door, Chun asks which house it is in. This is confusing since neither has indicated that there is more than one house. Chun does not ask about Xue's photo; she just repeats information she gave earlier in line 7, that her house just has two windows and gives their locations. She never explicitly says whether her house has a tiny window by the door, nor does Xue pursue the matter.

4  Xue corrects Chun's use of the term 'the leaf' (singular) with a recast: 'Leaves?' Chun repeats 'leafs' – adding a plural marker but still not pronouncing the word correctly. Xue is consistent; she uses the correct word 'leaves' again in line 41. It seems likely that Chun has noticed that she needed to add a plural –*s*.

5  Catrine and Jeanne, and Antonio and Rodrigo, are not as successful in reaching the communicative goal of the task as Xue and Chun. Catrine and Jeanne must be prompted twice by the interviewer to explicitly identify three similar and three different things in the photos. They do not use a process of question–answer–repeat the answer. Antonio and Rodrigo speak only about their own photos without listening to the information being provided by their partner.

They only look at one another to signal when their own turn is over. Each one seems totally focused on the struggle to produce descriptive statements. In this way, they seem to lose focus on the goal of the task. They could be taught to use expressions that establish common ground, like 'I have X; do you?' and answers like 'Yes, I have X. Do you have Y?'

**EXERCISE 6.2**      **Who Did What?**

| | First mention of child | Second mention of women | Second mention of child |
|---|---|---|---|
| *Olivia* | a small child | they | the small child |
| *Victoria* | her young daughter | the two women | the little girl, she |
| *Rodrigo* | the child | they | the child |
| *Antonio* | a child | — | child, the kid, the little girl |
| *Xue* | a two-years-old girl | they Mrs A. and that lady | that girl, she, he, that girl |
| *Chun* | her granddaughter | they | the granddaughter |
| *Catrine* | her daughter | they | her friend's daughter, she |
| *Jeanne* | her baby | they | the baby, she |

*Table 6.1 Characters in the Narrative Task*

1 Standard English grammar (for example, Yule 1996, 1999) requires that, in choosing among the articles 'a', 'an', and 'the', the indefinite articles 'a' or 'an' be used for new information (for example, first mention of a character that the listener does not already know about), and the definite article 'the' for given information (for example, subsequent mentions of that character, or the first mention of any character that the speaker assumes the listener already knows about). In using exactly the same phrase 'small child' with 'a' in her introduction and with 'the' in subsequent mention of the child, Olivia makes it easier for the listener to know who she is referring to. Victoria's references first to 'young daughter' and later to 'little girl' referring to the same person give her story stylistic variety, but it might be harder for an L2 listener to follow because she uses two different lexical items to refer to the same character.

2 Rodrigo doesn't mention the girl until she suddenly appears in the bottle-moving event, and then he uses the definite article 'the', which implies that the listener already is aware of her. He needs to learn the rule for English article usage described in 1 above.

3 They use the personal determiner (a possessive pronoun) 'her', a demonstrative determiner 'that', and the pronouns 'she' and 'he'. The first two are helpful in tracking reference. However, the pronouns can be less helpful, particularly since all the characters in the story are female, and so 'she' could in theory refer to any of them. Use of the pronoun 'he' is an error since there are no male characters in the story. Catrine uses different lexical items to differentiate the two adult women: 'woman' for the older woman, and 'friend' for the younger one.

4 Xue provides a detailed answer. Tarone and Yule (1989: 107) describe learners' use of 'over-elaboration' to provide more detail than NSs do on the same task,

apparently to build in more redundancy, send a bigger signal, to ensure that their message gets across. This can account for Xue's use of several linguistic expressions to refer to the little girl in the exercise above.

**EXERCISE 6.3**

### What Did the Child Do with the Bottle?

1 The learners' responses are longer than the NSs', with more false starts and repetitions of the sort described above in Exercise 6.2 (4). Most of the learners use vocabulary that is not as precise as that used by the NSs, and they omit some of the elements the NSs include, such as reference to the 'shelf'; possibly this is because they do not know the relevant vocabulary item, but also it could be because the entity is not culturally relevant to them. Asking you to compare the learners' responses to the NSs' responses is one way of asking, how would someone respond to this task if they had all the linguistic resources they needed? We might assume the NSs communicate their intended meanings better than the learners because they have better linguistic resources in English. Another way to establish the intended meanings of these speakers (because it would keep cultural assumptions and references constant) would be to ask the learners to also do the task in their NLs, and compare those NL responses to their responses in learner language.

2 Antonio and Rodrigo do not seem to know the word 'put'. Rodrigo uses the word 'introduce', from the Spanish *introducir*, but this is not the right verb to use in either English or Spanish; in Spanish, it is typically used in a more formal register. Antonio does not use any verb to directly refer to the girl's action, referring instead to the outcome, or result, of the girl's action: the final location of the bottle in the old lady's purse. This is a clever way of getting around not knowing the verb.

3 Xue produces 'put' twice in a row as a one-place verb. First she supplies the object but not the location ('he put out a bottle of vinegar'), and then she refers to the location with no object ('and put into Mrs. Anderson's basket').

4 It seems likely that Catrine misunderstands what is going on in the pictures. Her comments suggest she cannot figure out what is going on in the pictures, and her use of the verb 'take' could mean she thinks that the little girl is removing the bottle out of the lady's bag, in essence stealing it. It is also possible that Catrine does not understand the semantics of the verb 'take', and assumes it means something like 'put'.

5 The learners have varying degrees of difficulty indicating whose purse it is. Antonio and Rodrigo first refer to the bag and then the person whose bag it is: 'in the bag, in the nother person' and 'in the bag, … the, … this person'. This is the word order that would be used in Spanish, something like 'in the bag *of* this person'. But neither of these English expressions includes any marker of possession. Both Catrine and Jeanne start out saying 'her bag' but 'her' could refer to either woman. Jeanne self-corrects with 'in her mom friend's bag' – which is clearer – but still lacks one 's ('her mom's friend's bag'). Xue and Chun have no problem with indication of possession using correct English linguistic

expressions. All six learners' written versions of the bottle transfer are clearer and more accurate than their oral versions. So for example, Rodrigo refers in writing to 'the bag of the older woman' and Antonio to 'mom's bag'. Asking learners to do a task more than once may be a useful pedagogical tool in getting learners to attend both to clarity of reference and to problematic new linguistic expressions. In the video, the learners do the oral task first, and then the written one. Teachers might prefer to order the tasks in reverse: the written task first, and then the oral, in order to encourage learners to focus on accuracy in the oral task.

**EXERCISE 6.4**     **The Shopping Cart**

1  Three learners avoid mentioning the cart, in both the oral and written versions. This suggests that sometimes task repetition does not help improve all aspects of task performance; if learners don't know a word the first time, they are unlikely to know it the second time. Something has to happen in between to stimulate acquisition.

2  Rodrigo uses word coinage. He creates a new word out of other words he knows. In this case it seems like a good strategy in that it is easy to guess what he means.

3  Chun and Xue both use approximation and call it a 'car'. This is not a very effective strategy, since it is hard for a listener to guess what they mean without looking at the pictures. (This is especially true given that in the US, shopping carts in grocery stores may have plastic cars that are attached to them to entertain children while their parents shop.) We would say this is approximation, or possibly omission of the final consonant on 'cart'.

4  Xue follows her use of the word 'car' with a question to the interviewer 'Car? No'. This functions as an appeal for assistance and succeeds in getting the interviewer to supply the correct word 'cart', which Xue then repeats. The sequence is likely to lead to Xue's acquisition of a new vocabulary item.

1

**EXERCISE 6.5**     **Communication Strategies Referring to Entities**

| Produced | Intended | CS type | Acquisition? |
|---|---|---|---|
| **R:** market car | Shopping cart | Word coinage | Maybe |
| **A:** First there are adjective and after noun | Word order | Circumlocution | Unlikely |
| **A:** gesture (g) | the other way around | Mime | Yes |
| **A:** What is that? | Scarf | Appeal | Yes |
| **X:** what's that thing? | Scraper | Appeal | Yes |
| **X:** basket | Purse, bag, or cart | Approximation | No |
| **C:** secretarary; secretaire | Secretary | Literal translation | Yes |
| **J:** /yalon/ | Unclear | Word coinage? | No |
| **C:** woods | Fence | Approximation | No |
| **J:** out | Exterior, outside | Approximation | No |

*Answers to Exercise 6.5, (1)*

2 In general, it seems that when any strategy elicits input from the interlocutor, it is more likely to foster acquisition. Appeals, gestures, and literal translation seemed most effective in getting the interviewer to provide input by supplying an appropriate word. Approximation, word coinage, and circumlocution in general do not seem to lead the interviewer to supply input. The speakers may, however, solidify their knowledge of core vocabulary by using communication strategies.

**EXERCISE 6.6** **Communication Strategies Referring to Actions and Events**

1 Rodrigo and Antonio both refer to the consequence of the action of missing the bus, rather than referring directly to the action itself; the consequences are 'don't take your class' and 'the bus it's far'. This is a form of approximation. Their strategies are clever, but do not lead to supply of the needed verb in the input. Xue and Catrine both use circumlocutions, describing in detail what happens. In the process, they produce more complex sentences that aim to express a causal relationship. Antonio's and Rodrigo's learner grammars do not permit them to do this yet.

2 Rodrigo:   Avoidance. Does not help acquisition.

Antonio:   Circumlocution. Describes parts of event.

Chun:   Circumlocution and mime.

Xue:   Approximation.

Catrine:   Avoidance. Does not help acquisition.

Jeanne:   Avoidance. Does not help acquisition.

Xue's use of 'hike' as an approximation, together with her nonverbal appeal to the interview for help, succeed in getting the interviewer to supply the word 'hitchhike', which Xue then tries to use. This could lead to acquisition. Circumlocutions and avoidance do not lead to supply of the target word, and do not appear to be likely to lead to acquisition.

3 a 'Clean' and 'wash'. 'Wash' is understandable, but is not really an acceptable substitute since washing usually entails use of a liquid rather than a hand, a scraper, or snow. 'Clean' is in fact the term the interviewer uses, but she uses the word with an object (it sounds better here to say 'clean the snow' or 'clean the car').

b Both Rodrigo and Antonio provide a cause for the cleaning, although Rodrigo's is so syntactically simple that the relationship of causality is hard to see. Antonio's use of 'because' followed by a fairly clear statement of the problem is comparatively effective; as before, he focuses on causes or results of the action when he cannot name the action itself. Jeanne also uses 'because' with a less detailed but still helpful reference to snow.

## Chapter 7

**EXERCISE 7.1**  **Sentence Complexity and Task Demand**

1 The Jigsaw Task elicits only three complex sentences – all from Catrine, while the Comparison Task elicits at least one complex sentence from each learner, with multiple complex sentences from the more proficient learners. For these two tasks, the task with lower cognitive demand results in fewer complex sentences while the task with greater cognitive demand results in more.

2 Classifying nouns as concrete or abstract according to task, shown in the table below.

| Learner | Jigsaw Task | | Comparison Task | |
|---|---|---|---|---|
| | **Concrete** | **Abstract** | **Concrete** | **Abstract** |
| *Catrine* | house, windows, door, garage, car, tree, woods, flowers, picture, Minnesota, summer, sun, grass, front | half, place, question, part | house, woods, front, person, people, money | culture, classes, job, kind, stuff |
| *Jeanne* | picture, fence, woods, windows, door, back, house, garage, tree, grass, neighbors, car, branch, flowers, town, suburb, fall, leaves, floor, front, back | access, things, difference | people, the out | life |

*Answers to Exercise 7.1 (2)*

There are many more concrete nouns than abstract nouns used in the Jigsaw Task. The directions for that task specifically ask about concrete entities such as 'windows'. In the Comparison Task, we find about the same number of concrete and abstract nouns. This makes sense when looking at the directions for the Comparison Task, which ask both about both concrete entities (how many people?) and abstract ones (social class?).

**EXERCISE 7.2**  **Impact of Task on AS-Units**

1 We chose to analyze Antonio's language. The samples have slightly different word counts so we could have complete AS-units. Line 10 in the Comparison Task is part of an AS-unit which he co-constructs with Rodrigo. False starts, hesitations, and repetitions were not included in the word count; they are underlined in the text below.

### *Jigsaw Task*

1 **A** || Eh, this house, there are, four window,|| and, there is a, one tree, in front.|| Mm,
2 there is a, a [rahs], in, in the garden.||

7 **A** || OK, um, to uh, this, this house, in front, there are, a car, green car.|| Eh, inside,
8 the same, there is a, other house, color is, is white.||

42 words

5 AS-units

1 subordinate clause: color is white

## *Comparison Task*

1  **A**  || Eh this house, eh eh show me, that that eh, the the the people, the property, are,

2     maybe eh they, eh, they had a a a good job, eh, because, eh the house, eh show it.||

3     It's it's it's big,|| it's it's clean,|| eh, there is a car, ||and and, this eh house it's it's it's

4     small,|| it's no clean, || em I I I think I think so.||

10  **A**  Different classes, different ...

43 words

7 AS-units + partial in line 10

2 subordinate clauses: 'that the people maybe they had a good job', 'because the house show it'

2  As we noted above, we skipped false starts, hesitations, and repetitions in the word count. One difficulty arises in determining what is a subordinate clause. For example, in the Jigsaw Task, we could reconstruct line 8 as 'there is a other house whose color is white' or 'there is a other house. Its color is white'. The length of the pause between the two clauses as compared to other pauses may give us a clue whether the second clause is intended to be a subordinate clause or an independent clause.

**EXERCISE 7.3**

### Lexical Complexity

1  The TTR for Jeanne's written narrative (WR 4.6) = 44/50 or .88. The TTR for her oral narrative (DVD 4.6) is 29/50 or .58. The words Jeanne chooses for her oral narrative are simpler and more repetitive than those she chooses for the written narrative. In the written narrative, she uses adjectives ('busy', 'happy', 'distracted') but there are no adjectives in the oral version. Her active vocabulary is larger than the oral narrative would indicate.

2  When we compared written versus oral TTRs for the NSs, we were surprised to see that their TTRs are *lower* in the written version than in the oral version of this task. Olivia told us that because she is bad at spelling, she usually relies heavily on a spell checker. We had asked her to write with pen and paper rather than a word processor with a spell checker, so she tried to only use words she knew she could spell. This is clearly a generational phenomenon for some individuals (Victoria could not remember having similar concerns, but she is a good speller). We wonder how often lexical complexity is affected when learners are asked to handwrite versus word process an essay.

3  A 50-word segment of Jeanne's speech from DVD 2.6: Question Task:

25  What is going on in this house? What a mess. What happen?

27  Oh. Where does, where did he leave it?

30  Is that is that the only place he is looking for or?

32  Is he going to find it?

34  Yeah.

36        So, is he the same guy?

38        OK. <u>He's a real</u> he's really in trouble.

39        So <u>he does have</u>, does he need to

Underlined words are hesitations, false starts, and repetitions. They were omitted from the word count. The TTR for this segment is 31/50 or .62, which is close to the TTR for her oral DVD 4.6 Narrative Task. The oral narrative and question task are similar because they both require language for concrete entities which are shown in pictures. It seems that the written task gives Jeanne more opportunity to display the vocabulary at her command.

**EXERCISE 7.4**        **The Language of Inference and Justification**

| Speaker | Inference | Signals for inference | Justification | Signals for justification |
|---------|-----------|----------------------|---------------|--------------------------|
| *Antonio* | the people, the property, are, maybe eh they, eh, they had a a a good job | show me | the house show it. It's it's it's big, it's it's clean, eh, there is a car this eh house it's it's it's small, it's no clean | because |
| *Rodrigo* | poor, poorer money there are very money | show | This house is, is, it's a good house, but, eh, is better this house. | — |
| *Antonio and Rodrigo* | different classes, different … different classes, social classes | show | — | — |

*Table 7.4 Inference and Justification – Learners*

4  Antonio and Rodrigo use the verb 'show' to indicate their inferences. Each of them has used the expression 'I think' in other contexts, so a teacher could scaffold the use of that phrase to express inferences by providing a card with the sentence stem 'I think that … ' on it or by modeling it for the students. Antonio uses 'because' to signal his justification while Rodrigo uses no oral signal. Since these learners are trained as lawyers, a signal phrase they may find helpful is 'the evidence is … '. They could also be taught the sentence stem 'I think X based on Y' when they are ready to include both inference and justification in one sentence.

# TRANSCRIPTS AND WRITTEN NARRATIVES

## DVD 0.1 INTRODUCTION

### Narrator

Hi! And welcome to our exploration of learner language. You know, it's fascinating to take the time to really pay attention to the way learner language develops. No matter what sequence is followed by a teacher or textbook in presenting language structures, learners seem to have their own built-in syllabus. What they learn is different from what we teach.

Let's listen to the English that's spoken by Rodrigo. He's a beginning level learner just graduated from a Mexican university.

### Rodrigo

| 24 | **R** | the the more the more the most important, is write, |
| 25 | | write and, I don't know, and, grammar, maybe |
| 26 | **I** | Grammar. |
| 27 | **R** | But, no is good, in Mexico no is good. … |

### Narrator

So why did Rodrigo say 'no is good, in Mexico no is good'? His books and his teacher surely did not say it that way. Is it because of his native language, Spanish? Sometimes we say that language learners 'have an accent' from their native language. For example, their pronunciation may be different. Listen now to Jeanne, a native speaker of French, as she describes a photo of a house. How would you describe her pronunciation?

### Jeanne

| 5 | **J** | the back of |
| 6 | | the house got i, a small garage, and, there is tree around the house, and, that's it. |

### Narrator

As a more advanced speaker of English, Jeanne's pronunciation is really pretty good. But she does still have problems with one word: 'house.' She says 'ouse'. Why would a simple sound like 'h' prove to be such a problem for her? Now if you think you know the answer to that one, consider this: in the next segment, you will hear Chun, Catrine, and Antonio, native speakers of Chinese, French, and Spanish, use the same incorrect word order when they ask English questions.

### Chun

| | | |
|---|---|---|
| 1 | **C** | Is the man is a student? |
| 2 | **I** | Yes, he is a student. |

### Catrine

| | | |
|---|---|---|
| 26 | **C** | Why, the, bus driver can't, stop for him? |

### Antonio

| | | |
|---|---|---|
| 48 | **A** | Why, this guy, say, the uh s-stop? |

### Narrator

How can native speakers of such different native languages be in such agreement about how to incorrectly ask English questions? Their books and their teachers did not ask questions this way. So where did this pattern come from? Sometimes learners do learn from their teachers. Listen to Xue when she runs into problems finding the right English vocabulary word.

### Xue

| | | |
|---|---|---|
| 16 | **X** | It seems, like, he wants to hike, hi-, hi-, hi-. What, what he is doing? |
| 17 | **I** | He's hitchhiking. |
| 18 | **X** | Yeah, hitchhiking. |
| 19 | **I** | Hitchhiking, right. |

### Narrator

So a 'teacher' has taught Xue a new vocabulary word: 'hitchhiking'.

Do you think she knows it now? And do you think she'll know it tomorrow? What can a teacher do to help her remember? We can learn a lot when we take the time to pause, and look at learner language. Your insights are unique and important. Join us in our exploration of learner language.

## RODRIGO

### DVD 1.1 Interview (Rodrigo)

| | | |
|---|---|---|
| 1 | **I** | So let's start by saying, ah, what your native language is. |
| 2 | **R** | Um, no, sorry, I |
| 3 | **I** | What is your native language? |
| 4 | **R** | Ah, wha, my, first language? |
| 5 | **I** | Your first language. |
| 6 | **R** | Eh, Spanish. |

| | | |
|---|---|---|
| 7 | **I** | Spanish. And what other languages do you speak? |
| 8 | **R** | English. |
| 9 | **I** | English. |
| 10 | **R** | Yes. (laughs)… because yes, I need to speak English because I I I I would like |
| 11 | | to study the master's degree. And for |
| 12 | **I** | You need English because why? |
| 13 | **R** | Because I I would like, to st, to study the master's degree. |
| 14 | **I** | What does the teacher do? |
| 15 | **R** | The teacher he are, not interact in, speak, or, with, eh eh students. |
| 16 | **I** | He doesn't interact. |
| 17 | **R** | No, no. |
| 18 | **I** | So what do the students do? |
| 19 | **R** | Uh write. They write in the [naybor] they write in the book in the notebook, |
| 20 | | write, only write. |
| 21 | **I** | Only writing. |
| 22 | **R** | Yes. |
| 23 | **I** | OK. So you don't work on pronunciation? |
| 24 | **R** | Mm, no. No, no, no, no, is, the the more the more the most important, is write, |
| 25 | | write and, I don't know, and, grammar, maybe |
| 26 | **I** | Grammar. |
| 27 | **R** | But, no is good, in Mexico no is good. |
| 28 | **I** | Can you tell me some things you do now, to learn English? |
| 29 | **R** | When I, I, go in Minnesota, I, I, for me, eh I was very difficult speak English. |
| 30 | | I nerv, for, I I I I can't, eh, eh, talk when American people difficult, I I I can't, eh, |
| 31 | | take, the food, I I (laughs) the more language |
| 32 | **I** | You, you can't eat the food? |
| 33 | **R** | Yes, no, it it it it's is ah it was, difficult. But now, in the fourth, s, s, s, week, is |
| 34 | | more easy. I I I I I feel, to learn, more English vocabulary, eh, grammar, eh |
| 35 | | compo, eh speak. So I think, the most important, is, eh, think, in English. |
| 36 | **I** | Think in English. |
| 37 | **R** | Yes. |
| 38 | **I** | So you said it's easier now. |
| 39 | **R** | More ease, yes. |
| 40 | **I** | More easy |
| 41 | **R** | Yeah, yeah, I I I I |
| 42 | **I** | It's easier now. |
| 43 | **R** | Yes (laughs) yes uh I I think my English is is, no is, is not good but I, I, feel, I |
| 44 | | feel that, 'n maybe, I don't know [k] four, [k], four, four months or six months I I, |
| 45 | | my English is is, ve, is, I don't know I I I will, feel very very good. … |
| 46 | | If if I don't speak English, I never never, I I don't learn English. |
| 47 | **I** | So, when do you speak English with your siblings? |
| 48 | **R** | When. Hm, all time, in in in, I don't know in maybe, in in in Mexico. In |
| 49 | | Mexico, maybe in high school I I I start learn English, but, never speak English |
| 50 | | in Mexico. Now, in, in September 4 I I I now start. … |

### DVD 2.1 Question Task (Rodrigo)

1  **R**  Why he he's eh eh an- anxious, anxious or?
2  **I**   He's anxious because he's late for school.
3  **R**  Oh, who is he?
4  **I**   He's Ahmed, he's a friend of mine.
5  **R**  OK, eh what, what's, what is your name?
6  **I**   His name is Ahmed.
7  **R**  Ahmed. Oh. Where where is, where are the the school, your school?
8  **I**   Well, it's here in Minnesota.
9  **R**  Minnesota.
10 **I**   He goes, he goes to a college in Minnesota.
11 **R**  College. What level?
12 **I**   What's he learning?
13 **R**  Yeah no, level. What lev-
14 **I**   Oh, what level? It's a community college
15 **R**  Community college.
16 **I**   First year.
17 **R**  Oh, OK. Yes, uh He, he seem very, anxious.
18 **I**   Mm hm, he is because his clock didn't work.
19 **R**  Yes. Yes, y, y, your class, eh, is wha- what time?
20 **I**   Uh, what time is his class?
21 **R**  What time is his class, yes.
22 **I**   His class is at nine.
23 **R**  Oops. Who is he?
24 **I**   That's Ahmed again.
25 **R**  Ahmed. What what is, what is, eh, he doing?
26 **I**   Um, he's looking for his car keys.
27 **R**  Lost? The keys?
28 **I**   He lost his car keys.
29 **R**  Oh, OK. Uh in, is, is t today, is, is, cold? Is winter?
30 **I**   Yeah. It's winter. I it's winter in Minnesota.
31 **R**  Why What, what's, he, doing?
32 **I**   Well, he couldn't find his car keys and so he tried to take the bus.
33 **R**  The bus. The bus. Why? Why?
34 **I**   Why did he take the bus?
35 **R**  Yes.
36 **I**   Because he couldn't find his car keys.
37 **R**  Ah, Wh Where where, eh, going, [unclear]
38 **I**   He's trying to go to school. He's trying to go to his class at nine o'clock.
39 **R**  OK. Ah, OK.
40 **R**  What are you doing?
41 **I**   Well, Mohammed stopped the car to clean off the windshield.
42 **R**  Ah OK.
43 **I**   [Can you ask me another question?]

| 44 | **R** | [And and and ... ] And Ahmed? Wha- what what he's doing? What |
| 45 | | he's doing? |
| 46 | **I** | Well, Ahmed thought that Mohammed stopped because he was hitchhiking but |
| 47 | | Mohammed didn't see him. |
| 48 | **R** | ...think so, they, they are, happy? |
| 49 | **I** | Um. |
| 50 | **R** | I don't know. (laughs) |
| 51 | **I** | Can you ask a question? |
| 52 | **R** | Yes eh, why, why they are, happy? Is is cold, is winter, is late. (laughs) |
| 53 | **I** | Well, you can be happy in Minnesota even if it's cold in winter. |
| 54 | **R** | (laughs) Yesss. |

## DVD 3.1 Retell Task (Rodrigo)

| 1 | **R** | This eh he is Ahmed. Eh he he is he, he's late, uh uh because he, eh, have he |
| 2 | | he he has to, uh school. And, your class, is nine o'clock and, he, eh, he, he he's, I |
| 3 | | don't know es, sleeping, yeah. |
| 4 | **I** | Mm hm. |
| 5 | **R** | And, he is, n- anxious. |
| 6 | **I** | Mhm. |
| 7 | **R** | Mm and uh in this picture he lost, the [kay], the [kay]? And, is, la- he is very, |
| 8 | | eh, anxious because it's late. |
| 9 | **I** | Mm hm |
| 10 | **R** | And and, he, eh, eh, don't, he don't, don't take, your class, and now is, it's OK, |
| 11 | | is all ... |
| 12 | **R** | In this picture (laughs) in the, Mohammed, eh, smile, beca because, eh, |
| 13 | | Ahmed, eh, eh he is inside the car and he, clean, cleanest, eh up the window, and, |
| 14 | | the winter and cold (laughs) and and, they, they are, happy, in this picture, I don't |
| 15 | | know. |

## DVD 4.1 Narrative Task (Rodrigo)

| 1 | **R** | In, in the first picture and, she, take, her food maybe is, eh chicken or is eh I |
| 2 | | don't know is is is eh, meat no I don't know, and, she, eh, she, eh, go (sigh) and |
| 3 | | and and I don't know the the the, she ha-, sh she has, eh, in your hand, [esta, ba ba] |
| 4 | | bag, |
| 5 | **I** | Mm hm. |
| 6 | **R** | and eh put on the the this, c car, eh market car or eh I I don't know, and, eh, |
| 7 | | she walk in the market and, for buy, more products, uh I think so. And in the |
| 8 | | second picture eh she, eh she, talk, with your, with your friend and, and, they, |
| 9 | | they are, talking, about, your, mm your mm I don't know, your sh-, shopping? |
| 10 | **I** | Mhm. |
| 11 | **R** | And z- z third picture, eh, she she, no they, they are continue talking and, the |
| 12 | | ch-, children, eh, the chi the child, eh, is a, th take, she take, eh [wa] one, maybe |
| 13 | | red, eh, red w-, bottle wine. I don't know, is is is (laughs) dangerous, because is is |
| 14 | | is, eh, eh she, she can, eh, I don't know she can, n, she can cut in your hand, in, |
| 15 | | your, fingers, I don't know. |

| | | |
|---|---|---|
| 16 | **I** | Mhm. |
| 17 | **R** | And they are, continue talking and, in the, the four, picture, ah, oh, the the the |
| 18 | | the child, eh, in, introduce the, the, I don't know, introduce in in the bag, in the |
| 19 | | nother person, in the in the friend your mom, and, eh, they are continue talking |
| 20 | | and, she, eh, she can, she can't, eh, and the child, and, she can't, see, your bag. |
| 21 | **I** | Mm hm. |
| 22 | **R** | And, maybe, she, she wi-, was, ah, she was, arre-, uh, no she she will, eh she |
| 23 | | will be arrest. |
| 24 | **I** | Oh, arrested? |
| 25 | **R** | (laughs) Maybe, yes arrested, I don't know, I think so, maybe. |

## WR 4.1 Narrative Task Written (Rodrigo)

1 One day in the supermarket at 12:00 o'clock, two women and a little child, to talk
2 about of the shopping in this momet. They are friends and good persons. But they
3 lost to attention in the child, so, the child is takeing a bottle milk and she's
4 introducing in the bag of the older woman. Probably the older woman will be
5 arrested because she don't know that in your bag is a bottle milk and she will has
6 to pay for her.

## ANTONIO

### DVD 1.2 Interview (Antonio)

| | | |
|---|---|---|
| 1 | **I** | And what other languages do you speak? |
| 2 | **A** | Eh um only Spanish I, I I study er, a little bit, French. But I, natural language is |
| 3 | | Spanish. |
| 4 | **I** | Mmhm, OK. And can you tell me when you started learning English? |
| 5 | **A** | Eh um, I, I study English three years ago. |
| 6 | **I** | Mhm. |
| 7 | **A** | Eh, mm, but, this this language, is is necessary, practice. And I, I I can't do it. |
| 8 | **I** | You can't practice. |
| 9 | **A** | (Pause) Yeah, yeah … two, weeks ago, I, I more practice |
| 10 | **I** | Mhm |
| 11 | **A** | in university, and friends, an … |
| 12 | **I** | Did you learn English in school, at all, in Mexico? |
| 13 | **A** | Yeah, eh, in in high school, I I study English, very ea, it's English, uh, very |
| 14 | | easy. |
| 15 | **I** | It was easy. |
| 16 | **A** | Yeah, its, el-elemental |
| 17 | **I** | I'm sorry, it's what? |
| 18 | **A** | Elemental? It's it's it's easy for example, eh, "My name", eh, "He is", it's it's it's |
| 19 | | easy. |
| 20 | **I** | Oh, elementary. |
| 21 | **A** | Elementary, [ok, it' all right,] yeah, elementary. |
| 22 | **I** | [Elementary.] |
| 23 | **I** | OK. Can you describe a typical English class in Mexico? So, when you were |

| 24 | | learning English in high school, what was the class like? |
|----|---|---|
| 25 | **A** | Yeah, the the typical class it's, eh, it's easy. It's boring! |
| 26 | **I** | (laughs) It's boring. |
| 27 | **A** | Yeah, it's boring. |
| 28 | **I** | What makes it boring? |
| 29 | **A** | Yeah uh the the teacher, um, don't use, the, the the tools? |
| 30 | **I** | The teacher doesn't use the tools? |
| 31 | **A** | T, Tools, necessary, for the for the students. |
| 32 | **I** | What does that mean? |
| 33 | **A** | Yeah, um for example, in in university, U of M, the teacher, explain the class, |
| 34 | | eh, with, eh with tools, that, eh that, um that the student can't, learn the more, easy. |
| 35 | **I** | Mhm? |
| 36 | **A** | Mm, games, mm, and the and the other, other things. In in Mexico no. |
| 37 | **I** | No. |
| 38 | **A** | In Mexico the teacher only, teach in the book and, it's it's, it's tough. (laughs) |
| 39 | **I** | And do you speak English with your siblings? |
| 40 | **A** | Ehh (quizzical look and shrug) |
| 41 | **I** | Do you speak English with your siblings? |
| 42 | **A** | Siblings. |
| 43 | **I** | Siblings. (pause) Brothers and sisters. |
| 44 | **A** | Ah! oh, okay! Yeah! Yeah, I try it. Yeah. I try it. |
| 45 | **I** | And how does that go? (pause) Does, does that work? |
| 46 | **A** | Yeah. Yeah … |
| 47 | **A** | I think that for, for learn, very well, any language, it's, it's important, eh, eh |
| 48 | | learn, eh grammar, learn, listening, but for me, eh on, on my job, |
| 49 | **I** | Mhm |
| 50 | **A** | it's, more important, s speak. |
| 51 | **I** | Mhm. Can you say a little bit about your job, and why speaking is important |
| 52 | | with your job? |
| 53 | **A** | Yeh I, I work in, in human rights. In Mexico, I, I, I worked in human rights. |
| 54 | **I** | Mhm |
| 55 | **A** | eh so, I, I need speak, eh because, the people, throughout, my office, and, don't, |
| 56 | | eh eh, in, I, how you say in, m, don't use Spanish, eh fo-for all, there are, eh |
| 57 | | people, the the other, other countries, so, I need speak English. |
| 58 | **I** | So the people in your office come from other countries? |
| 59 | **A** | Yeah. |
| 60 | **I** | I see. |
| 61 | **A** | Yeah. |
| 62 | **I** | OK. And, um, What's easy for you to learn about English? |
| 63 | **A** | Mm, I don't know, it's difficult. |
| 64 | **I** | (laughs) It is difficult, OK. |
| 65 | **A** | It's difficult. |
| 66 | **I** | So tell me what's difficult. |
| 67 | **A** | Eh um, maybe, it's it's it's difficult, grammar. |
| 68 | **I** | Grammar. |

69  **A**  Grammar, yeah.
70  **I**  Anything in particular?
71  **A**  It it's difficult because eh in in in my language, for example, eh first, in in the
72        structure in the sentence, first eh there are uh uh adjective, and, eh after, noun. Uh
73        No. It's it's (gestures)
74  **I**  The other way around?
75  **A**  Yeah, the other way first noun and and second an adjective, Here no. Here it's
76        first adjective, it's difficult.
77  **I**  It's difficult. Yeah, OK.

## DVD 2.2 Question Task (Antonio)

1   **A**  Who is he?
2   **I**  That is my, my friend Ahmed.
3   **A**  Ah, your friend?
4   **I**  Yeah, my friend Ahmed.
5   **A**  Ahmed. Eh Where is he from?
6   **I**  He's from Somalia.
7   **A**  Somalia. Oh. That's really interesting. Eh What is, what is he?
8   **I**  What did you say? What is he?
9   **A**  What is he?
10  **I**  He's a student.
11  **A**  A student. Oh, uh, Where, uh, Is, is, is in the bed? He sit in the bed?
12  **I**  Yeah he's in bed.
13  **A**  In bed. Is, is, Ah, Ahmed?
14  **I**  Ahmed? That's [Ahmed.] Yeah, again.
15  **A**  [Ahmed?] Oh, eh, What is he, he doing?
16  **I**  He's looking for his car keys. He can't find his car keys.
17  **A**  What is, what is that?
18  **I**  That's a scarf.
19  **A**  A scarf.
20  **I**  He's wearing a scarf.
21  **A**  It's it's it's cold, I I I think so.
22  **I**  Yeah. It's cold outside. It's Minnesota in the winter.
23  **A**  Ah in the winter.
24  **I**  Yeah.
25  **A**  It's rea, It's very cold.
26  **I**  It's very cold. (laughs)
27  **A**  What is he, in the, in the, in the sta, bus station, or …?
28  **I**  Well he's on the corner outside his apartment building,
29  **A**  Oh. Ah.
30  **I**  and he was trying to catch the bus to school but he missed the bus.
31  **A**  Is, is your friend? or…
32  **I**  This guy? Or that guy?
33  **A**  Yeah, this guy.
34  **I**  This guy is Ahmed's friend.

| 35 | **A** | Ah. OK. It's, uh, it's it's your, uh your car? … the Ahmed, Ahmed's friend? |
| 36 | **I** | Yeah Ahmed's friend has a car and he's driving to school. |
| 37 | **A** | What are they doing? |
| 38 | **I** | Well Ahmed's friend stopped to clean off the windshield. |
| 39 | **A** | What are, what are they, what is he doing? This guy. |
| 40 | **I** | This guy? |
| 41 | **A** | Yeah. |
| 42 | **I** | He was cleaning the windshield. And all of a sudden he saw Ahmed inside the |
| 43 | | car and said, "What are YOU doing there?" He was surprised because he didn't see |
| 44 | | him before. |
| 45 | **A** | Yeah, uh, the the the the snow it's, uh its, uh, it's very difficult for, for to see. |
| 46 | **A** | Why, he, say stop? |
| 47 | **I** | Why, why what? |
| 48 | **A** | Why, this guy, say, the uh, s-stop? |
| 49 | **I** | Oh he's waving at him. He's saying "Hi! I'm here!" And he's saying "What are |
| 50 | | you doing there? How did you get there?" |

## DVD 3.2 Retell Task (Antonio)

| 1 | **A** | This guy is, Ahmed, |
| 2 | **I** | Mhm |
| 3 | **A** | Uh, Ahmed, eh, try wake up, uh, because he, he's he's late, uh, This, uh y- your |
| 4 | | watch, uh it's, eight, uh uh one five. And, I don't know I can't I can't see. This |
| 5 | | clock |
| 6 | **I** | This says five, fifteen. |
| 7 | **A** | Five fifteen. I, I think that I, I am late. |
| 8 | **I** | Mhm. OK, you can do it. |
| 9 | **A** | OK, he, he finded, uh, his his money. He, uh, he have to, to take a, a bus, uh for |
| 10 | | to go the the school and, uh he, don't, don't find. |
| 11 | **A** | Uh, He's late. The the bus, it's uh, it's far. Uh, It's, it's, it's winter, in |
| 12 | | Minnesota, It's cold. Poor Ah, Ahmed? |
| 13 | **I** | Mhm. (laughs) |
| 14 | **A** | It's it, it's a, lucky, it's, a, a, Ahmed friend? |
| 15 | **I** | Mhm |
| 16 | **A** | Uh, He, Ahmed, he, eh, he say the, a, a ride? M It's, it's a lucky. Lucky man. |
| 17 | **A** | Mm, his his friend, clean, the the window, um, because, the snow, no allow the |
| 18 | | see? |
| 19 | **I** | Mhm |
| 20 | **A** | And next, eh, Ahmed is say, hello, and, his friend's, "What are you doing?" |

## DVD 4.2 Narrative Task (Antonio)

| 1 | **A** | OK, I think, that, uh, she, trying t to buy, anything. Mmm sh, uh, Maybe, she, |
| 2 | | she is thinking, eh, "What about, what about, buy it?" I I don't know. |
| 3 | **A** | Uh, In this picture, I I can see, that, uh, the the the, miss, uh, find finded, the, |
| 4 | | other, other person. Maybe, her friend, or, I don't know. Eh uh, the, the this person, |
| 5 | | uh, mm, has a, a child, and, and child try, the the the take a, a bottle, bottle, milk or |

| 6 |   | wine, I don't know. |
|---|---|---|
| 7 | **A** | In this picture, eh, the kid, the little, little girl, eh, take the the bottle, and, eh uh, |
| 8 |   | OK in this picture, eh, the bottle, is in, is in the bag, the bag, the, this, this person. |
| 9 | **I** | What do you think happens after this? |
| 10 | **A** | I don't know. Maybe, eh, eh, poor little girl, maybe, eh, your, his, her her her |
| 11 |   | mom, mm, tell, eh, "You, don't do that". |

### WR 4.2 Narrative Task Written (Antonio)

| 1 | One upont a time, there is a old lady. She went to market because she need to buy |
|---|---|
| 2 | some things. In the market, she talked with another lady who has a little girl. The |
| 3 | little girl take it a bottle and she introduced in mom's bag. Her mom doesn't |
| 4 | didn't know the fact. Obviosly, wasn't pay it. I think that the little girl's mom tell |
| 5 | her "Don't do that." |

## RODRIGO AND ANTONIO

### DVD 5.1 Jigsaw Task (Rodrigo and Antonio)

| 1 | **A** | Eh, this house, there are, four window, and, there is a, one tree, in front. Mm, |
|---|---|---|
| 2 |   | there is a, a [rahs], in, in the garden. |
| 3 | **R** | This house, is, eh, white, uh, there are, three windows, and, two, doors. There're |
| 4 |   | eh, mm, in in front, are a street, and there a small, eh garden. And, back, uh maybe, |
| 5 |   | I, many, I don't know what is, three or four er four er street, and two, two, I don't |
| 6 |   | know |
| 7 | **A** | OK, um, to uh, this, this house, in front, there are, a car, green car. Eh, inside, |
| 8 |   | the same, there is a, other house, color is, is white. There are many walks too, 'rare |
| 9 |   | many flowers, eh, rose, roses, maybe, I I don't know. Mm, what else? … It's, OK. |

### DVD 6.1 Comparison Task (Rodrigo and Antonio)

| 1 | **A** | Eh this house, eh eh show me, that that eh, the the the people, the property, are, |
|---|---|---|
| 2 |   | maybe eh they, eh, they had a a a good job, eh, because, eh the house, eh show it. |
| 3 |   | It's it's it's big, it's it's clean, eh, there is a car, and and, this eh house it's it's it's |
| 4 |   | small, it's no clean, em I I I think I think so. |
| 5 | **R** | Yes, is correct, I think so, too. Eh, this house eh eh eh, show, eh, the the the, |
| 6 |   | poor, poorer money, I don't know, I I, this house, show, there are very money and |
| 7 |   | this house no. This house is, is, it's a good house but, eh, is better this house and |
| 8 |   | and and, and the and are worth in Mexico, in United States, in other countries, yes |
| 9 |   | I I I eh, um, I am, m, is is, em, show, eh, different … |
| 10 | **A** | Different classes, different … |
| 11 | **R** | Different classes, social classes … |
| 12 | **A** | Yeah. |
| 13 | **R** | Is in United States, is the same in in other countries. |

140

## XUE

### *DVD 1.3 Interview (Xue)*

1  **I**  Why did you start learning English?

2  **X**  Mm, because our school force us to learn English because um it's, it's a trend

3      to learn English in China.

4  **I**  Your sch-, your school did what?

5  **X**  Force us.

6  **I**  Forced you.

7  **X**  Yup.

8  **I**  Mm hm. I see. Can you say a little bit more about the trend?

9  **X**  Um, because I think English is the biggest language in the world and of course

10     in, because Chinese, China enter the WTO organization so it's our duty to learn

11     English and also because um Beijing 2008 Olympic Games and Chine-, China has

12     a lot of chance to, uh, to communicate with uh other countries from the, all over

13     the world.

14  **I**  Mmhm. And how do you feel about learning English? Do you see it as a duty or

15     something that you like or?

16  **X**  Um, actually when I was in the elementary school, when I started to learn

17     English and most of our classmates, they didn't like to learn English because um

18     it's hard for them to learn language, another language, uh and also because

19     English is too different from Chinese and so when we troo- took English classes

20     and many of them are, they don't really to, listen to that teacher, but I just like to

21     um adjust a language and I feel it's um a new experiment to learn English because

22     it's too different and I like to challenge this kind of difficult, so I am the, at that

23     time I am the, the um greatest student in the, in my class. And I li-, I like to learn

24     English. Yeah. …

25  **X**  We have a big classroom and o-, often in class teacher always stand in the um

26     in front of the blackboard and uh he or she will begin to talk about um English

27     grammars because Chinese are always focus on grammars. And actually I don't

28     like grammars at all.

29  **I**  The class focuses on grammar?

30  **X**  Yup, and because we have took a lot of examinations and of course um for

31     Chinese student um the most important thing when we are in elementary school,

32     middle school, and high school, the most important thing is to take a college

33     entrance examinations, so there, there's a lot of pressures on us and so we have to

34     learn those grammars, boring grammars, and uh we have to take a lot of

35     examinations to enter college and it's hard for us because um there's so many

36     students who are um, you know, they want to take a chance to go into the

37     university and they will have um, have a bright future so we have to learn the

38     grammars.

39  **I**  So you have to learn grammar.

40  **X**  Yeah, but when I enter the university, I don't usually learn grammars because I

41     don't like them. Yup.

42  **I**  And when do you speak English with your host siblings?

43  **X**  Host siblings, what's that?
44  **I**  Siblings means brothers and sisters.
45  **X**  Oh, uh, when?
46  **I**  Yeah, do you speak English with your host brothers and sisters?
47  **X**  Mm, yup, of, of course.
48  **I**  OK.
49  **X**  So, when. Actually our host blings?
50  **I**  Siblings.
51  **X**  Siblings, host siblings they are adults right now and they all get married and
52      so they didn't really um live in our house right now so
53  **I**  Mm, I see.
54  **X**  When, when they come to our house, then we will talk with them. …
55  **X**  Yeah, um, when I learn grammar, I will focus on those uh hard parts and, but I
56      don't like that, but I have to learn that, um if you are my English teacher, and I
57      would like to ask you a lot of questions and about those something I don't really
58      understand mm, but I like to speak and listen so I would like to mm, I would like
59      to talk with you, chat with you when you have free times and I would like to um
60      maybe go to your house and and watch movies with you, yup.

## DVD 2.3 Question Task (Xue)

1   **X**  What's the name's name?
2   **I**  Oh, that's my friend Ahmed.
3   **X**  Wh-, Can you say that?
4   **I**  Ahmed.
5   **X**  Ahmed?
6   **I**  Mm hm. He's Somali.
7   **X**  Oh. Um it seems that he get up late but what's the reason?
8   **I**  Um, his alarm clock didn't work. Something happened; either the clock didn't
9       work or the power went out, but yeah, he got up late.
10  **X**  What, what do, what does he do?
11  **I**  He has to go to school. He's late for school.
12  **X**  So he is a student?
13  **I**  He's a student.
14  **X**  Mm hm. And what day is it today?
15  **I**  Oh, I don't know but it's a school day.
16  **X**  It seems, like, he wants to hike, hi-, hi-, hi-. What, what he is doing?
17  **I**  He's hitchhiking.
18  **X**  Yeah, hitchhiking.
19  **I**  Hitchhiking, right.
20  **X**  Um, who is that man in the car?
21  **I**  Well, he's lucky because that's a friend of his.
22  **X**  Oh, grea-.
23  **I**  Yeah.
24  **X**  And where he is standing at?
25  **I**  He's standing outside his apartment building.

| 26 | **X** | So you mean that there is a bus stop just in front of their apartment? |
|----|-------|----------------------------------------------------------------------|
| 27 | **I** | Yeah. |
| 28 | **X** | Does he live in that campus? Dormitories? |
| 29 | **I** | No, no, he lives in Minneapolis but he doesn't live in the dormitory. |
| 30 | **X** | Um, is that apartments far away from the university? |
| 31 | **I** | Mm, it's a couple of miles. |
| 32 | **X** | How, how long will he take the bus to the school? |
| 33 | **I** | Oh, only maybe fifteen minutes or something like that. |
| 34 | **X** | Um, wh-, what's wrong with that man? Why he wave something? |
| 35 | **I** | Well, this is Ahmed's friend and he stopped to clean the snow off the |
| 36 |       | windshield. That's the scraper to clean the snow off the windshield. |
| 37 | **X** | Scraper? |
| 38 | **I** | Mm hm. But Ahmed thought that his friend stopped for him because he was |
| 39 |       | hitchhiking. |
| 40 | **X** | Oh. |
| 41 | **I** | So he got in the car. |
| 42 | **X** | Oh, what's name of her, his friend? |
| 43 | **I** | Mohammed. |
| 44 | **X** | Mohammed. Oh. They are, they are – Why? What are they doing, right now? |
| 45 | **I** | Well, Mohammed is cleaning the snow off the windshield and then he looks inside and said, "What are you doing in there?". |

## DVD 3.3 Retell Task (Xue)

| 1 | **X** | One day, Ohamek ... |
|---|-------|---------------------|
| 2 | **I** | Ahmed. |
| 3 | **X** | Ahmed, Ahemed was late for his school and it almost eight-fifteen and he |
| 4 |       | thought he must find his car to go to school so he, he tried, try to get up and dress |
| 5 |       | up all his clothes and hat and gloves but he can't he can't find his car keys um in |
| 6 |       | his sofa and because his his room is so messy and and then he go go outside. He |
| 7 |       | found that it's snowing outside and he wants to take bus to school but he wants |
| 8 |       | to find some change and he looking for change in his pocket but the bus just went |
| 9 |       | up and go go and keep going so he can't catch the bus. Um it was snowing so he |
| 10 |      | was kind of poor so he stand beside the road and wait for hike ... |
| 11 | **I** | Hitchhike. |
| 12 | **X** | Hitchhike, thank you, and then he found a car which is blue and he found that |
| 13 |       | car coming toward him so he just um thumb up his hand and waiting for there |
| 14 |       | and then he found that car stop and he thought that was for him. Um he thought |
| 15 |       | um that man, that man saw him and then stop for him to hitchhike so he go into, |
| 16 |       | go inside the card. Mm but that man was just stand up and pull outside uh what's |
| 17 |       | that thing? |
| 18 | **I** | A scraper? |
| 19 | **X** | Scraper. And he begin to clean the windshield. |

### DVD 4.3 Narrative Task (Xue)

| | | |
|---|---|---|
| 1 | **X** | Yeah, in, this is, this madam, who is my neighborhood and whose name is |
| 2 | | Anderson, Mrs. Anderson ... |
| 3 | **I** | Uh uh. |
| 4 | **X** | I'm sorry, Mrs. Anderson, she is shopping in a, in the Cub, Cub Foods. |
| 5 | **I** | Mm hm. |
| 6 | **X** | And she wants to find some great foods for his, uh for her um daughters and |
| 7 | | sons because that was weekend so she wants to make a feast for her daughters and |
| 8 | | sons and her granddaughters. Mm, so when, when she just shopping in the Cub |
| 9 | | Foods, and he, he met, he came across, met another ladies who has a a two-years- |
| 10 | | old girl and who is sitting in his car, is that? Car? No. |
| 11 | **I** | Mm hm. Cart. |
| 12 | **X** | Cart. So um that girl was very naughty and she, she is looking around and she |
| 13 | | wants to find something to play with but she, she can't find anything to play, but |
| 14 | | she saw that Mrs. Anderson's um blank, basket and so he put out a bottle of |
| 15 | | vinegar and put into Mrs. Anderson's basket. And, and he, they um Mrs. |
| 16 | | Anderson and that lady was chatting each other with um her her her |
| 17 | | granddaughters and uh her daughters so they didn't find that girl was doing that |
| 18 | | kind of naughty things and and they didn't notice, notice that that girl was just put |
| 19 | | the vinegar into her basket and then just sit there and pretend that anything, |
| 20 | | everything was good and and nothing's going to happen. Um so then um when the |
| 21 | | Mrs. Anderson who go to the cashier to to pay for the bills um they didn't notice |
| 22 | | that she has a vinegar, a bottle of vinegar in her basket, so he put in into the desk |
| 23 | | and the cashier check all those things and and and let her pay his bill, her her |
| 24 | | bill ... |
| 25 | **X** | So um he, when he back home, he found that there is more more more things |
| 26 | | that out of her budget so he check out what is going on here so she found that |
| 27 | | there is a bottle of vinegars. She didn't want that so she go back to the Cub Foods |
| 28 | | and and just um how to say? She wants that money back. |
| 29 | **I** | Oh, she tried to exchange it or get her money back. |
| 30 | **X** | Yeah, yeah. She get her money back. That's all. |

### WR 4.3 Narrative Task Written (Xue)

| | |
|---|---|
| 1 | There was a sunny day. Mrs. Anderson's daughters and sons were going to |
| 2 | come back home to get together with her. She wanted to prepare a feast for them. |
| 3 | So she went to Cub Foods. |
| 4 | Inside the store, she was seach searching for some good food that her kids |
| 5 | would love, then she came across a lady, who has a daughter siting in her pushing |
| 6 | car. The lady stopped and talked with Mrs. Anderson about Mrs. Anderson's |
| 7 | daughter because she was her classmate couple years ago. When they were |
| 8 | chatting, the girl who was 2 years old felt really boring, and she wanted to find |
| 9 | something to play with, she looked around and find Mrs. Anderson had an open |
| 10 | basket, then this nauthy girl seized a bottle of veniger putt it into Mrs. |
| 11 | Anderson's basket slightly and pretended that there was nothing happened. |

12    Both of the adults didn't notice that, after their chatting, Mrs. Ande
13    went to the cashier paid for the bill, however, the bill was beyond he
14    bardget, she didn't pay much attention to it. When she went back h
15    checked her bill and found out there is a bottle of veniger that she di
16    all, so she went back to Cub Food and got her money back.

## CHUN

### DVD 1.4 Interview (Chun)

1  **I**  Why did you start learning English?
2  **C**  Oh, actually, in the very beginning, it's, it's because of the, uh, we have the
3    kind of class, so we have to attend the class because they they they told us you
4    have to learn English, so we go to learn English, and then we found it's very
5    important, because now China is uh is ah have a good trade trade um connection
6    between the China and America so I I taink it's and other English countries so I
7    think it's very important so I studied very hard. That's the reason.
8  **I**  And why did you start?
9  **C**  Because we have the class. The English class. And the the teacher told us that
10    that um we have the class so you should attend the class.
11  **I**  [Mm]
12  **C**  [Yeah] so I learn I begin the learning of English.
13  **I**  OK.
14  **C**  Yeah.
15  **I**  Thank you.
16  **I**  Can you describe a typical class in China when you were 12?
17  **C**  Uh it's the English English teacher on the stage and the way it's just they uh
18    they told us the the pronunciation the words the vocabulary the words and the
19    pronunciation and we repeat his his pronunciation. And then it's we do a lot [prateks]
20  **I**  A lot, a lot of what?
21  **C**  Mm [pratek] um what's that uh, practice.
22  **I**  Practice.
23  **C**  Yeah yeah [practice]
24  **I**  [you did a lot] of practice.
25  **C**  Yeah.
26  **I**  Mhm. With the pronunciation.
27  **C**  Yeah and with with uh grammar. Yeah.
28  **I**  So can you say a little more about what the students did?
29  **C**  Um we will do um examination not the not very mm it's it's just uh the practice
30    and just like examinations. Paper.
31  **I**  Mhm.
32  **C**  And then they have the the choice the the have a lot of, things to, cloze? And uh
33    reading and about listening
34  **I**  Mhm.
35  **C**  Yeah.
36  **I**  When you say "cloze" … you mean

37  C  Cloze uh uh there is a article and have lots of words was pick up and we have
38     to choose the right one to, yeah.
39  I  The right one to put in the blank.
40  C  Uh yeah.
41  I  Yeah. And did you say you write you wrote in English?
42  C  Yeah. Wrote. Yeah.
43  I  Can you say a little bit more about that?
44  C  Mm we have the in the in the end of the paper we have the the mm they ask us to
45     write an article uh with English uh about maybe about your parents or your study
46     of English or ask some kind all kinds of (nods).
47  I  So at the end of the paper they asked you
48  C  Yeah. Yeah as they will they will uh ask me ask us to write in English. Yeah.
49     Maybe about one hundred and, twenty, words. It's OK yeah.
50  I  Mhm? OK.
51  I  Can you tell me some things you do now to learn English?
52  C  Uh now. Uh actually I do a lot of about my vocabulary because, um before I
53     came I I came here I think my vocabulary is enough but when I arrived here I
54     think I have a lot of words I don't know. So every night I will I will uh write
55     wrote the words I don't know and and then I will recite it and then will pronounce
56     will mm make sense make mm to remember it and then I will yeah just do this
57  I  You make you make sentences to remember them.
58  C  Mm yeah.
59  I  When do you speak English with your host siblings?
60  C  Host what?
61  I  Siblings.
62  C  What that mean?
63  I  That means brothers and sisters.
64  C  Oh. We don't have host brother and sisters.
65  I  Hm.
66  C  Yeah but because they all grew up uh [edet] and they all work in others place
67     of America so they just come back once or [twels] in one month maybe yeah so
68     we just say something that not very important yeah say "Nice to meet you" or yeah.
69  I  (laughs) Make small talk with them.
70  C  Yeah.

## DVD 2.4 Question Task (Chun)

1  C  Is the man is a student?
2  I  Yes, he is a student.
3  C  Yeah.
4  I  That's my friend Ahmed.
5  C  Oh. Yeah and … it's in the morning?
6  I  Mhm.
7  C  And so I have no question about this picture.
8     Abou, ne, next.
9  C  Who's who's that man?

*[Handwritten annotations in margins:]*

*Recast correctn* (lines 41–42)

*Recast* (line 47)

*doesn't correct uses future with "they will ask"* (lines 48–49)

*time marker* (line 51)

*before* (circled, line 52)

*Repeat* (line 57)

*Indicate → time markers "before" → conversation "they will, etc."*

| 10 | **I** | That's Ahmed again. |
|----|-------|---------------------|
| 11 | **C** | Oh. It's so it's in the winter? |
| 12 | **I** | It IS in the winter. |
| 13 | **C** | Yeah and what's what's he doing? |
| 14 | **I** | Well, it turns out that he's late for school. |
| 15 | **C** | Yeah? |
| 16 | **I** | And so he's looking for his car keys, he's in a real hurry. He's look he can't find |
| 17 | | his car keys. |
| 18 | **C** | Car key? |
| 19 | **I** | Car keys? |
| 20 | **C** | Oh. |
| 21 | **I** | And um so then since he can't find his car keys he's also looking for money to |
| 22 | | take the bus to school. |
| 23 | **C** | Mm yeah. OK. |
| 24 | **C** | Yeah and so he missed the bus. Or |
| 25 | **I** | He missed the bus. |
| 26 | **C** | Oh and so next. |
| 27 | **I** | Sure. |
| 28 | **C** | Does he want to take the taxi? |
| 29 | **I** | No he's trying to hitchhike. |
| 30 | **C** | Oh. Hitchhike? |
| 31 | **I** | Hitchhike. Put his thumb out and get somebody to give him a ride? |
| 32 | **C** | Oh. Yeah. Hitchhike. And is that way work? Is that way work? |
| 33 | **I** | Does that way work? |
| 34 | **C** | Yeah. |
| 35 | **I** | Well I don't do it but (laughs) it does sometimes work for Ahmed. |
| 36 | **C** | Oh. OK (laughs) What's what's that man doing? |
| 37 | **I** | Well actually |
| 38 | **C** | The driver? |
| 39 | **I** | The driver |
| 40 | **C** | Yeah |
| 41 | **I** | stopped the car to clean the snow off the windshield? |
| 42 | **C** | Oh |
| 43 | **I** | so he's here with his scraper and he stopped to clear the snow off the car? |
| 44 | **C** | Yeah |
| 45 | **I** | But Ahmed thought that the driver stopped for him |
| 46 | **C** | Oh |
| 47 | **I** | so he got into the car. |
| 48 | **C** | Oh yeah and mm OK. |
| 49 | **C** | Yeah. So, when the the driver get off the the car he didn't found the the boy? |
| 50 | **I** | He was surprised. (laughs) |
| 51 | **C** | Oh yeah he's surprised. |
| 52 | **I** | What are you doing in my car? (laughs) |
| 53 | **C** | Oh yeah |
| 54 | **C** | Yeah and what what's what is he's thinking? |

| | | |
|---|---|---|
| 55 | I | Well he's actually Ahmed is saying hi because this turns out it's his friend |
| 56 | | Mohammed. |
| 57 | C | Oh. Ah. |
| 58 | I | So he knew him and he thought well he just stopped to give me a ride |
| 59 | C | Oh yeah |
| 60 | I | but Mohamed actually stopped to clean off the windshield |
| 61 | C | Yeah |
| 62 | I | so he was surprised when he saw Ahmed in his car. He never saw him hitch |
| 63 | | hiking. |
| 64 | C | Oh OK. OK so so his friend is very surprised and, OK, next. |
| 65 | I | Nope that's it, that's the last picture. |
| 66 | C | So would would his friend will uh take him to the school? |
| 67 | I | Yeah he goes to the same school so it worked out just fine. |
| 68 | C | So he isn't [lake]. |
| 69 | I | Well he's a little bit late but he got there OK. |

### *DVD 3.4 Retell Task (Chun)*

| | | |
|---|---|---|
| 1 | C | Uh so it's a winter morning and and the boy is a student and when, when he |
| 2 | | got up and he found he's [lake], uh, he's late because uh and then he's very hurry, |
| 3 | | to find the money and other things to go to the school, to find money to take the |
| 4 | | bus and and he very hurry to to catch the bus and then found that he missed the |
| 5 | | bus and then he want to he want to uh take a take a ride? (looks at I) |
| 6 | I | Mhm. |
| 7 | C | Ride? Right? Uh yeah take a ride but and he just do this (gestures with thumb) |
| 8 | | then uh gesture and then he found he found there is a car and then stopped at |
| 9 | | before at before him and then he think the car was, agree, the driver want to take |
| 10 | | him to the school so he get in the car. He get in the car but the driver mm the driver |
| 11 | | uh get off the car because the driver mm didn't saw, don't saw him but but he want |
| 12 | | to, he just want to clean the windshield uh and then but but he think he the driver |
| 13 | | want to take him to the school |
| 14 | I | Mhm |
| 15 | C | and then and then the driver just clean the the windshield and then uh she uh he |
| 16 | | he was surprise to find the boy in his car and and the boy said s-said "Hi" (laughs) |
| 17 | | and then, The driver was his, was one of his friends. And then he took him to |
| 18 | | the school and he's a little bit late. |

### *DVD 4.4 Narrative Task (Chun)*

| | | |
|---|---|---|
| 1 | C | This is [a, uh] old lady and she wants to buy something in the in the sho-, in |
| 2 | | the uh supermarket and then she uh take a car and then she go into the |
| 3 | | supermarket and she happen to meet his her her daughter, yeah, her doctor, her |
| 4 | | dau- her daughter and the and and her granddaughter. And her her daughter was |
| 5 | | also finding something maybe a be beer or wine. Then they talk to each other and |
| 6 | | and then the granddaughter uh was was, oh, yeah, her her granddaughter is, |
| 7 | | curious about all the things and she grab, one one bottle of wine and put it in the |
| 8 | | in the old lady's bag. |

| 9  | **I** | (laughs) |
|----|-------|----------|
| 10 | **C** | (laughs) Yeah. |
| 11 | **I** | And what do you think would happen after that? |
| 12 | **C** | The old lady will will get in trouble to to to uh get off get out of the |
| 13 |       | supermarket, yeah. |

## WR 4.4 Narrative Task Written (Chun)

| 1 | One day, an old lady wants to buy something in the supermarket. |
|---|----------------------------------------------------------------|
| 2 | When she is looking for what she wants, she come up happens to meet her |
| 3 | daughter and her granddaughter. And then they keep talking with each other. |
| 4 | Her granddaughter is curious about the bottles beside her so she graps a bottle and |
| 5 | put it into her grandma's bag. But the old lady just doesn't realize it. So, I think |
| 6 | the old lady will be trou get in trouble when she gets out of the market. |

## XUE AND CHUN

### DVD 5.2 Jigsaw Task (Xue and Chun)

| 1  | **X** | Is is that a sunny days? And they have a a straight trees outside a house? |
|----|-------|---------------------------------------------------------------------------|
| 2  | **C** | Yeah. It's a sunny day, and it has street trees but but in the picture they're just |
| 3  |       | have the leaf. |
| 4  | **X** | Leaves? |
| 5  | **C** | Yeah. Leafs. |
| 6  | **X** | In my picture there's four windows in the house. How about you? |
| 7  | **C** | Um I have I just have two windows. |
| 8  | **X** | The house has two floors, what about yours? |
| 9  | **C** | Yeah, yeah, me too. And my house is white. The roof is brown. |
| 10 | **X** | Mm. I think the second floor of my house is white but the first floor is like |
| 11 |       | brown and and the roof is grey. |
| 12 | **C** | Oh. OK. |
| 13 | **X** | And there's a door. |
| 14 | **C** | Yeah. |
| 15 | **X** | The door was white. |
| 16 | **C** | Yeah. Me too. |
| 17 | **X** | And it have a it has a garage. Do you have a garage in your picture? |
| 18 | **C** | No. No. I don't have garage. |
| 19 | **X** | And |
| 20 | **C** | And what about the grass? |
| 21 | **X** | Grass? |
| 22 | **C** | Grass, the lawn? |
| 23 | **X** | Uh huh. |
| 24 | **C** | Uh yeah do you have the lawn? |
| 25 | **X** | Yeah. I have. |
| 26 | **C** | Oh. And what's the color? |
| 27 | **X** | Green? |
| 28 | **C** | Green yeah |

| 29 | X | Of course. |
|---|---|---|
| 30 | X | But in my in my house there is a tiny window beside a door. Do you has do |
| 31 | | you have that? |
| 32 | C | You mean the, which house, you mean the |
| 33 | X | The oh |
| 34 | C | the first house or |
| 35 | X | The main house. |
| 36 | C | OK Uh, no. I just have I just have two windows. |
| 37 | X | Two windows? |
| 38 | C | Yeah. One floor is have one and the second floor have one. |
| 39 | X | Mhm. |
| 40 | C | And what about the sky? Is cloudy? Or sunny? Do you have the cloud? |
| 41 | X | No because the the sky was covered by the trees leaves and I can't really see it. |
| 42 | C | Oh OK. So. We have got three three different and three same part. |
| 43 | X | Well what's three different? |
| 44 | C | The three different is the roof, the color of the house and the road before the |
| 45 | | house and the car. |
| 46 | X | Mhm yep. |
| 47 | C | And the same is is a the same is the the sunny day, the tree, and the … |
| 48 | X | The door? |
| 49 | C | Ah. Yeah. The door. |

### DVD 6.2 Comparison Task (Xue and Chun)

| 1 | C | I think this house will have four people to live in, one mother, one father and a |
|---|---|---|
| 2 | | brother, a sister. Yeah, maybe it's a middle class family, what about you? |
| 3 | X | In my pictures, I think they might be have five people in the house, one father, |
| 4 | | one mother and one sister and two brothers, little, younger brothers. And there |
| 5 | | might be a little dog live in that house and they have, they have a car. Um |
| 6 | | and they are the middle classes in the United States. |
| 7 | C | Yah, and I think it's a typical house in Minnesota. |
| 8 | X | Typical house. (whisper) |
| 9 | C | Yah, because when we go back home on the bus, we s-, we saw a lot of this |
| 10 | | kind of houses. |
| 11 | X | Yeah. |
| 12 | C | Yeah. |
| 13 | X | But a lot of house they don't have fence around them. |
| 14 | C | Oh, yeah. That's true, but I think the house is very typical. |
| 15 | X | House is typical. |
| 16 | C | Yeah, yeah. And some of them have, some of these houses have the fence. |
| 17 | X | Mmhm. |
| 18 | C | Yeah. |
| 19 | X | About American cultures, I think it's more focus on the privacy space, private |
| 20 | | space … |
| 21 | C | Mm. |
| 22 | X | And they, they are a family so they have a big house and fence and the garage |

23   mm they don't have, they didn't want to live in that apartment so they, they don't
24   want to share um the garage with others, other peoples and like um and in that
25   kind of house they have, they have lawns belongs to them and a little yard and
26   they can mow the lawn themselves ...
27 **C** Yeah. And they can barbeque outside, I think that's, that's a way they enjoy their lives.

# CATRINE

## *DVD 1.5 Interview (Catrine)*

1  **I** Can you tell me when you started learning English, and how old you were?
2  **C** I started learning English a long time ago but, it was different from, learning
3     English in USA. We used to learn English at school and, we most write, than,
4     speaking. So I really learn English when I came here speaking but writing I used
5     to learn in my country.
6  **I** Why did you start learning English, in your country?
7  **C** Because, in my country, the school require, me to take English.
8  **I** The school what?
9  **C** Like it was require for me to take English.
10 **I** Mhm.
11 **C** Yeah. Like, if you are, if you start high school, depend on what you want to do
12    when you grow up, then you, have to take English.
13 **I** So can you tell me about a typical class, in your country? Learning English. A
14    typical English class.
15 **C** OK. If you want to be a secretarary, I don't know, secretaire
16 **I** Secretary?
17 **C** Yeah. If you want to be a secretary, you need to learn English, and, if you want
18    to be a business you want to major in business when you grow up, they, talk, they
19    will tell you that you have to learn English.
20 **I** Mhm.
21 **C** Yep.
22 **I** Do you do anything else by yourself or with your friends to practice English?
23 **C** No. Like I have friends, American friends.
24 **I** Mhm.
25 **C** Like, um, I stay after school for a lot, a lot of stuff like sport, and that's help me
26    learn a lot of things from them, learning and practicing my English, yeah. That's
27    how, I ca- I think that's how I learn my English.
28 **I** Yeah?
29 **C** Yeah.
30 **I** From your friends.
31 **C** Yes from my friends.
32 **I** And when do you speak English with your siblings?
33 **C** My family?
34 **I** Your sib[lings?]
35 **C** [Like] ... what do you mean by my siblings?
36 **I** Your brothers and sisters.

37   **C**   Mm I don't speak English with my brothers and sister but sometimes, um, like, I
38          can say like a word in English to them but not it's like speaking for long time. Yes.
39          I don't speak, really English with my brothers.

## *DVD 2.5 Question Task (Catrine)*

1   **C**   Why, who's the boy, in the bed?
2   **I**   That's my friend Ahmed.
3   **C**   Why he looks so sad?
4   **I**   Well, he's late for school.
5   **C**   But, um Why is he holding, some, what what is he holding in his hand?
6   **I**   He's holding his watch in his hand.
7   **C**   OK. Mm What, Why didn't he, put his alarm? Like, why didn't he set, his alarm?
8   **I**   Well, he did set his alarm but something happened. Either the clock didn't work
9          or the power went out so the alarm didn't go off.
10   **C**   OK. Umm. Why can't he stay and, look for a ride right now?
11   **I**   Yeah, well he's going to have to figure out how to get to school. He's late.
12   **C**   OK. What is he looking for?
13   **I**   He's looking for his car keys and he can't find them.
14   **C**   Mm. Is he mad?
15   **I**   He's upset. He's kind of upset with himself.
16   **C**   OK. Why is he wearing a jacket?
17   **I**   Because it's Minnesota in the winter.
18   **C**   OK.
19   **C**   What is he, is he running?
20   **I**   Yeah he's running after the bus.
21   **C**   I thought he knew already that he missed the bus. He was late, for the bus.
22   **I**   Well he was going to drive?
23   **C**   Oh yeah.
24   **I**   But he couldn't find his car keys.
25   **C**   OK.
26   **C**   Why, the, bus driver can't, stop for him?
27   **I**   He was too late.
28   **C**   OK.
29   **I**   He was too late.
30   **C**   Who's the person in the, blue car?
31   **I**   The person in the blue car is Ahmed's friend Mohammed.
32   **C**   OK. Is he going to give him a ride?
33   **I**   Well, Ahmed wants him to give him a ride. He's trying to hitchhike.
34   **C**   OK. Is he going to, go? Is he, going to be OK? His friend give him a ride or, is
35          he still mad because, wake up late?
36   **I**   Well, we'll see, won't we?
37   **C**   OK. What's happen to the car right now? What is happening?
38   **I**   Well, Mohammed stopped the car to clean the snow off the windshield.
39   **C**   OK. Is he helping, ah, his friend?
40   **I**   No. Ahmed thought that Mohammed stopped to give him a ride so he just got in

41     the car without saying anything.
42   **C**   Oh OK. Why are they happy now?
43   **I**   Well, Ahmed is happy because he's got a ride. And then when Mohammed
44     cleaned off the windshield, he said, "Hey! How'd you get in my car? I didn't see
45     you before."
46   **C**   (laughs) Why can't he help, his friend clean, the, remove the snow on the car?
47   **I**   Well he probably should, shouldn't he?
48   **C**   Yeah, he should.

### DVD 3.5 Retell Task (Catrine)

1   **C**   This is Mohammed.
2   **I**   No, that's Ahmed.
3   **C**   Oh, yeah this is Ahmed. He just, wake up late for school, and then, he didn't
4     set he just realized that he didn't set his alarm.
5   **C**   Now he's looking for the keys, but he can't find the keys, and he's wearing his
6     jacket because, it's, cold. It's Minnesota. And, now, uh, he miss the bus, and
7     he's, trying to catch the bus but it's too late, and the bus driver can't, hear, or
8     see him. He left. And now, he find his friend, he see his friend in the car, and he
9     think his friend can give me a ri-, can give him a ride. And, his friend stop to
10     clean, the snow, from the car, and he, get in the car, so he can have a ride. And
11     now, he is happy because he has a ride now. And his friend, is, asking him, "What
12     are you doing in my car?" (laughs)

### DVD 4.5 Narrative Task (Catrine)

1   **C**   OK, there is a woman, is going to a store, and then, in her way she finds a
2     friend's, in the store, buying stuff too, with her daughter, and then, they decide
3     they're they going to shop together. And then, they start talking about how's,
4     how life was, and, um because they didn't see each other for a long time ago, for a
5     long time ago. And, here there is the, her friend's daughter, trying, to take
6     something, I can't really see. She trying to take something, in the, bag, in her bag.
7     And sh, she can't see. She can't see if in her bag, like she can't see if there's
8     someone's who's taking something in her bag. And there is a lot of stuff they
9     bought, like, they buy from the store? In the, shop.
10   **I**   What do you think will happen next?
11   **C**   Um, I think the woman will find out, what is going on, with, her friend's
12     daughter? And they might, leave together and go somewhere else.

### WR 4.5 Narrative Task Written (Catrine)

1   There is a woman in a store: She is coming to shop. And she meets her friend, and
2   her daughter's friend in a store. They start talking and happy to see each other
3   because it has been long time since they saw each other. And her friend's
4   daughter reach in her bag. She maybe took something in the bag. After they finish
5   shopping they might go somewhere else together.

151

# JEANNE
## *DVD 1.6 Interview (Jeanne)*

| | | |
|---|---|---|
| | **I** | Can you tell me why you started learning English? |
| | **J** | It was like require in my school back in c-, back in my country. |
| 3 | **I** | It was what? |
| 4 | **J** | It was like a class, a course we c-, we were supposed to take, like, I don-, like |
| 5 | | French and other language, so. |
| 6 | **I** | I see. |
| 7 | **J** | Like social study, yeah, it was like a class like that too, so we're required to take it. |
| 8 | **J** | First, like in seventh grade, you start with the ABCs and, um numbers, and, just a little |
| 9 | | bit and then, when you, get like in eighth, ninth grade, we start learning grammar and, |
| 10 | | more stuff k- like, how how to use the verb in the sentence and, all that stuff, grammar. |
| 11 | **I** | So in one of the classes where you were learning grammar, what did the teacher do? |
| 12 | **J** | Um they would give us like, some exercise how to use, use the verb in a sentence, with, |
| 13 | **J** | how to, maybe if she say yeah gave an example about "I", what verb, and what tense, |
| 14 | | how are you going to use the verb, like if I would give you the verb, and, use it in the |
| 15 | | sentence you have to know like its end with 's', or it doesn't and, maybe, with the time, |
| 16 | | so you know how to use them maybe in the past with, the time she would give like |
| 17 | | 'yesterday', 'tomorrow', so you know how to use, kind of that, yeah. |
| 18 | **I** | Were they speaking exercises … |
| 19 | **J** | Mm mm. |
| 20 | **I** | or written exercises or … |
| 21 | **J** | No, just grammar. Writing let me see uh no, I never write in in English. I just |
| 22 | **I** | You never wrote in English. |
| 23 | **J** | No, never wrote in English. |
| 24 | **J** | We had like some speaking too but not every day. |
| 25 | **I** | Mm hm. |
| 26 | **J** | It was like if the teacher say, "Today you're going to speak in English," uh we're like, |
| 27 | | "No way, we're not going do it," because we did not know a lot of word, and, maybe, a |
| 28 | | little bit, verbs and stuff, so. It was hard, so really hard to, to speak in English so it was |
| 29 | | like, "Yeah, today you're going to do like conversation with," he's going to give us, what |
| 30 | | kind of conversation you guys are going to do, and, memorize it and say it in front of the |
| 31 | | student and stuff. It wasn't every day. |
| 32 | **I** | When do you speak English with your siblings? |
| 33 | **J** | Where? |
| 34 | **I** | When do you speak English with your siblings? |
| 35 | **J** | Mm, we don't usually speak English; we speak French. |
| 36 | **I** | Oh, OK. |
| 37 | **J** | Yeah, we don't, really, I speak English in school with my friends at school, and, people |
| 38 | | that I don't know so, I don't usually speak English with my siblings. Yeah. |
| 39 | **I** | Is there something about learning English that you find excruciating? |
| 40 | **J** | Mm, uh, not really, that was, it's such a good experience though. Yeah, it's different, |
| 41 | | but, there's nothing, nothing. |
| 42 | **I** | So if I were your English teacher, what would you want me to know about you, |

Handwritten annotations (margin):
- First - then Present not past
- Present
- past Time marker
- recast
- correct use after past after recast
- * when she pretends to be teacher → present
- Indication → time markers → conversation say… present

| | | |
|---|---|---|
| 43 | | and how you learn a language? |
| 44 | J | If you were my English teacher? Um, I would say that, I am a fast learner, yeah. I like |
| 45 | | l-, I like, knowing new, new language learning new language and stuff. So, I don't know |
| 46 | | I think I'm a fast learner though when I want to, yeah. |
| 47 | I | And so what could I do to help you learn fast? |
| 48 | J | Mm, I think, its depend I don't know, maybe, give me some books and, and, give me |
| 49 | | some grammar books and stuff, just, when I say, something bad, just help me out and, |
| 50 | | because I know I'm learning, I still have, to learn English so, its depend everything, you |
| 51 | | can do, it's going to be welcome though. |

## DVD 2.6 Question Task (Jeanne)

| | | |
|---|---|---|
| 1 | J | So what is going on with this guy? Is he late for school? |
| 2 | I | Yeah, he is; he's late for school. |
| 3 | J | How come he's, he woke up so late? |
| 4 | I | Well, he's not really sure; he doesn't remember if he forgot to set the alarm or the |
| 5 | | power went off or ... something's wrong with his alarm clock though. |
| 6 | J | Why, didn't, does he have to, does he need the alarm to wake up? |
| 7 | I | Yeah, he needs the alarm to w-; he was up, he was up late studying last night so he |
| 8 | | needs the alarm to wake up. |
| 9 | J | Oh, so he seems really tired. Does, his head hurt? |
| 10 | I | I'm sorry, what? |
| 11 | J | His head hurt? |
| 12 | I | Oh, his head hurts. |
| 13 | J | Yeah. |
| 14 | I | Yeah, his head hurts because he's worried about being late for school. |
| 15 | J | Where does he go to school? |
| 16 | I | He goes to one of the local community colleges. |
| 17 | J | Oh. Does he live near the school? |
| 18 | I | Um, he lives far enough away that he has to either drive or take the bus. |
| 19 | J | Mm, so, he has a car? |
| 20 | I | He does; he has a car. |
| 21 | J | Oh. What class did he miss? |
| 22 | I | Well he hasn't missed a class yet because it starts at nine o'clock but he's worried that |
| 23 | | that he will miss it. |
| 24 | J | Oh. |
| 25 | J | What is going on in this house? What a mess. What happen? |
| 26 | I | Well, he can't find his car keys. |
| 27 | J | Oh. Where does, where did he leave it? |
| 28 | I | Well, he doesn't know and you can see he's pretty desperate because he's looking in |
| 29 | | the couch. |
| 30 | J | Is th-, is is that the only place he, is looking for or? |
| 31 | I | No, he looked all over the place; I think this is the last place he's looking. |
| 32 | J | Is he going to find it? |
| 33 | I | Well, we'll see in the next picture, won't we. |

| 34 | J | Yeah. |
|----|---|-------|
| 35 | I | Do you want to ask something else? |
| 36 | J | So, is he the same guy? |
| 37 | I | Yes, this is, this is Ahmed; it's the same guy. |
| 38 | J | OK. He's a real, he's really in trouble. |
| 39 | J | So he does have, does he need to go, today is he taking the bus? |
| 40 | I | Well, he didn't find his car keys. But he did find some money for the bus so he was |
| 41 |   | going to try to get the bus. |
| 42 | J | Is he late for the bus? |
| 43 | I | He is late for the bus. |
| 44 | J | Oh. What he's going to do? |
| 45 | I | Ah, he's going to hitchhike. |
| 46 | J | OK. Is he going to run? |
| 47 | I | No, he's going to hitchhike. |
| 48 | J | OK. |
| 49 | J | So what happened to the car again? |
| 50 | I | Well, Mohammed couldn't see very well so he stopped to clear the snow off the |
| 51 |   | windshield. |
| 52 | J | So is he helping him or he's just getting in the car? |
| 53 | I | Ahmed is just getting in the car he thinks that Mohammed stopped to give him a ride |
| 54 |   | but Mohammed didn't see him. |
| 55 | J | Oh, Mohammed didn't see him. |
| 56 | I | No. |
| 57 | J | So what is Mohamed going to say about it? |
| 58 | I | Well, in the next picture ... Mohammed says, "Hey, what are you doing in my car?" |

## DVD 3.6 Retell Task (Jeanne)

| 1 | J | Ah, but you did not tell me the name of this guy. |
|---|---|---|
| 2 | I | Oh, his name is Ahmed. |
| 3 | J | Ahmed. So, Ahmed is, wake up, late for school today. He did not set the alarm. And |
| 4 |   | then, but he he wasn't really late for school. He had to wake up and dress up quick, to go |
| 5 |   | to school. In his way to, go to school, and, he find out that, he lost his keys, and then he |
| 6 |   | started looking for the key everywhere all over the place and, in his coach, and then, he |
| 7 |   | did not find it. It was snowing outside, when he went out, out there. He run, he he went |
| 8 |   | out he went out, and he was late for the bus, because he was looking for his key, and |
| 9 |   | then, good luck his friend, Mohammed came up, but Mohammed did not see him. He |
| 10 |   | came, he was washing the windshield because of the snow. It, he couldn't see where he |
| 11 |   | was going, but, Ahmed, jump in the car without even telling him. And his friend |
| 12 |   | Mohammed ask him, "What are you doing in my car?" and he say, " I thought you stop |
| 13 |   | for me" and then, they went to school. They did no- did not get late. |

## DVD 4.6 Narrative Task (Jeanne)

| 1 | J | This is, a lady, she went to the grocery, and then, she met her friend, her friend I don't |
|---|---|---|
| 2 |   | know the name, with her baby. And then the baby put, um, something in her bag that she |
| 3 |   | took from, the grocery, and she put it in her, bag, in the, in her mom friend's bag. And |

4   then they went. But she did not know about it, when they went out, the [yalon], I don't
5   know how they call that.
6  **I**  Mmhm.
7  **J**  So they say that she she, I don't know she took it or stole it, I think so.
8  **I**  What do you think will happen after that?
9  **J**  Mm, in the, in the way out from the store, um, they're going to, say that she stole it,
10   and she's going to say, "Oh, I did not know. It's maybe, maybe the baby, I don't know
11   how it's got there." That's what she's going to say but, she's not going to know that it
12   was the, baby who put it in her, bag.
13  **I**  Mmhm.
14  **J**  So, that's what is g-, she, she does, she won't know about it. She won't know who put
15   it there and, they're going to ask her to pay, for it.

### WR 4.6 Narrative Task Written (Jeanne)

1   This morning when she went to the store, Anna met her friend Elizabeth who came with
2   her daughter Lisa. They were buzy talking because they met each other for long ago. The
3   women were so happy and distracted when Elizabeth daughter's take the bottle of lotion
4   and put it in Ann's buek.
5   They went to cashier and pay for everything but in their way out the detector (alarm)
6   sounded. They were astonished because they don't know what happened. So, the had to
7   pay for it.

## CATRINE AND JEANNE
### DVD 5.3 Jigsaw Task (Catrine and Jeanne)

1  **J**  My pic, my picture is, uh, fence in woods, it's got green, um, it is white, and got two
2   windows.
3  **C**  Mm, mine, has, mine has, something that could help me, um, go to another place,
4   and something that can help me, climb, and has, yep. It's pretty.
5  **J**  Um, on my picture I can see one, one, door? And there is the back, the back of
6   the house got i, a small garage, and, there is tree around the house, and, that's it.
7  **C**  Mm, my house have windows, four of them and, oh five, and, a door, and a
8   garage. And there's another house next to the house. But I can see [o] I can't see the
9   whole house but I only can see half of the house.
10  **J**  There is some, grass, in t, in front of the, house, and, two, neighbors, two, two
11   big houses too that's look, like the same, I think.
12  **C**  Does, your house have a car?
13  **J**  A car? No. There is no car. There is no access to the car in my, on my, I
14   think.
15  **C**  Does your house have a, tree?
16  **J**  Yeah, [but] I cannot see, the tree, the, branch, or I can see. I cannot see the,
17  **C**  [trees?]
18  **J**  I can just see the branch of the trees, like through trees. And, that's it.
19   And, does your house got a fence? In wood?
20  **C**  No, my house, doesn't have a, doesn't have woods. There, there's flowers.

| 21 | **J** | Flowers? |
|---|---|---|
| 22 | **C** | In my picture. |
| 23 | **J** | Mm how many windows do, does your house have? |
| 24 | **C** | My house have five windows, but there is another house next door the house |
| 25 | | that have I can see only four windows but I, cannot see the other part of the |
| 26 | | house. |
| 27 | **J** | OK. So where do you think your house is, in, the town, or, in the big town or, |
| 28 | | in, suburb? That's, never mind. |
| 29 | **C** | Um, I think my house, ma- might be, Minnesota, in Minnesota. During the summer, |
| 30 | | because it's shiny, and there is sun too. |
| 31 | **J** | Mm I think mine is in, fall. Cause there are some, leaves on the floor it's, |
| 32 | | yellow. And, kind of that's it. |

### *DVD 6.3 Comparison Task (Catrine and Jeanne)*

| 1 | **C** | The, the, this house looks like, it's more fancy than the other house because the |
|---|---|---|
| 2 | | woods in front of the house it's, kind of old, old, so I will say, the, there's a lot of classes, |
| 3 | | by this I can understand that the culture by the culture of the American, there's classes |
| 4 | | like, different people, depend on how, um, um, how they job are, to have a hou- like, to |
| 5 | | have the kind of house they have. Don't know if you understand what I say. |
| 6 | **J** | Mm you mean, uh its depend on how much they earn? |
| 7 | **C** | Yeah. It depend on, how much they earn, that's, um, like, this house, looks more, |
| 8 | | beautiful than the other, so I, think, this house maybe, the person earn ma- more than the |
| 9 | | other, the people living in the other house. And, I think in the other house, the second |
| 10 | | one, there's, more people living because looks big, and the oth- the other house I think |
| 11 | | maybe there is, not much people living in, the house. |
| 12 | **J** | Mm mm. In the other house, no, the other one, I think, there may be, people who, got, |
| 13 | | enough, like, I don't know, they got a good life and, in this one it seems thats people |
| 14 | | don't really, care about, how, about the out. |
| 15 | **C** | About renewing her like stuff, |
| 16 | **J** | Yeah. |
| 17 | **C** | and, [make it new]. |
| 18 | **J** | [Clean up.] |
| 19 | **C** | Maybe there's nobody living in that house. Um doesn't really mean that the other |
| 20 | | house has more money, doesn't really but, maybe, there's no one living in the other |
| 21 | | house. No one to take care of the house. |
| 22 | **J** | They may be busy people, they go to work, and, they are tired to, wash and clean up |
| 23 | | and, kind of putting, everything clean. |

## OLIVIA

### *DVD 2.7 Question Task (Olivia)*

| 1 | **O** | Is, um, is this something he does normally? |
|---|---|---|
| 2 | **I** | No, no, uh, he usually drives and if he can't drive, then he takes the bus and so this is |
| 3 | | the last resort. |
| 4 | **O** | Mm, kay. Does he, does, is he late for w-, for class a lot? Is that why he's so desperate |

| 5 | | to get there, even through the snow and … |
|---|---|---|
| 6 | **I** | I think it's just he feels it's important for him to be there on time. |
| 7 | **O** | OK. Is, do we know whether or not he's going to get a ride yet or is that in the next |
| 8 | | picture? |
| 9 | **I** | Well, it turns out that this is a friend of his… |
| 10 | **O** | Oh. |
| 11 | **I** | who just happened to come along at the right time. |
| 12 | **O** | Lucky. |
| 13 | **I** | Ready for the next picture? |
| 14 | **O** | Mm hm. OK, so he is getting a ride obviously from his friend? |
| 15 | **I** | Well, he is, but uh actually the friend stopped to clean the snow off the car window and |
| 16 | | Ahmed thought that his friend had stopped but he didn't actually see him. |
| 17 | **O** | Uh oh. So now he's going to surprise his friend by being in the car when he gets there. |
| 18 | **I** | I'm afraid so. |
| 19 | **O** | Oh, that could be scary. But he does know him? |
| 20 | **I** | Yeah, yeah, that's a friend of his. |
| 21 | **O** | OK. |
| 22 | **I** | Ready for the next picture? |
| 23 | **O** | Sure. OK. Um, is he, why is Ahmed sitting in there when he could be out helping, |
| 24 | | I guess is what I'm thinking. |
| 25 | **I** | Well, that's a good question. I don't know the answer to that one. |
| 26 | **O** | I guess if I were in there, I would probably ask if they wanted help. |

### DVD 3.7 Retell Task (Olivia)

| 1 | **O** | OK. Ahmed woke up um and he realized his alarm clock somehow didn't work and |
|---|---|---|
| 2 | | he's late for school. Um he couldn't find his keys, so he's trying to find either his keys or |
| 3 | | change for the bus, just madly rushing around… |
| 4 | **I** | Mm hm. |
| 5 | **O** | trying to find it. Um he finally obviously found some change because he is now trying |
| 6 | | to catch the bus, but he just misses the bus um and then he sees his friend, who is driving |
| 7 | | down the street and tries to flag him down um so that he can get a ride. Um his friend |
| 8 | | stops to brush off his car because there's snow all over the car um in the blizzard and he, |
| 9 | | so he thinks his friend is stopping to uh pick him up but he actually doesn't even see Ha-, |
| 10 | | Ahmed. Until he looks into his car where Ahmed is and um then they go to school. |

### DVD 4.7 Narrative Task (Olivia)

| 1 | **O** | Let's see, um, a woman came into the store um, obviously she looks like an older |
|---|---|---|
| 2 | | woman um, oh! She, she sees somebody maybe that she knows but somebody that she |
| 3 | | wants to talk to, at any rate. Um, that person has a small child. The, uh, while they're |
| 4 | | talking, um and not paying attention to the small child, who is in the shopping cart of the |
| 5 | | other lady, um, the child picks up a bottle of what looks like probably wine and um puts it |
| 6 | | in the other, older woman's purse. |
| 7 | **I** | And what do you think happens next? |
| 8 | **O** | My guess is that because it's an older woman and the bottle looks small enough to |
| 9 | | conceal the bottle of whatever it was put into the purse, that she probably makes it home, |

| 10 | | well, she either makes it home or she makes it to the cash register and finds it and gets |
|---|---|---|
| 11 | | very embarrassed and very confused about finding it in her purse. |

## VICTORIA

### *DVD 2.8 Question Task (Victoria)*

| 1 | **V** | Um so does he have an alternative plan if he misses the bus? |
|---|---|---|
| 2 | **I** | Well, now his plan is to hitchhike. |
| 3 | **V** | OK. Does he think that's a good plan? OK, um … |
| 4 | **I** | Yeah, he does because he sees this friend of his coming along. |
| 5 | **V** | So he knows this person. |
| 6 | **I** | He knows the person driving the blue car. |
| 7 | **V** | OK, but he didn't, he … Did he know this person was coming or is he, was he just |
| 8 | | randomly going to hitchhike? |
| 9 | **I** | He was just randomly going to hitchhike. |
| 10 | **V** | OK. |
| 11 | **I** | He didn't know his friend was coming. |
| 12 | **V** | OK. Does this friend go to school with him? |
| 13 | **I** | Yeah, yeah, he does. |
| 14 | **V** | OK. Is this, is he on his way to school? |
| 15 | **I** | Yeah. |
| 16 | **V** | OK. So his friend was also late for whatever reason? |
| 17 | **I** | Yeah, I guess so. |
| 18 | **V** | OK. |
| 19 | **I** | Well, probably the snow. |
| 20 | **V** | Probably the snow. Looks like he didn't have time to brush off his car. |
| 21 | **I** | He didn't. |
| 22 | **V** | Too bad. |
| 23 | **I** | Um. |
| 24 | **V** | Are they stopping to brush the snow off the car? |
| 25 | **I** | Well… |
| 26 | **V** | What is in his hand? |
| 27 | **I** | Yeah, that's a snow brush… |

### *DVD 3.8 Retell Task (Victoria)*

| 1 | **V** | So our main character has woken up um on a school morning but unfortunately he's |
|---|---|---|
| 2 | | late because his alarm clock is broken. He looks at his watch and sees the actual time and |
| 3 | | sees that he's late so he gets out of bed, puts on his coat and is about to go outside; he's |
| 4 | | frantically looking for his car keys, which he can't find so he's looking under the couch |
| 5 | | cushions to see if they're there or to get some spare change so that he can take the bus. |
| 6 | | Uh, finds some change, goes outside into the snow, um but unfortunately misses his bus |
| 7 | | so he's still looking for a way to get to school, decides to stand on the side of the road |
| 8 | | and hitchhike and then as luck would have it, one of his friends is driving by uh in a car |
| 9 | | and he decides that since that friend is going to school anyway, he'll probably be able to |
| 10 | | give him a ride. The friend pulls over um and our main character thinks that the friend is |

| 11 | | pulling over to let him in. The main character gets into the car without saying anything |
| 12 | | but the driver had just pulled over to scrape the snow off of his windshield and doesn't |
| 13 | | notice that his friend has gotten into his car. Um but then after scraping the snow off the |
| 14 | | windshield, looks in and sees his friend sitting in his car and that's the end. |

### DVD 4.8 Narrative Task (Victoria)

| 1 | V | An older lady was walking through the grocery store and has her purse in her grocery |
| 2 | | cart. She walks down an aisle and runs into a friend who is shopping and has her young |
| 3 | | daughter sitting in the, sitting in her shopping cart um sort of looking at the things that are |
| 4 | | on the shelf and the two women are talking and don't really notice what the little girl is |
| 5 | | doing and she reaches over onto a shelf and grabs a bottle of something, possibly wine, |
| 6 | | possibly, you know, something that looks like wine, um, but the story's funnier if it is |
| 7 | | wine because it's a very strait-laced looking older lady, and she takes the bottle and drops |
| 8 | | it in the elderly woman's purse um without the woman noticing and that's where it ends. |
| 9 | I | And what do you think happens next? |
| 10 | V | Well, quite possibly what happens is the woman does her shopping and tries to leave |
| 11 | | without paying for whatever's in her purse, not knowing that it's there and sets off the |
| 12 | | store alarm, they think she trying to steal or you know, going through her purse to pay for |
| 13 | | her groceries, she notices that it's in there and is not sure how it came to be in her purse, |
| 14 | | so… |
| 15 | I | OK. |

## OLIVIA AND VICTORIA

### DVD 5.4 Jigsaw Task (Olivia and Victoria)

| 1 | V | So the three similarities between our houses, I suppose, if we were to list them, would |
| 2 | | be they're both two-story houses, … |
| 3 | O | They both have white siding. |
| 4 | V | Right. |
| 5 | O | Um. |
| 6 | V | And they're both in residential areas. |
| 7 | O | That works. Or they both have green lawns, depending… |
| 8 | V | Right, more than three similarities. |
| 9 | O | I suppose that… |
| 10 | V | Um. |
| 11 | O | That works for me. |
| 12 | V | OK, and uh the three differences uh one, I suppose would be that there's a fence in |
| 13 | | front of this house and not in front of yours. |
| 14 | O | Mm hm. Um, there's brick on this house and not on yours. |
| 15 | V | Mm hm. Correct. And uh… |
| 16 | O | There's an attached garage on mine. |
| 17 | V | Exactly and not on this house that you can see unless it's only in the very back in a |
| 18 | | really inconvenient place, so I would assume not. |
| 19 | O | Mm hm. |

### DVD 6.4 Comparison Task (Olivia and Victoria)

1  V  All right. Well, I think that these are both family homes, so I would assume that
2     there's a family living in both of these houses um but your house strikes me as a m-, like
3     a upper-middle class family whereas my house is more of a lower-middle class um home,
4     just based on, it just doesn't look quite as kept up, um and also just not quite as big, so,
5     that's my impression.
6  O  I get the same impression. Um, my thoughts also um just from looking at these that
7     it's possible that the house that I, that my house has one or two children but if you saw
8     the other house, even though they're the same size, you would expect them to have more
9     children.
10 V  Yeah.
11 O  Because people in lower-class families can't afford large houses.
12 V  Right.
13 O  And and I guess sort of says something about our culture is that richer people tend to
14    have less children and that's sort of a stereotype anyway.

# SAMPLE CONSENT FORM

You are invited to be in a research study on second language learning. I would like your help because you are learning another language. Please read this form and ask questions before agreeing to be in the study. This study is being conducted by _____, who is a [teacher/student] at [name of institution].

The purpose of this study is to learn more about the way in which people learn a second language. After you have completed the study, we will tell you the precise focus of this study, and ask you for your insights into your own language learning.

*Procedures:* If you agree to be in this study, you will be asked to do the following things: [clearly explain tasks or procedures, and length of time they will take. For example, 'I will ask you to do some tasks and record your responses; it will take 30 minutes.']

*Risks and Benefits of Being in the Study:* This study has [no/few] risks to you. [Usually there are no risks. If there are risks, clearly explain them.]

*Confidentiality:* The records of this study will be kept private. In any sort of written report, no information will be included that will make it possible to identify you. Research records will be kept in a locked file; only [names] will have access to the records.

*Voluntary Nature of the Study:* You do not have to be in this study. If you decide to participate, you are free to withdraw at any time with no penalty [no effect on your grade in the class or your relationships with your teachers].

*Contacts and questions:* The researchers conducting this study are _____ and _____ . You may ask any questions you have now. If you have questions later, you may contact them at _____; phone: _____ . [The researcher's advisor/supervisor is name/address/phone].

You will be given a copy of this form to keep for your records.

**Statement of Consent:**

I have read the above information. I have asked questions and received answers. I consent to participate in the study.

Signature _____          Date _____

Signature of researcher _____          Date _____

# PHOTOCOPIABLE RESOURCES

## Prompt Cards for Question Task and Retell Task

1

2

3

4

5

6

# Prompt Cards for Narrative Task

1

2

3

4

# Prompt Cards for JigsawTask and Comparison Task

1

2

# GLOSSARY

*academic language function:* in an academic setting, use of language to perform a cognitive function, for example, comparing and contrasting, sequencing, inferring, or synthesizing.

*acquisition:* according to *Monitor model*, the unconscious internalization of a new TL linguistic form or rule.

*affective filter:* in *Monitor model*, a metaphorical barrier that prevents input from becoming intake.

*article:* determiners identifying a noun; in English: 'a', 'an', 'the'.

*AS unit:* a single speaker's utterance consisting of an independent clause or subclausal unit, together with any subordinate clause(s) associated with it; also Analysis of Speech unit (Foster, Tonkyn, and Wigglesworth 2000: 365).

*auxiliary verb:* a verb that combines with a main verb to help express tense or voice; examples include 'be', 'have', 'do', 'will', 'may'. Also called a 'helping verb'.

*avoidance:* a type of communication strategy in which an individual does not refer to an entity or action because they do not know or cannot access the relevant lexical item.

*behaviorism:* a psychological theory that learning, including language learning, takes place through habit-formation.

*circumlocution:* a type of communication strategy in which a learner describes an entity in terms of its components, function, or purpose.

*clarification request:* an indication that the interlocutor's utterance has been misunderstood or is incorrect in some way and that the interlocutor should repeat or rephrase it. May be part of *negotiation of meaning* or *corrective feedback*. See *recast* and *prompt*.

*clinical elicitation task:* a task designed to get the learner to produce 'language of any sort' (Corder 1981).

*co-construction:* in *sociocultural theory*, the support provided in the ZPD for a conversational partner who encounters difficulty in expressing meaning or producing forms.

*cognitivism:* in SLA, the hypothesis that language learning is accomplished by cognitive processes that are not specific to language.

*communication strategy:* linguistic expressions used jointly by speakers to resolve difficulties in agreeing on an intended meaning (Tarone 1980). Includes paraphrase, circumlocution, gesture, literal translation from the NL.

*connectionist model*: a cognitivist SLA model which views language learning as part of general learning (i.e. it is not *innatist*), and conceptualizes language as an interconnected network of units in the mind.

*content-based instruction* (CBI): teaching academic content through the medium of the L2, accompanied by supporting language instruction.

*contrastive analysis* (CA): comparison of linguistic expressions in a learner's NL and TL in order to predict learning difficulty.

*copula:* a verb, usually 'be', that identifies a subject with a predicate, as in 'He is a teacher'. Sometimes called a 'linking verb'.

*corrective feedback:* any indication to a learner that his or her use of a TL linguistic expression is inaccurate (for example, explicit correction, recast, prompt).

*critical period:* age range during which the brain is predisposed to success in language learning.

*determiner:* member of a group of adjectival words that can precede descriptive adjectives in a noun phrase; includes the articles 'a', 'an', 'the', and words that can replace them like 'this', 'her', and 'some'.

*dictogloss:* an activity in which a short text is read aloud to learners who take notes and who later work in groups to reconstruct the text from their notes.

*discourse:* a unit of speech or writing that is longer than a sentence.

*discourse community:* a group of people who share the same communicative purpose, such as members of the same academic discipline or profession.

*discrete-point test:* a test format that presents the learner with choices (for example, multiple choice, fill-in-the-blanks).

*elicitation:* any of three techniques that teachers use to get students to produce language: (1) eliciting completion of the teacher's utterance ('Kim is not go-...'), (2) asking about the correct form ('What is the present progressive form of "go"?'), and (3) eliciting a self-correction from the student ('Can you say "Kim is not go" another way?').

*error:* incorrect linguistic expression that is systematically produced by a learner; it is assumed to result from an IL rule that differs from the TL rule.

*error analysis:* process of identifying errors learners have made in speaking or writing a TL.

*essential task structure:* the set of entities, events, and relationships that must be referred to in a referential communication task for a successful outcome.

*explicit correction:* a direct indication that a student made an error together with explicit provision of the correct form.

*extrinsic motivation:* motivation that is imposed on the learner by outside forces (for example, grades, job requirements).

*first language:* see *native language.*

*Focus on Form:* an approach to language teaching where, in a mainly meaning-focused interaction, the teacher or students occasionally switch briefly to focusing on linguistic form.

*foreign language learning:* classroom learning of a TL in a place where that language is not spoken outside the classroom (for example, French in the U.S.); contrasts with *second language learning.*

*fossilize:* (of a non-target like linguistic form, feature or rule) to become permanently established in an interlanguage, impervious to the influence of input or instruction.

*given information:* information that the speaker or writer assumes that the listener or reader already knows or can uniquely identify from what is being said. In English, given information is often signaled by using pronouns, demonstratives ('this', 'that', 'these', 'those') or the definite article 'the'. (Contrast with *new information.*)

*independent clause:* a clause that contains a tensed verb and can stand alone as a sentence.

*innatism:* theory that humans are born with a property of the human mind that is dedicated specifically to the acquisition of language.

*innatist SLA theories:* cognitivist theories based on the hypothesis that language learning results from an innate property of the human mind that is dedicated to language acquisition.

*input:* linguistic forms and rules presented to the learner aurally or in writing, and available for SLA.

*instrumental motivation:* motivation that arises from practical goals for language learning such as program or career requirements.

*intake:* linguistic forms and rules in the input that are incorporated into the learner's IL and can be used in generating utterances.

*integrative motivation:* motivation for language learning that arises from a personal affinity for the people and culture related to the L2.

*interaction:* the exchange and *co-construction* of turns between individuals in the course of communication.

*interactional modification:* change that occurs in discourse when a communication breakdown occurs or is anticipated: change in the way the discourse is managed (repetition, comprehension checks) or repair of the discourse when a breakdown occurs (negotiation of meaning, self-correction, abandoning the message).

*interactionist:* theory that SLA is accomplished through a learner's interaction with others, who may modify their speech to meet the learner's communicative and learning needs.

*interlanguage (IL):* linguistic system evidenced when a L2 learner tries to express meanings in the second language.

*interlanguage phonology:* patterns of pronunciation in learner language.

*interlocutor:* the person the learner is interacting with.

*International Phonetic Alphabet (IPA):* set of symbols comprising a universally understood system for transcribing the speech sounds of the world's languages, devised by the International Phonetic Association.

*interpersonal communication:* interactive communication primarily intended to maintain social relationships; compare with *referential communication*.

*intralingual:* developmental factors other than NL transfer that shape learner language, including cognitive processes such as *overgeneralization*.

*intrinsic motivation:* motivation that comes from within the learner (desire for personal growth or cultural enrichment).

*Joseph Conrad phenomenon:* post-critical period success in acquiring native-like syntax, lexis, and discourse while retaining a foreign accent.

*learning:* in the *Monitor model*, the conscious internalization of a TL linguistic form or rule. Such forms or rules become part of the monitor, only useful for editing utterances but not generating them.

*learning strategy:* specific activity a learner undertakes in order to learn the TL, such as repeating a new word aloud.

*learning style:* overall learner preference in learning a TL, such as a preference for visual as opposed to auditory input.

*lexicon:* vocabulary of a language.

*linguistic expression:* language form functioning syntactically as a unit.

*main verb:* word denoting an action, occurrence, or state of being; the main verb comes first in a verb plus complement structure, as in 'She likes to walk'.

*metalinguistic feedback:* a comment on a learner's utterance that provides information about the correct form (for example, if a learner says 'two parrot', metalinguistic feedback might be 'You need the plural –s'.)

*mistake:* a non-systematic deviation in learner language; caused by processing problems blocking access to a linguistic expression the learner knows. Compare to *error*.

*Monitor:* in the *Monitor model*, the learned language system, which acts as an editor by making changes in what the acquired language system produces.

*Monitor model:* an *innatist* SLA theory claiming that the cause of successful 'acquisition' is exposure to comprehensible target language input.

*morpheme:* smallest meaningful unit of a language. Free morphemes like 'see' can stand alone; bound morphemes are prefixes and suffixes like *un–* or *–able*.

*morphology:* the structure and content of word forms in a language.

*motivation:* the intensity and persistence of a learner's desire to succeed in learning a language.

*native language (NL):* the language first learned. Children who first learn two languages at once have two native languages.

*native language (NL) transfer:* use in learner language of linguistic elements drawn directly from the NL. In negative transfer, this results in error, and in positive transfer, it corresponds to a correct TL form.

*native speaker (NS):* someone who learned a language at an early age and retains full mastery of the language.

*natural order:* in the *Monitor model*, the order in which linguistic elements of a L2 are acquired (not learned).

*negotiation of meaning:* the interaction that occurs when interlocutors try to prevent or repair a communication breakdown.

*new information:* information that the speaker or writer assumes the listener or reader does not already know. In English, new information is typically signaled by using the indefinite article 'a' or colloquially with an indefinite 'this', as in 'I saw this funny-looking cat today'. (Contrast with *given information*.)

*noninterface:* the claim that there is no relationship between a learner's conscious knowledge about L2 and knowledge the learner unconsciously uses to generate utterances.

*noticing:* a conscious focus on 'elements of the surface structure of utterances in the input' (Schmidt, 2001).

*noun phrase:* a pronoun or a noun and its modifiers (for example, determiners, descriptive adjectives), typically functioning as a subject or object in a sentence.

*obligatory context:* a linguistic context that requires a specific language form for grammaticality (for example, the *–s* in 'Tom drinks coffee').

*overgeneralization:* using a TL grammar rule in a context where it does not belong; for example, using an *–ed* ending with irregular verbs, as in 'buyed' and 'runned'.

*personality:* an individual's mental, emotional, and social characteristics.

*phoneme:* smallest meaningful sound segment in a language.

*phonology:* the sound system, or pronunciation, of a language.

*Processability Theory:* a *cognitivist* theory which claims that processing constraints on permissible changes in word order can account for developmental sequences in SLA.

*prompt:* a type of *corrective feedback* that does not provide the learner with a correct form; examples include *elicitation*, *clarification request*, or repetition.

*recast:* a form of corrective feedback that provides a correct form. If a learner says 'She don't play', a recast would be 'She doesn't play'.

*reference:* process by which entities are identified (by naming or description), are located or moved relative to other entities (by giving instructions or directions), or followed through sequences of events and locations (in narratives).

*referential communication:* communication in which information is exchanged between two speakers, by means of successful acts of reference.

*relative clause:* a clause that modifies a noun or pronoun, as in 'The house that Jack built'.

*repair:* a learner's self-correction, often as part of uptake in response to corrective feedback. See *uptake*.

*repetition:* a type of *corrective feedback* in which a teacher repeats a student's *error*, typically with stress or intonation indicating where the error is.

*risk-taking:* in SLA, willingness to act or speak despite possible loss of face because of incorrect language forms.

*scaffolding:* language support that an interlocutor provides for the communicative success of another speaker with a structure, word, etc. that the speaker is not able to produce without support.

*second language:* any language acquired subsequent to the native language.

*second language learning:* classroom learning of a TL in a place where that language is spoken outside the classroom (for example, French in France). Contrasts with *foreign language learning*.

*sociocultural theory:* interactionist SLA theory based on the work of Vygotsky (1978, 1987), which says that language development is socially mediated.

*sociolinguistic theory:* interactionist SLA theory based on the work of Labov (1972) that traces variation in learner language to social and linguistic variables that systematically encourage or discourage the production of particular linguistic forms. Also known as Variationist Theory.

*subclausal unit:* a segment of speech or writing that can be elaborated into a complete clause by recovering elements which were omitted or a minor utterance such as 'Thank you'.

*subordinate clause:* a verb (either tensed or not tensed) plus at least one other element such as a subject or object; a sentence fragment if used alone (as, 'if it is raining').

*syllabus:* the sequence in which items of course content will be presented in a class, as allied with class goals.

*syntax:* rules for constructing sentences in a language, such as permissible word orders.

*target language (TL):* a language additional to a NL that is being learned.

*target-like use (TLU) analysis:* analysis of learner language that tabulates both correct and incorrect instances in a learner's production of a target-language form.

*task:* activity with a communicative outcome in which a learner attends to meaning, not linguistic structure.

*task motivation:* interest and willingness to expend effort on a classroom task.

*tense:* verb element indicating time of occurrence of a state or action, such as past or present.

*third person singular morpheme:* the *–s* affix attached to a present tense verb with a third person subject in English, as in 'He plays baseball'.

*transfer of training:* a cognitive process by which some IL elements result from the way the L2 learner was taught.

*trigger:* an utterance that contains an error or causes a misunderstanding.

*type-token ratio (TTR):* the total number of different words (types) divided by the total number of words (tokens) in a section of discourse; a measure of vocabulary breadth or complexity.

*unanalyzed 'don't':* 'don't' functions for the learner as a single lexical item (not a combination of 'do' + 'not') that does not change with person.

*uptake:* a learner's immediate response to corrective feedback. This response may or may not be to repair the error. See *repair*.

*variation:* shift in the form of a linguistic feature of learner language due to different tasks, listeners, topics, or other contextual factors.

*verb phrase:* a verb and its modifiers and objects; functions like a verb in a sentence.

*word coinage:* a type of communication strategy in which a learner creates a lexical item, as in 'air ball' for 'balloon'.

*Zone of Proximal Development (ZPD):* in *sociocultural theory,* an area of potential language development defined as those language forms or functions that are beyond a learner's ability to produce alone but that can be produced by the learner with *scaffolding* support from other people.

# BIBLIOGRAPHY

**Adamson, H.D.** 1993. *Academic Competence, Theory and Classroom Practice: Preparing ESL Students for Content Courses.* New York: Longman.

**Allwright, D.** 2001. 'Three major processes of teacher development and the appropriate design criteria for developing and using them' in B. Johnston and S. Irujo (eds.). *Research and Practice in Language Teacher Education: Voices from the Field.* Minneapolis, MN: Center for Advanced Research on Language Acquisition.

**Allwright, D.** 2003. 'Exploratory practice: Rethinking practitioner research in language teaching'. *Language Teaching Research* 7: 113–41.

**Allwright, D.** 2005. 'Developing principles for practitioner research: The case of Exploratory Practice'. *The Modern Language Journal* 89: 353–66.

**Allwright, D.** and **J. Hanks.** 2009. *The Developing Language Learner: An Introduction to Exploratory Practice.* Basingstoke: Palgrave Macmillan.

**Bardovi-Harlig, K.** 1992a. 'The telling of a tale: Discourse structure and tense use in learners' narratives' in L. Bouton and Y. Kachru (eds.). *Pragmatics and Language Learning* Vol. 3. Urbana-Champaign, IL: DEIL.

**Bardovi-Harlig, K.** 1992b. 'The use of adverbials and natural order in the development of temporal expression'. *International Review of Applied Linguistics* 30: 199–220.

**Bardovi-Harlig, K.** 2000. *Tense and Aspect in Second Language Acquisition: Form, Meaning and Use.* Malden, MA: Blackwell.

**Barnes-Karol, G.** and **M. Broner.** 2008a. 'Introduction to CBI at St. Olaf: Intermediate French/Spanish I'. Unpublished workshop handout. Northfield, Minnesota: St. Olaf College.

**Barnes-Karol, G.** and **M. Broner.** 2008b. 'Uso de postales y fotografías en Span 231'. Unpublished workshop handout. Northfield, Minnesota: St. Olaf College.

**Bayley, R.** 1994. 'Interlanguage variation and the quantitative paradigm: Past tense marking in Chinese-English' in E. Tarone, S. M. Gass, and A. D. Cohen (eds.). *Research Methodology in Second-Language Acquisition.* Hillsdale, NJ: Lawrence Erlbaum Associates.

**Beebe, L.** 1977. 'The influence of the listener on code-switching'. *Language Learning* 27: 33–39.

**Berdan, R.** 1996. 'Disentangling language acquisition from language variation' in R. Bayley and D. Preston (eds.). *Second Language Acquisition and Linguistic Variation.* Amsterdam: John Benjamins.

**Bernach, C., K. Galinat,** and **S. Jimenez.** 2005. 'Co-teaching in a sheltered model: Maximizing content and language acquisition for beginning-level English language learners' in D. Kaufman and J. Crandall (eds.). *Content-Based Instruction in Primary and Secondary School Settings*. Alexandria, VA: TESOL.

**Biber, D.** 1988. *Variation Across Spoken and Written English*. Cambridge: Cambridge University Press.

**Biber, D.** 2006. *University Language: A Corpus-Based Study of Spoken and Written Registers*. Amsterdam: John Benjamins.

**Bigelow, M., R. DelMas, K. Hansen,** and **E. Tarone.** 2006. 'Literacy and the processing of oral recasts in SLA'. *TESOL Quarterly* 40: 1–25.

**Bigelow, M., S. Ranney,** and **A. Dahlman.** 2006. 'Keeping the language focus in content-based ESL instruction through proactive curriculum-planning'. *TESL Canada Journal* 24: 40–58.

**Brière, E. J., R. Campbell,** and **M. Soemarmo.** 1968. 'A need for the syllable in contrastive analysis'. *Journal of Verbal Learning and Verbal Behavior* 7: 384–89.

**Brinton, D., M. Snow,** and **M. Wesche.** 2003. *Content-Based Second Language Instruction*. Ann Arbor, MI: University of Michigan Press.

**Brown, G.,** and **G. Yule.** 1983. *Teaching the Spoken Language*. Cambridge: Cambridge University Press.

**Brown, H. D.** 2007. *Principles of Language Learning and Teaching* (5th edn.). White Plains, NY: Addison Wesley.

**Bunch, G., R. Lotan, G. Valdés,** and **E. Cohen.** 2005. 'Keeping content at the heart of content-based instruction: Access and support for transitional English learners' in D. Kaufman and J. Crandall (eds.). *Content-Based Instruction in Primary and Secondary School Settings*. Alexandria, VA: TESOL.

**Cazden, C.** 1992. *Whole Language Plus: Essays on Literacy in the United States and New Zealand*. New York: Teachers College Press.

**Center for Advanced Research on Language Acquisition.** 2009. *Content-Based Language Teaching with Technology*. University of Minnesota. Accessed on January 5, 2009, from http://www.carla.umn.edu/cobaltt/.

**Center for Advanced Research on Language Aquisition.** 2009. *Language Immersion Education and Research*. University of Minnesota. Accessed on January 5, 2009 at http://www.carla.umn.edu/immersion.

**Chang, J.** 2001. 'Chinese Speakers' in M. Swann and B. Smith (eds.) *Learner English: A Teacher's Guide to Interference and Other Problems*. Cambridge: Cambridge University Press.

**Chomsky, N.** 1957. *Syntactic Structures*. The Hague: Mouton.

**Chomsky, N.** 1959. 'Review of B.F. Skinner, Verbal Behavior'. *Language* 35: 26–58.

**Clahsen, H.** 1988. 'Critical phases of grammar development: A study of the acquisition of negation in children and adults' in P. Jordens and J. Halleman (eds.). *Language Development*. Dordrecht: Foris.

**Coe, N.** 2001. 'Speakers of Spanish and Catalan' in M. Swann and B.Smith (eds.). *Learner English: A Teacher's Guide to Interference and Other Problems*. Cambridge: Cambridge University Press.

**Coffin, C.** 1997. 'Constructing and giving value to the past: An investigation into secondary school history' in F. Christie and J. R. Martin (eds.). *Genre and Institutions: Social Processes in the Workplace and School*. London: Cassell.

**Content-Based Language Teaching with Technology.** 2009. Center for Advanced Research on Language Acquisition, University of Minnesota. Accessed on January 5, 2009, from http://www.carla.umn.edu/cobaltt/.

**Cook, V. J.** 1993. *Linguistics and Second Language Acquisition*. New York: St. Martin's Press.

**Corder, S. P.** 1967. 'The significance of learners' errors'. *International Review of Applied Linguistics* 5: 161–70.

**Corder, S. P.** 1974. 'Error analysis' in J. Allen and S. Corder (eds.). *The Edinburgh Course in Applied Linguistics Vol. 3: Techniques in Applied Linguistics*. Oxford: Oxford University Press.

**Corder, S. P.** 1981. *Error Analysis and Interlanguage*. Oxford: Oxford University Press.

**Cummins, J.** 1981. 'The role of primary language development in promoting educational success for language minority students' in California State Department of Education (ed.). *Schooling and Language Minority Students: A Theoretical Framework*. Los Angeles: California State University Evaluation, Dissemination and Assessment Center.

**Cummins, J.** 2000. 'Putting language proficiency in its place: Responding to critiques of the conversational/academic language distinction' in J. Cenoz and U. Jessner (eds.). *English in Europe: The Acquisition of a Third Language*. Clevedon: Multilingual Matters.

**deBot, K., W. Lowie,** and **M. Verspoor**. 2005. *Second Language Acquisition: An Advanced Resource Book*. New York: Routledge.

**Dörnyei, Z.** and **J. Kormos**. 2000. 'The role of individual and social variables in oral task performance'. *Language Teaching Research* 4: 275–300.

**Doughty, C.** 1991. 'Second language instruction does make a difference: Evidence from an empirical study of SL relativization'. *Studies in Second Language Acquisition* 13: 431–69.

**Doughty, C.** 2001. 'Cognitive underpinnings of focus on form' in P. Robinson (ed.). *Cognition and Second Language Instruction*. New York: Cambridge University Press.

**Doughty, C.** and **M. Long.** 2005. *Handbook of Second Language Acquisition.* Oxford: Blackwell.

**Doughty, C.** and **J. Williams** (eds.). 1998. *Focus on Form in Classroom Second Language Acquisition.* Cambridge: Cambridge University Press.

**Eckman, F.** 1977. 'Markedness and the contrastive analysis hypothesis'. *Language Learning* 27: 315–30.

**Eckman, F., L. Bell,** and **D. Nelson**. 1988. 'On the generalization of relative clause instruction in the acquisition of English as a second language'. *Applied Linguistics* 9: 1–20.

**Ellis, N.** 2002. 'Frequency effects in language processing: A review with implications for theories of implicit and explicit language acquisition'. *Studies in Second Language Acquisition* 24: 143–88.

**Ellis, R.** 1984. 'Can syntax be taught? A study of the effects of formal instruction on the acquisition of WH questions by children'. *Applied Linguistics* 5: 138–55.

**Ellis, R.** 1994. *The Study of Second Language Acquisition.* Oxford: Oxford University Press.

**Ellis, R.** 1999. *Learning a Second Language Through Interaction.* Amsterdam: John Benjamins.

**Ellis, R.** 2003. *Task-Based Language Learning and Teaching.* Oxford: Oxford University Press.

**Ellis, R.** and **G. Barkhuizen**. 2005. *Analysing Learner Language.* Oxford: Oxford University Press.

**Ellis, R., S. Loewen,** and **R. Erlam.** 2006. 'Implicit and explicit corrective feedback and the acquisition of L2 grammar'. *Studies in Second Language Acquisition* 28: 339–68.

**Ellis, R.** and **Y. Sheen.** 2006. 'Reexamining the role of recasts in second language acquisition'. *Studies in Second Language Acquisition* 28: 575–600.

**Faerch, C.** and **G. Kasper.** 1983. *Strategies in Interlanguage Communication.* New York: Longman.

**Foster, P., A. Tonkyn,** and **G. Wigglesworth.** 2000. 'Measuring spoken language: A unit for all reasons'. *Applied Linguistics* 21: 354–75.

**Freeman, D.,** and **D. Johnson.** 1998. 'Reconceptualizing the knowledge-base of language teacher education'. *TESOL Quarterly* 32: 397-418.

**Gardner, R. C.** and **W. E. Lambert.** 1972. *Attitudes and Motivation in Second Language Learning.* Rowley, MA: Newbury House.

**Gass, S. M.** and **L. Selinker.** 2008. *Second Language Acquisition: An Introductory Course* (3rd edn.). New York: Routledge.

**Gass, S. M., A. Sorace,** and **L. Selinker.** 1999. *Second Language Learning Data Analysis* (2nd edn.). Mahwah, NJ: Lawrence Erlbaum Associates.

**Guiora, A., B. Beit-Hallahami, R. Brannon, C. Dull,** and **T. Scovel.** 1972. 'The effects of experimentally induced changes in ego states on pronunciation ability in a second language: An exploratory study'. *Comprehensive Psychiatry* 13: 421–28.

**Hakuta, K.** 2000. *Testing English-language Learners in U.S. Schools: Report and Workshop Summary*. Washington, DC: National Academies Press.

**Kaufman, D.** and **J. Crandall** (eds.). 2005. *Content-Based Instruction in Primary and Secondary School Settings*. Alexandria, VA: TESOL.

**Klee, C.** and **G. Barnes-Karol.** 2006. 'A content-based approach to Spanish language study: Foreign languages across the curriculum' in M. R. Salaberry and B. Lafford (eds.). *The Art of Teaching Spanish: Second Language Acquisition from Research to Praxis*. Washington, DC: Georgetown University Press.

**Krashen, S.** 1977. 'Some issues relating to the Monitor Model' in H. Brown, C. Yorio, and R. Crymes (eds.). *On TESOL '77*. Washington, DC: TESOL.

**Krashen, S.** 1981. *Second Language Acquisition and Learning*. Oxford: Pergamon Press.

**Krashen, S.** 1982. *Principles and Practice in Second Language Acquisition*. Oxford: Pergamon Press.

**Krashen, S.** 1985. *The Input Hypothesis: Issues and Implications*. London: Longman.

**Labov, W.** 1972. *Sociolinguistic Patterns*. Philadelphia PENN: University of Pennsylvania.

**Lado, R.** 1957. *Linguistics Across Cultures*. Ann Arbor, MI: University of Michigan Press.

**Lantolf, J.** 2000. 'Introducing sociocultural theory' in J. Lantolf (ed.). *Sociocultural Theory and Second Language Learning*. Oxford: Oxford University Press.

**Larsen-Freeman, D.** 2001. 'Teaching grammar' in M. Celce-Murcia (ed.). *Teaching English as a Second or Foreign Language* (3rd edn.). Boston, MA: Heinle and Heinle.

**Larsen-Freeman, D.** and **M. Long.** 1991. *An Introduction to Second Language Acquisition Research*. New York: Longman.

**Lightbown, P.** 1983a. 'Acquiring English L2 in Quebec classrooms' in S. Felix and H. Wode (eds.). *Language Development at the Crossroads*. Tubingen: Gunter Narr.

**Lightbown, P.** 1983b. 'Exploring relationships between developmental and instructional sequences in L2 acquisition' in H. W. Seliger and M. H. Long (eds.). *Classroom Oriented Research in Second Language Acquisition*. Rowley, MA: Newbury House.

**Lightbown, P.** and **N. Spada.** 2006. *How Languages Are Learned* (3rd edn.). Oxford: Oxford University Press.

**Liu, G.** 1991. 'Interaction and Second Language Acquisition: A case study of a Chinese child's acquisition of English as a second language'. Unpublished PhD dissertation, La Trobe University, Melbourne.

**Liu, G.** 2000. *Interaction and Second Language Acquisition: A Longitudinal Study of a Child's Acquisition of English as a Second Language.* Beijing: Beijing Language and Culture University.

**Long, M.** 1996. 'The role of the linguistic environment in second language acquisition' in W. Ritchie and T. Bhatia (eds.). *Handbook of Second Language Acquisition.* San Diego, CA: Academic Press.

**Lyster, R.** 2007. *Learning and Teaching Languages Through Content: A Counterbalanced Approach.* Amsterdam: John Benjamins.

**Lyster, R.** and **H. Mori.** 2006. 'Interactional feedback and instructional counterbalance'. *Studies in Second Language Acquisition* 28: 269–300.

**Lyster, R.** and **L. Ranta.** 1997. 'Corrective feedback and learner update: Negotiation of form in communicative classrooms'. *Studies in Second Language Acquisition* 19: 37–61.

**Mackay, R.** 1981. 'Developing a reading curriculum for ESP' in L. Selinker, E. Tarone, and V. Hanzeli (eds.). *English for Academic and Technical Purposes: Studies in Honor of Louis Trimble.* Rowley, MA: Newbury House.

**Mackey, A.** (ed.). 2007. *Conversational Interaction in Second Language Acquisition.* Oxford: Oxford University Press.

**Mackey, A., S. M. Gass,** and **K. McDonough.** 2000. 'How do learners perceive interactional feedback?' *Studies in Second Language Acquisition* 22: 471–97.

**Major, R. C.** 2001. *Foreign Accent: The Ontogeny and Phylogeny of Second Language Phonology.* Mahwah, NJ: Lawrence Erlbaum Associates.

**Mehan, H.** 1979. *Learning Lessons: Social Organization in the Classroom.* Cambridge, MA: Harvard University Press.

**Mohan, B. A., C. Leung** and **C. Davison** (eds.). 2001. *English as a Second Language in the Mainstream: Teaching, Learning and Identity.* New York: Longman.

**Norris, J.** and **L. Ortega.** 2000. 'Effectiveness of L2 instruction: A research synthesis and quantitative meta-analysis'. *Language Learning* 50: 417–528.

**Ortega, L.** In press. *Understanding Second Language Acquisition.* Hodder Arnold Publications.

**Paul, M.** 1999. *Success in Referential Communication.* Dordrecht: Kluwer Academic Publishers.

**Pavesi, M.** 1984. 'The acquisition of relative clauses in a formal and informal context' in D. Singleton and D. Little (eds.). *Language Learning in Formal and Informal Contexts.* Dublin: IRAAL.

**Pavesi, M.** 1986. 'Markedness, discoursal modes and relative clause formation in a formal and informal context'. *Studies in Second Language Acquisition* 8: 38–55.

**Pica, T.** 1983. 'Adult acquisition of English as a second language under different conditions of exposure'. *Language Learning* 33: 465–97.

**Pica, T.** 1996. 'The essential role of negotiation in the communicative classroom'. *JALT Journal* 18: 241–68.

**Pienemann, M.** 1987. 'Determining the influence of instruction on L2 speech processing'. *Australian Review of Applied Linguistics* 10: 83–113.

**Pienemann, M.** 1989. 'Is language teachable? Psycholinguistic experiments and hypotheses'. *Applied Linguistics* 10: 52–79.

**Pienemann, M.** 1998. *Language Processing and Second Language Development.* Philadelphia, PA: John Benjamins.

**Pienemann, M.** 2005. *Cross-Linguistic Aspects of Processability Theory.* Amsterdam: John Benjamins.

**Pienemann, M.** and **M. Johnston.** 1987. 'Factors influencing the development of language proficiency' in D. Nunan (ed.). *Applying Second Language Acquisition Research.* Adelaide: National Curriculum Resource Centre, Adult Migrant Education Program.

**Pienemann, M., M. Johnston,** and **G. Brindley.** 1988. 'Constructing an acquisition-based procedure for second language assessment'. *Studies in Second Language Acquisition* 10: 217–43.

**Pienemann, M.** and **A. Mackey.** 1993. 'An empirical study of children's ESL development' in P. McKay (ed.). *ESL Development – Language and Literacy in Schools: Vol. 2.* Canberra: National Languages and Literacy Institute of Australia and Commonwealth of Australia.

**Preston, D.** 1989. *Sociolinguistics and Second Language Acquisition.* Oxford: Basil Blackwell.

**Preston, D.** 2002. 'A variationist perspective on SLA: Psycholinguistic concerns' in R. Kaplan (ed.). *Oxford Handbook of Applied Linguistics.* Oxford: Oxford University Press.

**Ravem, R.** 1978. 'Two Norwegian children's acquisition of English syntax' in E. Hatch (ed.). *Second Language Acquisition.* Rowley, MA: Newbury House.

**Ravid, D.** and **L. Tolchinsky.** 2002. 'Developing linguistic literacy: A comprehensive model'. *Journal of Child Language* 29: 417–47.

**Robinson, P.** 1995. 'Attention, memory, and the "noticing" hypothesis'. *Language Learning* 45: 283–331.

**Salaberry, M. R.** 2000. 'The acquisition of English past tense in an instructional setting'. *System* 28: 135–52.

**Saville-Troike, M.** 2006. *Introducing Second Language Acquisition*. Cambridge: Cambridge University Press.

**Schleppegrell, M.** 2004. *The Language of Schooling: A Functional Linguistics Perspective*. Mahwah, NJ: Lawrence Erlbaum Associates.

**Schmidt, R. W.** 1990. 'The role of consciousness in second language learning'. *Applied Linguistics* 11: 129–58.

**Schmidt, R. W.** 2001. 'Attention' in P. Robinson (ed.) *Cognition and Second Language Instruction*. Cambridge: Cambridge University Press.

**Schumann, J.** 1979. 'The acquisition of negation by speakers of Spanish: A review of the literature' in R. Andersen (ed.). *The Acquisition and Use of Spanish and English as a First and Second Language*, Washington, DC: TESOL.

**Scovel, T.** 1969. 'Foreign accents, language acquisition, and cerebral dominance'. *Language Learning* 28: 129–42.

**Scovel, T.** 2001. *Learning New Languages: A Guide to Second Language Acquisition*. Boston, MA: Heinle and Heinle.

**Selinker, L.** 1972. 'Interlanguage'. *International Review of Applied Linguistics* 10: 209–41.

**Shapira, R. G.** 1978. 'The non-learning of English: Case study of an adult' in E. M. Hatch (ed.). *Second Language Acquisition: A Book of Readings*. Rowley, MA: Newbury House.

**Snow, M. A.** 2001. 'Content-based and immersion models for second and foreign language teaching' in M. Celce-Murcia (ed.). *Teaching English as a Second or Foreign Language* (3rd edn.). Boston, MA: Heinle and Heinle.

**Sorace, A., S. M. Gass,** and **L. Selinker.** 1994. *Second Language Learning Data Analysis*. Hillsdale, NJ: Lawrence Erlbaum Associates.

**Spada, N.** and **P. Lightbown.** 1993. 'Instruction and the development of questions in L2 classrooms'. *Studies in Second Language Acquisition* 15: 205–24.

**Swain, M.** 1995. 'Three functions of output in second language learning' in G. Cook and B. Seidlhofer (eds.). *Principle and Practice in Applied Linguistics*. Oxford: Oxford University Press.

**Swain, M.** 2000. 'The output hypothesis and beyond: Mediating acquisition through collaborative dialogue' in J. Lantolf (ed.). *Sociocultural Theory and Second Language Learning*. Oxford: Oxford University Press.

**Swain, M.** and **S. Lapkin.** 1998. 'Interaction and second language learning: Two adolescent French immersion students working together'. *Modern Language Journal* 82: 320–37.

**Swan, M.** and **B. Smith** (eds.). 2001. *Learner English: A Teacher's Guide to Interference and Other Problems*. Cambridge: Cambridge University Press.

**Tarone, E.** 1980. Communication strategies, foreign talk, and repair in interlanguage. *Language Learning* 30, 417-31.

**Tarone, E.** 1983. 'On the variability of interlanguage systems'. *Applied Linguistics* 4: 43–63.

**Tarone, E.** 1988. *Variation in Interlanguage*. London: Edward Arnold.

**Tarone, E.** 2000. 'Still wrestling with "context" in interlanguage theory'. *International Review of Applied Linguistics* 20, 182–98.

**Tarone, E.** In press. 'Equipping teachers to be language explorers' in M. E. Anderson and A. Lazaraton (eds.). *Bridging Contexts, Making Connections: Selected Papers from the Fifth International Conference on Language Teacher Education.* Minneapolis, MN: Center for Advanced Research on Language Acquisition.

**Tarone, E.** and **D. Allwright.** 2005. 'Language teacher-learning and student language-learning: Shaping the knowledge base' in D. J. Tedick (ed.). *Second Language Teacher Education: International Perspectives.* Mahwah, NJ: Lawrence Erlbaum Associates.

**Tarone, E., M. Bigelow,** and **K. Hansen.** 2009. *Literacy and Second Language Oracy.* Oxford: Oxford University Press.

**Tarone, E.** and **G. Liu.** 1995. 'Situational context, variation and SLA theory' in G. Cook and B. Seidlhofer (eds.). *Principle and Practice in Applied Linguistics: Studies in Honour of H.G. Widdowson.* Oxford: Oxford University Press.

**Tarone, E.** and **G. Yule.** 1989. *Focus on the Language Learner.* Oxford: Oxford University Press.

**Teemant, A.** and **S. Pinnegar.** 2002. *The second language acquisition case: A video ethnography of second language learners, Parts I, II and III.* Provo, UT: BEEDE Program, Brigham Young University. http://creativeworks.byu.edu/office.

**Thomas, W. P.** and **V. Collier.** 1997. *School Effectiveness for Language Minority Students.* Washington, DC: National Clearinghouse for Bilingual Education. Accessed on January 2, 2009 at www.ncela.gwu.edu/pubs/resource/effectiveness/.

**VanPatten, B.** 1990. 'Attending to form and content in the input: An experiment in consciousness'. *Studies in Second Language Acquisition* 12: 287–301.

**Vygotsky, L. S.** 1978. *Mind in Society.* Cambridge, MA: Harvard University Press.

**Vygotsky, L. S.** 1987. *The Collected Works of L. S. Vygotsky. Vol. I: Thinking and Speaking.* New York: Plenum.

**Walther C.** 2001. 'French Speakers' in M. Swann and B. Smith (eds.) *Learner English: A Teacher's Guide to Interference and Other Problems.* Cambridge: Cambridge University Press.

**White, J.** 1998. 'Getting the learners' attention: A typographical input enhancement study' in C. Doughty and J. Williams (eds.). *Focus on Form in Classroom SLA*. Cambridge: Cambridge University Press.

**Yule, G.** 1996. *Pragmatics*. Oxford: Oxford University Press.

**Yule, G.** 1997. *Referential Communication Tasks*. Mahwah, NJ: Lawrence Erlbaum Associates.

**Yule, G.** 1999. *Explaining English Grammar*. Oxford: Oxford University Press.

**Yule, G.** 2006. *Oxford Practice Grammar: Advanced*. Oxford: Oxford University Press.

**Yule, G.** and **D. Macdonald.** 1990. 'Resolving referential conflicts in L2 interaction: The effect of proficiency and interactive role'. *Language Learning* 40: 539–56.

**Yule, G.** and **E. Tarone.** 1997. 'Investigating communication strategies in L2 reference: Pros and cons' in G. Kasper and E. Kellerman (eds.). *Communication Strategies: Psycholinguistic and Sociolinguistic Perspectives*. New York: Longman.

**Zwiers, J.** 2008. *Building Academic Language: Essential Practices for Content Classrooms, Grades 5–12*. San Francisco, CA: Jossey-Bass.

# INDEX

# DVD TRACKLIST

**Introduction**

**Segment 1: Interviews**

| | |
|---|---|
| 1.1 | Rodrigo |
| 1.2 | Antonio |
| 1.3 | Xue |
| 1.4 | Chun |
| 1.5 | Catrine |
| 1.6 | Jeanne |

**Segment 2: Question Task**

| | |
|---|---|
| 2.1 | Rodrigo |
| 2.2 | Antonio |
| 2.3 | Xue |
| 2.4 | Chun |
| 2.5 | Catrine |
| 2.6 | Jeanne |
| 2.7 | Olivia |
| 2.8 | Victoria |

**Segment 3: Retell Task**

| | |
|---|---|
| 3.1 | Rodrigo |
| 3.2 | Antonio |
| 3.3 | Xue |
| 3.4 | Chun |
| 3.5 | Catrine |
| 3.6 | Jeanne |
| 3.7 | Olivia |
| 3.8 | Victoria |

**Segment 4: Narrative Task**

| | |
|---|---|
| 4.1 | Rodrigo |
| 4.2 | Antonio |
| 4.3 | Xue |
| 4.4 | Chun |
| 4.5 | Catrine |
| 4.6 | Jeanne |
| 4.7 | Olivia |
| 4.8 | Victoria |

**Segment 5: Jigsaw Task**

| | |
|---|---|
| 5.1 | Rodrigo and Antonio |
| 5.2 | Xue and Chun |
| 5.3 | Catrine and Jeanne |
| 5.4 | Olivia and Victoria |

**Segment 6: Comparison Task**

| | |
|---|---|
| 6.1 | Rodrigo and Antonio |
| 6.2 | Xue and Chun |
| 6.3 | Catrine and Jeanne |
| 6.4 | Olivia and Victoria |

---

The 'additional resources' on the DVD main menu refer to the transcripts pdf file, which can be opened in a separate window and used alongside the video material.